FROM FIELD TO FACTORY

COMMUNITY STRUCTURE AND
INDUSTRIALIZATION IN WEST BENGAL

FROM FIELD TO FACTORY

COMMUNITY STRUCTURE AND
INDUSTRIALIZATION IN WEST BENGAL

Morton Klass

ISHI

*A Publication of the
Institute for the Study of Human Issues
Philadelphia*

Manufactured in the United States of America

Library of Congress Cataloging in Publication Data:

Klass, Morton, 1927–
    From field to factory.

    Bibliography: p.
    Includes index.
    1. West Bengal—Rural conditions.   2. Villages—India—West
Bengal.   3. West Bengal—Industries.   I. Title
HN690.B4K53   301.35′2′095414   78–1552
ISBN 0–915980–34–7

A portion of the Introduction to this book was previously published in the
American Anthropologist 74(3): 606–609, 1972.

For information, write:

Director of Publications
ISHI
3401 Science Center
Philadelphia, Pennsylvania 19104
U.S.A.

For Sheila,
alone

Contents

PART III

THE VILLAGE AND THE FACTORY

Preface

Beginning points are never easily identified. I have been concerned with the issues and problems underlying this work for most of my professional life. The actual research, however, developed out of a continuing inquiry, at Columbia University in the early 1960s, on the effects of contemporary culture change upon South Asian social structure. Conrad M. Arensberg and Joan Mencher initiated the inquiry and drew many colleagues and students into the discussion, which ultimately became a research project funded by the National Institutes of Mental Health. I take this opportunity to express my gratitude to N.I.M.H. for the research support and to the American Council of Learned Societies for a grant that enabled me to complete the manuscript.

I am of course grateful to all my colleagues in the research project. From initial formulations, through fieldwork, through the various drafts of this manuscript, I have had the benefit of the advice, criticism, and friendship of such people as Joan Mencher, Owen M. Lynch, Doranne Jacobson, and Leon Swartzberg. Happily for us, Conrad Arensberg was—and remains—our Principal Investigator and gentle doyen.

There have been other colleagues, not part of the research group, who have also read all or part of the manuscript and have advised me in its preparation; I would like to express particular gratitude to Abraham Rosman, Suzanne Hanchett, Karen Kerner, and David Feingold. The advice was good, but the responsibility for the final manuscript is mine alone.

The world changes, and so—*pace* Tennyson—does Asia. When the fieldwork upon which this book is based was being conducted, the boundaries of many states of India were different. "Bangladesh" was a term all Bengalis used for the total territory in which dialects of their language were spoken. What is now the sovereign and independent nation of Bangladesh was then East Pakistan. Other changes have taken place—are taking place, even as I write. However, the

Indian state of West Bengal, the site of the research, has not changed its boundaries, and the Asansol subdivision of District Burdwan of West Bengal continues to be one of the most important industrial regions of India.

At the time research was being conducted, 4.76 Indian rupees were worth one dollar (U.S.), and monetary references throughout the text reflect that exchange rate. A rupee was, and remains, divisible into one hundred *naya paise*—officially. Unofficially, the countryman often prefers to think of the rupee as containing the traditional sixteen annas.

The Asansol area draws people in search of opportunity from all parts of India, and indeed of the world, and a wide range of tongues may be encountered in the streets of the town. In the countryside around Asansol, however, the primary language spoken is the local dialect of Bengali, the "standard" form of which is simultaneously the state language of West Bengal and the national language of Bangladesh. Bengali is customarily written in an Indic script related to, but by no means identical with, the Devanagari script in which both ancient Sanskrit and modern Hindi are usually written.

My sole interest in reproducing the speech of the villagers of the area north of Asansol is to enable *all* readers, familiar or not with Indic languages and scripts, to be able to determine the *local* pronunciation and usage. This may be a laudable objective; given the problems, it is not an easy one. To begin with, Bengali—like most Indian languages—is customarily simply transliterated from its own script into Roman letters. But Bengali orthography, like English and French, exhibits a wide range of words with "silent"(that is, unpronounced) letters, and when these are transliterated they tend to break their silence. A speaker of Bengali knows, of course, that the "r" of *sraddha* and the "m" of *atma* are pronounced exactly as are the "b" of *doubt* and the "n" of *monsieur,* but he is accustomed to the conventional transliteration and finds representations such as *śaddhô* and *atta* as disquieting as others might find *dowt* and *mersyer.* I crave his pardon and beg his indulgence.

Therefore, while I have stayed as close as I could to the orthography conventionally used for Indic languages—retroflex consonants are represented by a subscript dot ("ṛ" "ḍ" "ṭ") and aspirated ones by an "h"[1] (as in *bhat*)—there are some changes. Modern Bengali does not distinguish, except in orthography, between long and short vowels ("i" and "ī," "u" and "ū") and so I have not. I indicate the

1. Therefore, as is customary in Indic representation, the "ch" sound (as in English "church") is indicated by "c." Whenever "ch" is used it represents the aspirated form of the same consonant; in English "chh."

Bengali low central vowel with "a" (pronounced as in English "father") and the ubiquitous Bengali lower mid-back vowel with "ô" (pronounced as is the vowel sound in English "bought"). Written Bengali has characters for three different "s" sounds, as did Sanskrit, but in spoken Bengali almost all sibilants are alveopalatal or "hushing" (as in English "shut") and are represented here by "ś." Without the superscript accent mark, "s" is pronounced as in English.

There are additional problems. A reader familiar with Bengali and willing to accept my orthographic representation may still come upon some unwelcome surprises. The statement "I will give" in Standard Bengali is "*dobo.*" It appears in this book, in one quotation, as "*dubo.*" As I indicated earlier, my objective was to present *local* pronunciation and usage.

And finally, it has been difficult, perhaps impossible, to be consistent. Some words, particularly names, are familiar to English readers; they have, in other words, conventional English spellings. Shall I refer to "Hindu" or "Hindoo," to "Brahmin" or "Brahman," particularly when the villager is apt to say "Bamun"? The problem is particularly acute in the representations of Hindu divinities: who will recognize "Śiva" under the name of "Śibu" or, "Saraswatī" under the name of "Śôrôśôtti"? Where I thought it was necessary, therefore, the more familiar Sanskrit or Hindi (or even sometimes Standard Bengali) term is provided in the text. I urge the reader, of whatever specialty, to remember that the primary concerns in this work are ethnographic and not linguistic, or even Indological.

The anthropologist, like Blanche Du Bois, is forever dependent upon the kindness of strangers. In my own case, from the moment of my arrival in India to the day of my departure, my way was smoothed, my work facilitated, and my stay made delightful because of the efforts of people who had never met me before. India is truly a land of gracious and abiding hospitality, and the list of those to whom I feel indebted is endless; I can only name a few: Professor M. N. Srinivas, Professor N. K. Bose, Dr. D. Sen, and other scholars at universities and museums in Delhi and Calcutta; K. C. Sivaramakrishnan, A.D.M., and his hardworking staff; S. K. Bannerji and other officials of the Community Development Program; N. P. Vyas and other officers and members of the Asansol Lions and Rotary Clubs; Mr. S. C. Som and his family; Father John Turner, Ralph and Sally Segman, Dr. and Mrs. K. Sen, and Mr. and Mrs. Abraham Sirkin.

In my effort to respect privacy and protect confidences, I have used fictitious names for the villages I studied and for the factory in which many of the villagers are employed. I cannot, therefore, mention either factory officials or villagers by name (when names appear in the text they are not the real names of the individuals referred to). Without their endless patience and kindness the study would never have been completed, and I am grateful to all, and most particularly to the people of the village I have called "Gôndôgram": I have done my best to portray their village as they showed it to me.

I was particularly fortunate in obtaining the services of Mr. Sibamay Adhikari as research assistant. A young man endowed with many talents and the capacity for great industry, he worked at my side throughout the study, helping me—and teaching me.

There are others who have contributed to the completion of this work: Connie Budelis, who typed most of the manuscript; my students, who listened, argued, and clarified; and my children, who were remarkably forgiving through it all.

And last of all, and most of all, I thank my wife, Sheila, for all of all.

Leonia, New Jersey
February, 1978

Introduction:

In Search of Community

India, for many people, is an ancient and yet ageless civilization. It is a land where even today goats are sacrificed to mother goddesses, where in almost every home prayers are offered to divinities as old as any who dwelt on Olympus or in Asgard. Most of all, it is the land of the "caste system," that mystifying institution usually encompassed by bleak adjectives such as "brittle," "unchanging," "frozen."

Indians, of course, know better. They know they live in the present moment of time, along with everyone else in the world. Like everyone, they must cope with contemporary world problems, from overpopulation to strange new technologies. And, as in every nation, indeed in every village or band, conditions of life reflect the events that have gone before. Indians, like all of us, bear the burdens of the past as they wrestle with the present and attempt to survive into the future.

This work is a study of a contemporary village in India. The time is the first half of the seventh decade of the twentieth century. The village is imbedded in a particular district of a particular state. For the century and more since the founding of the village, its inhabitants had been occupied primarily, almost solely, with the production of rice. For more than a decade before this study begins, however, a modern factory has been in operation near this village and the inhabitants have been affected by it. Most adult men work in the factory or in occupations deriving from the presence of the factory in the countryside.

The original intent of the study, therefore, was to explore the relationships between factory and village, and to analyze the extent and nature of the factory's impact upon ongoing village life. What changes have occurred in economic transactions? In social relation-

5

INDIA

0   100   200   300
Miles

Indus R.

Delhi •

NEPAL

Ganges R.

BANGLADESH

West Bengal
Asansol •

Calcutta •

Bombay •

Madras •

N

ships? In values and beliefs? Put simply, it was to be a study of the
ways in which the *factory* has affected the *village*. Soon, however, it
began to appear that in important respects there really was no
"village."

The physical locality is there, of course; there are houses clustered
together containing people, and the locality has a history and even a
name. That name is replaced in this text, to provide a measure of
anonymic protection and privacy for living human beings, with the
fictitious name "Gôndôgram." As far as I know, there is no actual
village anywhere in India named Gôndôgram, for it is a Bengali expression for all villages, for *every-village*. The urban Bengali uses it to
express gentle contempt for country crudeness, for rural gaucherie.
The student at the university points at a confused newcomer who
speaks a barely intelligible dialect, wears the short *dhuti* (the traditional white nether wrapping of the Indian countryman), and is unfa-
miliar with coffee shops and classes. The urban sophisticate observes,
smiling, "He is real *Gôndôgram*." And the rural Bengali also uses the
expression, but with pride—if a touch of defensiveness. A villager will
inform a visitor that his community lacks—along with sanitation, electricity, and good drinking water—crime and caste conflict: "We are a
true *Gôndôgram*." "Gôndôgram" means "big village," but it glosses
more accurately as "small town" or "hick town" in American usage.

To repeat, then, our Gôndôgram is an actual locality. It is situ-
ated, in fact, a few miles north of one of the major industrial com-
plexes of all India, in the Asansol subdistrict of District Burdwan, in
the state of West Bengal.

Asansol forms part of the western border of West Bengal, where
that state ends as the hills of the Chota Nagpur range rise up to form
the eastern boundary of Bihar. The industrial town of Asansol itself
presides over the entire region, important now as in the past for
mining and industry. Though much of the once-extensive coal depos-
its have either been extracted over the past century or abandoned as
unproductive or uneconomic, active collieries may still be found from
Raniganj in the east through Asansol and its environs onward deep
into Bihar to the west.

With coal and good transportation facilities available, for both
the Great Eastern Railway and the Grand Trunk Road run parallel
through this area, much industry is present. By the time of Indian
Independence, Asansol was noted for the mining of coal and iron, for
the production of iron and steel, and for the manufacture of locomo-
tives and railway carriages. Steel tubing is produced in a town just to
the west of Asansol, and there are many other factories and industries
in the area.

Most industry (apart from mining) tends to be located in or very close to Asansol or one of the other towns, where there is good access to highway and railroad. As a result of this and related factors, the industrial centers tend to be overcrowded. They present problems of the usual kind for administrators: disease, crowded slums, filth, poor sanitation and water, crime, and so on. On the other hand, within a short distance to the north and south of the major arteries lie stretches of comparatively sparsely inhabited land, for neither the soil nor the undulating terrain is particularly suited for intensive rice cultivation. Much of this land (or the mineral rights thereto) belonged and still belongs to the collieries, and the natural disadvantages have been augmented by land subsidence (actual or potential) and by the draining of underground water into abandoned tunnels. The Asansol subdistrict may therefore be said to consist of badly overcrowded industrial centers, surrounded by square miles of poor farmland occupied by impoverished rural agriculturalists desperately trying to scratch a living from a hostile environment.

After Independence, representatives of industry and government gave attention to the possibilities of establishing light industry out in the countryside, away from the overcrowded centers but yet close enough to benefit from sources of raw materials and good transportation. In addition, it was hoped, such industry would find a labor source in the surrounding villages eager for employment and ready to be trained. Such laborers could reside in their home villages, walking or cycling to work. This would not only obviate any need to build extensive labor quarters around the factory; it would also, it was hoped, diminish the incidence of drunkenness and disease and the conflicts resulting from prostitution. The argument was that men living in crowded and dull workers' compounds around a factory, bored and miserable away from their homes and families, turn in their misery to liquor stalls, prostitutes, and fighting and gambling. The social "breakdown" is deplored, along with the concomitant absenteeism. But factories built in the countryside, it was felt, would experience no such problems, workers would be living in their original homes, with their families, and so apart from their new employment their lives would go on unchanged.

And, finally, the factory representatives were well aware that land in the industrial heart of Asansol was expensive, while the marginal farmland of the countryside could not but be cheaper.

One of the results of these deliberations was the establishment, in 1951, of a bicycle factory approximately four miles northwest of Asansol as the crow flies, and even farther from it along the one winding road that then traversed the distance. In this study, the ficti-

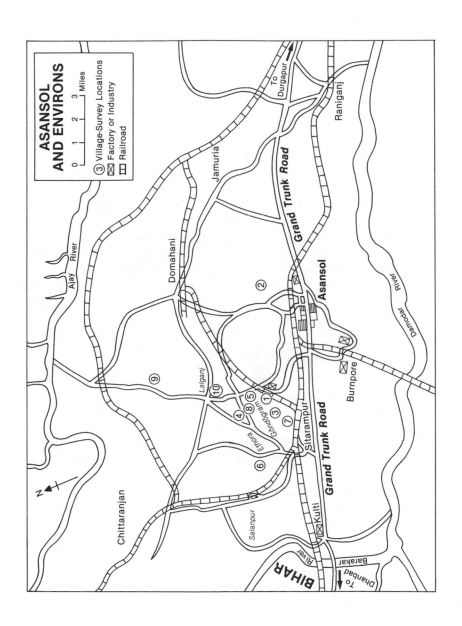

ASANSOL AND ENVIRONS

③ Village-Survey Locations
⊠ Factory or Industry
▦ Railroad

0   1   2   3
Miles

tious name "Das-Walters Company" has been assigned to the factory, just as "Gôndôgram" was assigned to the nearby village.

Whatever the original hopes and expectations of those who established the factory in its rural setting, the senior officials were unanimous in their expressions of resentment, puzzlement, and general unhappiness about the behavior of the inhabitants of Gôndôgram. Their views will be examined in some detail in a later chapter; for the moment, only a summary is needed.

In brief, the factory officials consider the villagers of Gôndôgram to be sickly, unindustrious, clannish, mendacious, whiningly importunate, and trouble-making. They would prefer not to employ them, and in fact do not, except for the minimum forced upon them by early agreements. Furthermore, they extend their distaste for the inhabitants of Gôndôgram to all the villages of the area, and seek their employees elsewhere, preferably from as far away as Bihar.

Does it not sound from all of this as if the village here identified as "Gôndôgram" does indeed exist? Is there not, in fact, an actual settlement, locatable on a map? Of course, but I would argue that geographical appearances and sociological assumptions can sometimes be misleading. The factory officials, for example, see a cluster of homes from their office windows, note that the cluster is separated from more distant clusters by intervening ricefields, and assume, quite reasonably, that it is a "village" and that all who live in it are therefore "villagers." They further assume, equally reasonably, that all the "villagers" who live together in such a small "village" share the same traits and can be characterized in common, and as we have just seen they do not hesitate to do so.

These factory officials, of course, are not social scientists, nor do they pretend to be. With one exception (British-born), they are all Indians. They are all urban-bred and educated, however, and share a cosmopolitan, European-oriented outlook. They know little of the Bengali countryside and its ways. Their views on life in the village around them reflect an absence of direct experience. They have read and loved the short stories of Rabindranath Tagore (and with music and song they celebrate his memory every year), and they are familiar as well with Western (particularly English) perceptions of village life. They imagine a village in India to be a place where independent egalitarian farmers dwell, each with his wife and children around him and his fields nearby. They believe that each such village farmer worships the ancient Vedic gods with offerings of songs and flowers.

To the limited extent that they are aware that the inhabitants of Gôndôgram do not conform to this image, the officials become dismayed and uncomfortable. They warn the visitor about the ignorant ways of the Gôndôgram inhabitants: these people perform animal sacrifices, they live in joint families, and—perhaps worst of all in the eyes of the officials—they still observe the strictures of the "caste system." The officials urge the visitor to believe that all such things are untypical, unfortunate, and most unlikely to withstand the forces of change abroad in the world.

Some persons may be tempted to speculate that the distaste the officials feel for the countryman's behavior contributes significantly to their unwillingness to employ him. Myself, I would give more weight to the implications of the officials' belief that Gôndôgram is a "village," inhabited by "villagers." But let me not anticipate too much; the examination of the interaction of Gôndôgram and factory will come later, along with a consideration of their respective reasons for being dissatisfied with each other.

For the moment, I merely note the factory officials' assumption of a Gôndôgram village, and therefore of a Gôndôgram "villager." I herewith challenge that assumption; if "village" must imply "villager" then we have no village because we will find no characteristic villager. Just to begin with, the inhabitants of Gôndôgram belong to a number of different *jatis*[1] and the members of each jati, we shall discover, have responded differently, and often in completely unrelated ways, to the coming of the factory.

For students of Indian society this should not come as a surprise; surely they know how separate the jatis keep from one another and how distinct each jati perceives its interests to be. Still, we are faced, if we think about it, with serious theoretical and methodological problems, and the literature is not as helpful as it ought to be. There are problems specific to India, and problems that are plaguing anthropologists wherever in the world they conduct research.

Once, the field ethnographer could study his village or band as an isolate. He felt little compulsion to relate it to any external place or person or event. The reader of his ethnography was often ignorant of the very name of the nearest other village or tribe. Today we know that few if any communities are isolates, or ever have been. Networks of interaction and interrelationship envelop the band or village, binding it to others. Goods and materials travel thousands of miles over oceans and through deserts and jungles; ideas and people move with equal facility.

We have long been alerted, therefore, to the need to view the local community in terms of the widest possible context of influence

1. "Jati" is usually translated as "caste." The meaning of "jati" will be explored later on in this chapter, and the nature of "caste" and "caste system" will be discussed throughout this work.

(cf. Steward 1950; Marriott 1955; Manners 1960; etc.). We can expect that, like the other half-million or more residential agglomerates of India commonly known as "villages," Gôndôgram has been substantially affected by political, social, and economic events in the wider nation. The British conquest of north India, indeed, is usually said to have begun with a military victory near another village in Bengal, named "Pôlaśi" (or, in the British annals, "Plassey"). The zemindari tax-farming system, in its British variant, flourished in this state, and modern forms of mining and industry had their origins, for India, in the region that stretches from Raniganj to the Chota Nagpur hills. Gôndôgram lies in the very center of this latter region.

One could go on endlessly; the problem is precisely that of endlessness. We might take as our point of departure the chaotic last decades of the eighteenth century, when the *Bôrgis,* or Mahratta raiders, swept plundering by, for they are still remembered in fearful legend. Or should we start still further back, with the Muslim conquests and conversions in Bengal? Certainly, the effects of those events are very much in evidence in West Bengal and Bangladesh.

Hindu villagers, in their *jatras,* or rural theatrical performances, prefer to gaze even further into the past to the coming of Sivaism to Bengal and its successful conflict with the earlier Buddhism. But if Buddhism was vanquished, it is not gone without a trace; on the day when Buddhists all over South and Southeast Asia commemorate the Buddha's attainment of nirvana, Hindu villagers in Gôndôgram and elsewhere in the region perform a religious ceremony in honor of a divinity known to them now as Dharmôraj, the *dharma*-king, lord of the right way.

Or shall we move in other directions? Santal "tribesmen," presumably descended from the aboriginal inhabitants of the area, sing songs of their unsuccessful wars against the British. The Hindu villagers, of course, remember the struggles for independence and will tell you proudly that Bengalis led the struggles from the first. Winds of change have blown through Gôndôgram, and village Brahmans will tell the visitor earnestly (if privately) that they are disciples of Gandhiji and hope to see an end to all caste-based discrimination in their lifetime.

The Independence of India in 1947 has affected the village in ways too numerous to recount in anything less than a work devoted entirely to that subject. The end of zemindari relationships and their replacement with other forms of taxation; land-distribution laws and laws affecting the traditional occupations of such folk as distillers and goldsmiths—all and more cry out for detailed examination.

And this is an industrialized area; a labor-saving device invented in Czechoslovakia can bring despair to a thatched cottage in Gôndô-gram before a year is out. The people of the countryside must adjust to economic and political decisions made in London, Moscow, and Peking as well as in Calcutta and New Delhi. While some in the village are eyeing Community Development programs and Union Board elections with a mixture of uncertainty and hope, others in the same village are attempting to relate to their own agonies the political and economic theories of Karl Marx.

None of the foregoing—and of much more like it—can properly be ignored if one is to penetrate the lives of the people of Gôndôgram. And yet I am simply not qualified to deal with all these issues adequately. I am not that latter-day Renaissance Man; economist-historian-political scientist cum whatever. I am a cultural anthropologist and I must get about my business, for I think I have information of some interest to impart. It is true that Gôndôgram is part of the total world around it and cannot be interpreted always and only in terms of itself. But it is also true that I am responsible primarily for the presentation of data about events in Gôndôgram and its neighbors, for where else can the reader learn of them?

So we return to the village. But a village, I have argued, is not simply a geographic locality; it is also (and more importantly) the people residing in it. Should we say then that an Indian village is in fact many villages? Or should we renounce the theory and method of community study and concentrate on neighborhoods or caste clusters within them? The issue is a knotty one, but I am happy to affirm that despite it anthropologists have been able to provide us with truly fine studies of the intricacies of village and caste life.

What they have not done, by and large, is assess their theoretical underpinnings. If they are studying communities in India, what exactly do they mean by "community," and is it the same in India as it is elsewhere in the world? Those few who have addressed themselves to this problem have apparently concluded that the approach to *community* developed by Robert Redfield in Yucatán and elsewhere in the New World is somehow adequately applicable to South Asia (cf. Singer 1976: 210). If only a few have taken this position explicitly, even fewer (of all those who have utilized the Redfield model in Indian community studies) have bothered to examine the implications of the model they were using. My own view is that Redfield's classic formulation—that a "little community" is characterized by "distinctiveness, smallness, homogeneity, and all-providing self-sufficiency" (1955: 4)—is a limiting one for India, however useful it may be elsewhere.

How can an Indian village be called "homogeneous" when it is made up of an assortment of ranked jatis? How can it be considered "all-providingly self-sufficient" when, *by its own rules,* it may not be able to provide its members with husbands and wives? Clearly, the Indian rural community is something other than Redfield's "Little Community," and if it is, then attempts to force it into that alien mold must inevitably lead to difficulties. Such a difficulty is exemplified by the "Great Tradition/Little Traditions" approach to religion in the Indian countryside, because—assuming a Redfieldian "folk-urban continuum," as if the variations in Indian religious practice are merely bipolar—it ignores and obscures the actual complexity of rural Indian religion.

This work is not intended as any sort of polemic. My desire is to explain what happened—and why—when a factory was established near a "village" in Bengal. But if we are to understand the changes that take place in the community of which the *village* of Gôndôgram is only one dimension, then surely it is necessary for us to consider first the nature of *community* itself in West Bengal, so that we can perceive clearly the parameters and subdivisions of the total community under study. With this guide we can then attempt to encompass the life of the people in the community before the coming of the factory, and that will be a major portion of this work. We must see the community in full richness and complexity—of social structure, of political and economic interaction, and most of all of value and belief—before we can hope to deal meaningfully with the agents and effects of change.

My approach is explicitly structural, and it is in terms of this approach that I will examine the minutiae of community life and the stresses that have come to bear on that life. My own view of the term "community," and my perceptions of the nature of community in India, must consequently be equally explicit. It is for the reader to determine whether my approach yields dividends of any value in the understanding of social structure, ideology, and—most importantly—of the effects of change in the Indian countryside.

I have argued on an earlier occasion (1972) that Redfield's "Little Community" formulation be replaced, at least for India, by one deriving from the theoretical writings of Conrad M. Arensberg, who urges us to view communities as: "basic units of organization and transmission within a society and its culture" (1961: 248). This approach, in my view, provides us with greater assistance in understanding rural life in India.

Since this present work constitutes, at least in part, an effort to utilize and therefore test the approach I have championed, it is obviously necessary for me to repeat some of the arguments and formulations of my earlier essay.[2]

The issue may be posed as follows: Is *community* a universal feature of culture, manifesting itself differently in different sociocultural systems? For Redfield, it is a ubiquitous if not universal organizational type; when present, it provides a favorable setting for anthropological research. For Arensberg, on the other hand, *community* is a universal human rubric:

> The human community, like that of any animal, is such a minimal unit of population as must coexist in order to insure the continuance of the species. In the human case, it necessarily counts among minimal personnel some instances of every kind of individual in which the species manifests itself: baby, child, adolescent, adult and oldster, of each sex. (*Ibid.*: 249–250.)

Further, he proposes:

> . . . The unit minimum population aggregate, the community, is a structured social field of inter-individual relationships unfolding through time. The community is not only a territorial unit and a unit table of organization; it is also an enduring, temporal pattern of coexistences, an ordered time-progress of individuals, from their births to their deaths, through roles and relationships of each kind known to their species or their culture. In short, it is the minimal common cast of characters supporting the drama of the biogram, in biology, or, in social science, its analogue, of the way of life. (*Ibid.*: 250–251.)

Let us note that "community," as Arensberg approaches it, is many things at once—a "territorial unit," a "table of organization," an "ordered time-progress of individuals"—but it need not be a single "village"! For once we mean by "community" for any given society its basic structural unit "of organization and transmission," there is obviously no reason it may not be represented by a village, a neighborhood, a cluster of villages, or whatever constitutes, in the culture under study, such a basic unit. This book, we have already noted, derives from a study of the differential effects of the presence of a factory upon the component jatis of a Bengal village; the advantages of Arensberg's approach must surely be immediately apparent.

Following Arensberg, then, I have noted five structural elements which, in their interrelationship, form "community" at least in the area of West Bengal studied. The Bengali countryman, indeed, is

2. The following discussion of community derives in large measure from my essay "Community Structure in West Bengal" (1972).

aware of all five, and their names in local dialect would be: *śôŋśar* (family circle), *paṛa* (neighborhood circle), *gram* (village), *jati* (circle of caste-mates), and *côkrô* (circle of villages).

(1) *Śôŋśar* (family circle): This is the subunit of community in which procreation and early socialization take place. In actual manifestation, śôŋśar may be observed within one *ghôr,* or household: an aggregate of people living under one roof, sharing a common kitchen, courtyard, and purse. It is not the same for all strata in the Bengali village, for there is a tendency for śôŋśar among the higher socioeconomic jatis of a village to be joint-family (specifically, brothers together with their wives and children), while for lower socioeconomic strata śôŋśar tends to be nuclear-family.

(2) *Paṛa* (neighborhood circle): This is the subunit, within the Bengali community, of residence, of later socialization, and of continuing informal association. Paṛa manifests itself in a neighborhood cluster of households. The composition of the paṛa, like that of the śôŋśar, is likely to vary among the different socioeconomic strata. The upper-stratum paṛa is inhabited by those who "dominate" the village; those who own or control most of the land. If they are all of one jati—and, even more, descended from one founding ancestor— their paṛa may indeed be quite unified. Otherwise, one is likely to observe distinct social, even physical, boundaries dividing the cluster into sub-paṛas. The middle-stratum paṛa tends to be inhabited primarily by artisans and others who provide special services. It is usually a fairly large, composite paṛa, for rarely are there enough households of any such jatis in a village to make up a paṛa of their own. Lower-stratum paṛas are those inhabited by agricultural laborers or those performing other services considered demeaning. A paṛa of this kind is likely to be physically separated from the other paṛas of the village, and thus is often referred to in the literature on Indian villages as a "hamlet." There seems to be no structural reason for such a distinction, and indeed none is made in the language of Bengal. Such paṛas tend to be small, made up usually of a few households of one jati.

(3) *Gram,* or *gā,* (village): This is the subunit, within the Bengali community, of economic activity, most particularly, the production of the crop for subsistence and market. Gram is manifested in a cluster of paṛas—those of landholders, artisans, and laborers—plus the land surrounding the paṛas on which the total crop is raised. All together, this is what the Western observer sees as the "village."

I am aware that some might object, not unreasonably, to my limitation of gram to "economic activity." There are, as we shall see in the chapters to come, religious and political activities that are village-wide. After all, continued residence within a shared area (use of common ponds, shrines, and so on) contributes to a sense of shared identity, as against inhabitants of a more distant settlement. There is shared scandal and shared memory of good and bad times. What I am arguing, however, is that all of that is structurally irrelevant, that none of it is necessary and in given cases may not occur. Rural economic activity, however—all that enters into the production and distribution of a crop—requires the total gram, at minimum. Those who own or control most of the land will not (often cannot) engage in the basic agriculture-production activities, and so laborers, sharecroppers, or tenant farmers are needed. Specialists are required to provide and repair the equipment needed for production and to provide necessary personal services for the personnel of the gram.

(4) *Jati* (circle of caste-mates): This is the subunit of the Bengali community within which formal social relationships are found—most specifically those of kinship and marriage—and within which we may effectively observe the total life cycle from birth, through marriage, to death. The new generation enters the community through the śôŋśar, but the śôŋśar cannot provide wives for its members and so is maintained over time only because males are provided with wives drawn from other śôŋśars. This distribution of females takes place *only* within the jati. Jati is manifested in a "marriage-circle" (in this part of Bengal called a *śômaj,* or sometimes a *mojliś,* a number of households scattered within a specific set of villages over a delimited geographical area. Within this śômaj (or at most a few contiguous ones of the same jati) the household head must search for spouses for his children. These, too, are the people who will join with him at the time of funereal and other special ceremonies. On economic matters, therefore, his behavior is governed by the nature of his relationships within the gram (particularly if he is not a landholder), but on questions having to do with propriety or morality or the rites of passage, the individual must bow to the authority of his śômaj. As a body, for example, it can exclude a household from the exchange of women.

(5) *Côkrô* (circle of villages): This is the "district" within which people from different villages interact; its boundaries may, but need not always, conform to the political ones. In other words, it is a unit of total resource, for it provides persons and events not otherwise available within the village.

The model of community in West Bengal, presented above, is represented in Figure 1 in order to indicate the relationship between the five structural elements.

It must be emphasized that the foregoing model is offered not as a representation of *any* actual community in West Bengal, but rather as a statement of the elements, and relationships between the ele-

FIGURE 1

Model of "Community" for West Bengal

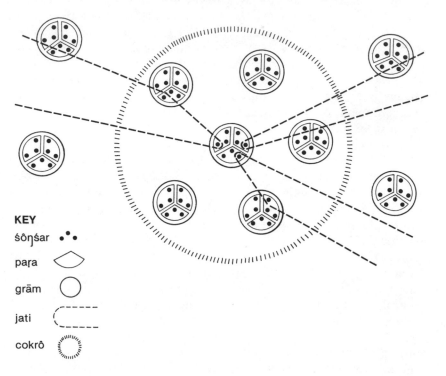

KEY

śôŋśar   •ᵉ•

paṛa   ◇

grām   ○

jati   ⌐-----

cokrô   ⟆⟆⟆

ments, of *community* in West Bengal. It has merit only if it is useful in research and analysis. In the succeeding chapters, with this model in mind, I shall explore social, economic, religious, and political dimensions of Gôndôgram. Then—still leaning upon this model—I shall pursue change and the effects of change upon the inhabitants of Gôndôgram and their community.

The reader must of course determine whether the use of this model has provided this work with any additional measure of merit, whether of perception or of analysis. For me, however, the approach has provided operational flexibility. Each structural element may be expected in actual manifestation to be subject to apparent variation depending upon the socioeconomic perspective selected; the perspective of a landholding Brahman, for example, differs substantially from that of a low-caste plowman. The perspectives of man and woman, of different age groups, are dissimilar, and certain activities and relationships ap-

importance. For me, then, the model assists perception and analysis, providing a multidimensional and multifaceted view of community.

* * *

In addition, use of the foregoing model has illuminated for me certain issues, often ambiguously treated by other writers, perhaps because of their somewhat traditional view of community. I can no longer be content, for example, with this question: Is the Bengali village I am studying "joint-family" or "nuclear-family"? I have noted that both "ideal family" and the statistical reality will vary from para to para and perhaps jati to jati.

Similarly, I have argued that we must seek to understand social relationships within the community not in terms of the village but in terms of the jati. Circumstances have brought representatives of different jatis together (but by no means completely together) in one village. As common residents, they inevitably share experiences and even interests. Their interpretations of those interests, and the implications of those shared experiences, may be widely divergent. Economically, and in a number of political and religious contexts, as we shall see, the lives of the villagers are nevertheless intertwined. It is only in the contexts usually thought of as "social"—the patterned relationships having to do with the life crises (particularly birth, marriage, and death), with commensality, and with the other manifestations of what we tend to think of as friendly association—that interaction between people of different jatis, even if they have lived side by side all their lives, is minimal to the point of non-existence.

And yet, to say that the villagers of different jatis do not associate with each other socially is as inadequate as is the notion that the village constitutes the Indian countryman's social universe. In other words, the relationships between people of the same village but of different jatis are remarkably complex. There are reciprocal economic obligations—usually referred to in the literature as "jajmani" or "jajman-kamin" relationships—along with, as we shall see, inter-caste godparenthood and ritual obligations. For now, let us observe that one avenue through the complexity has been provided by Louis Dumont (1970), who in turn drew upon earlier perceptions of Émile Senart (1894) and particularly of Célestin Bouglé (1908). From these scholars we learn that relationships between people of different castes reflect not one but *three* operative structural principles: that of "separation," that of "hierarchy," and that of "interaction."

Castes in India are "separate": their respective members may not marry members of the other groups, nor may they eat together or associate in most other ways. But they are not merely "separate"; castes in a village arrange themselves into a "hierarchy" in terms of ritual purity-pollution. This hierarchy is expressed, it has been pointed out (see, for example: Dube 1955, Marriott 1959, Freed 1963, etc.), in terms of prestation rules: those higher in the hierarchy will not accept water and certain kinds of cooked food from the members of any group lower than themselves in the hierarchy. Dispute between representatives of two jatis about relative position in the hierarchy is not an uncommon occurrence, according to the literature. Such conflict, however, is alleviated by the functioning of the former principle, that of "separation." For you and I may disagree bitterly as to which of our jatis is higher or lower, but in certain ways it doesn't matter, since we would never eat together or seek the other's children in marriage. Then why the "hierarchy" at all? Because though we are completely separate in terms of formal organization, still we do interact continually, and interaction between totally separate, autocephalous bodies requires some rules—and the principle of "hierarchy" provides a basis for such rules.

Furthermore, if these three principles underlie the "caste system" we must bear in mind that *intra*-caste relationships are very much part of that system, and we should not be surprised to find the principles operating within castes as well as between them. The manifestations, however of intra-caste "hierarchy," "separation," and "interaction" may be expected to vary considerably from jati to jati, and they do.

A particularly important arena of inter-caste interaction (*and* separation, *and* hierarchy!) is in economic activity, as has already been noted. The business of the village, normally, is the production of a crop or crops for sustenance and sale. I have argued here that the village is in fact a "unit of agricultural production" and Arensberg, similarly, has called the Indian village a "land-use corporation" (1961: 255). Certainly, such statements should not be interpreted as allegations that all the land is owned, or even worked, in common, for such is no more the case in the village under consideration here than it is elsewhere in India. The land of Gôndôgram is divided up among separate owners, who work their land independently and dispose of their produce each in his own way and time. The issue is, however, that Gôndôgram—again, like most Indian villages—is not an aggregate of independent egalitarian farmers. We will see farmers who can engage in *no* agricultural activities by themselves. The village contains, in addition to landholders, laborers, and sharecroppers, specialist-artisans and even some specialists (barber, distiller) whose connection with agriculture seems at first glance remote.

Yet we see that a crop is produced, and in principle all those in the village participate and share in that production. The participation and the sharing are very different, jati by jati, so we should not be surprised to find that attitudes toward the desirability or acceptability of certain occupations or goals vary among landholders, laborers, sharecroppers, and artisans as much as do roles. There are different views to be noted about the acceptability of certain foods, and equally about the advantages of living in a rural community. The village—to sum up—is one and many, separated and hierarchically arranged, and yet interacting and interrelated.

* * *

Still, it should be easy enough, one would certainly think, to categorize the religious persuasions of Gôndôgram. After all, there are no Christians among its inhabitants, and presumably no Buddhists. There are no Sikhs, Jews, Parsees, or other such. There is one Muslim, and the Santals are . . . well, Santals, but everyone else would be labeled—and would label himself—as a Hindu.

And even if it is true that many of the beliefs and most of the practices to be found in the village bear little resemblance to those given in the usual Western treatise on Hinduism (if we note, even, that a learned urban Brahman is likely to be surprised, perhaps even repelled, by what passes for Hinduism in Gôndôgram) for many of my readers this too should pose no problem. Hinduism in India, we have been taught, is manifested in a "Great Tradition" (Marriott 1955: 207; Singer 1958)—deriving from the massive body of Hindu religious literature beginning with the Vedas and continuing through the writings of contemporary Indian theologians and philosophers—and in innumerable "Little Traditions," each the composite of some local region's beliefs and practices. The Little Tradition, we know, is a mixture of folk misinterpretation, tribal survival, and syncretic cult.

This "Great Tradition/Little Tradition" conceptual framework has been of great service to scholars seeking to penetrate the complexity that is Indian religion, and I shall make use of it myself in the appropriate section of this work. The dichotomy expressed in this framework is indeed clearly present and must be taken into account in any analysis of religion in India. But is there only *one* dichotomy or opposition? Not in Gôndôgram, and I strongly suspect not in other villages in India. One must therefore be aware that the "Great Tradition/Little Tradition" approach is not sufficient *by itself* for the analysis of Indian religion: used alone it tends often to blur distinctions and obscure issues that would otherwise present themselves as in need of explication and analysis. "Great Tradition," for example, implies one system or body of belief for all the educated, all the elite, of Hinduism. Does such an all-pervasive body of beliefs for all India really exist? Did it ever? I do not profess to know, but certainly my observations in West Bengal have made me profoundly dubious.

The Brahmans of Gôndôgram do indeed articulate with an elite tradition, but it is one that seems to give greater place to female divinities such as Kali and Durga than to Śiva and Viśnu. True, such a statement is debatable, but the point is that it *is* debatable in Bengal, but hardly elsewhere in Hindu India. Further, a substantial portion of the Bengal Hindu elite has traditionally accepted animal sacrifice as a legitimate element in religious ceremony. In other words, we have a distinctive *regional* rather than pan-India Great Tradition.

On the other hand, the use of the plural for "Little Traditions" implies a number of variant folk belief-sets, each a response to some local set of circumstances and therefore peculiar to a district or locality. The elements of a given Little Tradition may reflect awareness of the Great Tradition and even be influenced by it, but they are distinctive, local, not pan-Indian. As an example, a local divinity—deriving from some particular tribal or low-caste divinity, or some regional saint—may be associated with some Great Tradition divinity; Viśnu, perhaps, or Śiva. The point is, of course, that such a divinity would not be known, by original name and original attributes, outside the region of provenience. In Gôndôgram, as in almost every village of India, however, there is a village guardian divinity, the genius of the village, propitiated from village to village by all strata in much the same way for much the same reasons at much the same times. Is this village guardian deity, then, Little Tradition but pan-Indian?

David Mandelbaum (1964) has proposed an alternative ordering of religious belief and practice. He suggests that Hinduism in the Indian village is manifested everywhere in two distinctive but complementary sets of beliefs, practices, and practitioners: the "transcendental" (concerned with the basic, or overriding, theological issues, such as the nature of the universe and the relationships between man and divine) and the "pragmatic" (concerned with response to mundane problems and crises, such as illness, natural disaster, barrenness, and so on). In this perspective, Brahmans and much of the beliefs and practices hitherto associated with Great Tradition Hinduism may be viewed as concerned with the "transcendental," while other village religious practitioners (shamans, in anthropological parlance), their beliefs, practices, and even divinities, all relate to "pragmatic" concerns. All villagers, elite and non-elite, may participate in either domain (a Brahman may offer up a goat to a snake-goddess to save a snake-bitten son, and a low-caste man listen in awe at a reading of the *Bhagavad Gita*), and we can avoid the knotty problems of what is elite, pan-Indian, local, or such.

For all the utility of Mandelbaum's approach (and it will be utilized throughout the appropriate sections), the framework is not helpful in dealing with two issues deriving from this study of Gôndôgram.

First of all, to note there are both transcendental and pragmatic practitioners, beliefs, and divinities side by side in the village does not really help us to understand *why* or *how* they can exist in such contiguity. One may acknowledge a belief structure, for example, that includes an explanation of misfortune as a punishment for misdeeds in a previous incarnation. Or, one may acknowledge a belief that in the event of misfortune the thing to do is to propitiate or otherwise gain the favor of some independent spirit or divinity with the power to prevent or alleviate the misfortune.

What is not explained by Mandelbaum is how the same individual may pursue *both* lines of reasoning at the same time; if my misfortune is a punishment for a previous misdeed, how may my offering to Kali alleviate it? And if misfortunes come and go at the whim of apparently independent divinities, then what price the concept of "karma" in Hinduism? Are we to assume that the Indian villager, the village Brahman even, lacks the intelligence or the insight necessary to perceive such an obvious paradox? After all, a rural Roman Catholic priest in a European village may be forced by circumstance to wink at what he considers superstition or pagan practice, but he knows exactly what is acceptable or permitted according to dogma and what is at variance with it.

The village Brahman in Gôndôgram, on the other hand, like his counterpart elsewhere in India, may indicate a degree of personal distaste for certain modes of belief and practice, but he quite obviously does not consider them *wrong*—they are simply not the way he prefers to go about it. And if he or a member of his family participates occasionally in the pragmatic mode (and they will!) he sees no compromise or contradiction whatever. An effort will be made to resolve this apparent contradiction after an examination of Gôndôgram ritual and belief.

There is a second problem we will have to face as we examine Bengali village religion. Mandelbaum's approach reflects a binary division: transcendental/pragmatic. Similarly, the Great Tradition/Little Tradition approach is a binary one. But Gôndôgram, I have argued, like most Indian villages does not exhibit any simple binary structural division, as, say, between elite and non-elite. There is a caste structure, a hierarchy if you will, involving in principle more than two divisions. Any binary division, therefore, must become at times overly simplistic because it cannot cope with the multiple distinctions between castes as well as within castes. This will become particularly

apparent when we attempt to construct a village
events.

This book, then, represents an effort to expl
complexities of community in West Bengal, Ind
nomic transactions, social relationships, religio
tices, and much else. In the course of the preser
ously held approaches to the nature of Indian vi
examined, and new approaches will be put fort
pose of all this, at least for this book, is to she
mechanisms, processes, and events of change—
and the West Bengal rural community come int
other.

Part I

ILLAGE A

OMMUNI

1

The Village of Gôndôgram

Let us seek a beginning point: the founding of the village. Records, like memories and family genealogies, are hazy, imprecise, full of gaps, and often contradictory. When the factory officials, for example, were in the process of buying up land on which to build the plant, as many as twenty men might show up with shadowy claims to the same third of an acre. And when all those claims were settled, one way or another, still more men with tattered, almost indecipherable deeds would arrive from distant villages. The past is obscured by haze and is difficult to penetrate.

Still, we can be reasonably certain that sometime in the first quarter of the nineteenth century, the earlier Santal[1] inhabitants of the region having been killed, subdued, or driven out, Bengalis were settling on the land north of the town of Asansol. By the second quarter of the nineteenth century the ancestors of many of the present inhabitants of the village had taken up residence.

It was certainly not the most desirable part of Bengal. Bengali rice farmers prefer land that is flat and well-watered. The land from Raniganj to the foothills of the Chota Nagpur Range is what Bengalis call in English, with a note of weariness, "undulating"; to grow rice on it requires sophisticated techniques of embankment construction, verging in places on true terracing. Rainfall, when compared to that of eastern Bengal, is barely sufficient, and other sources of water are uncertain at best. Worst of all, the soil is poor. Unlike much of deltaic Bengal to the east, where farmers hope for two harvests of rice in a

1. A so-called "tribal" people, speaking a language of the Munda-Kol linguistic family, and, as far as is known, the original inhabitants of the Chota Nagpur region.

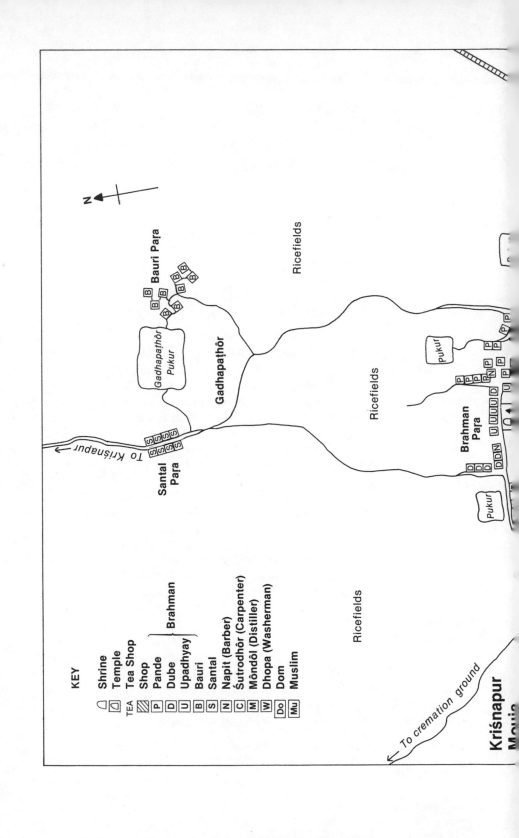

KEY

⌂	Shrine
⌂	Temple
TEA	Tea Shop
▨	Shop
P	Pande ⎫
D	Dube ⎬ Brahman
U	Upadhyay ⎭
B	Bauri
S	Santal
N	Napit (Barber)
C	Śutrodhōr (Carpenter)
M	Mōndōl (Distiller)
W	Dhopa (Washerman)
Do	Dom
Mu	Muslim

N

To Krisnapur →

Santal Para

Gadhapathōr Pukur

Gadhapathōr

Bauri Para

Ricefields

Ricefields

Ricefields

Pukur

Brahman Para

Pukur

Ricefields

To cremation ground →

Kriśnapur
Mauja

lized throughout the appropriate sections), the framework is not helpful in dealing with two issues deriving from this study of Gôndôgram.

First of all, to note there are both transcendental and pragmatic
practitioners, beliefs, and divinities side by side in the village does not
really help us to understand *why* or *how* they can exist in such contiguity. One may acknowledge a belief structure, for example, that
includes an explanation of misfortune as a punishment for misdeeds in
a previous incarnation. Or, one may acknowledge a belief that in the
event of misfortune the thing to do is to propitiate or otherwise gain
the favor of some independent spirit or divinity with the power to
prevent or alleviate the misfortune.

What is not explained by Mandelbaum is how the same individual
may pursue *both* lines of reasoning at the same time; if my misfortune
is a punishment for a previous misdeed, how may my offering to Kali
alleviate it? And if misfortunes come and go at the whim of apparently independent divinities, then what price the concept of "karma"
in Hinduism? Are we to assume that the Indian villager, the village
Brahman even, lacks the intelligence or the insight necessary to perceive such an obvious paradox? After all, a rural Roman Catholic
priest in a European village may be forced by circumstance to wink at
what he considers superstition or pagan practice, but he knows exactly what is acceptable or permitted according to dogma and what is
at variance with it.

The village Brahman in Gôndôgram, on the other hand, like his
counterpart elsewhere in India, may indicate a degree of personal
distaste for certain modes of belief and practice, but he quite obviously does not consider them *wrong*—they are simply not the way he
prefers to go about it. And if he or a member of his family participates
occasionally in the pragmatic mode (and they will!) he sees no compromise or contradiction whatever. An effort will be made to resolve
this apparent contradiction after an examination of Gôndôgram ritual
and belief.

There is a second problem we will have to face as we examine
Bengali village religion. Mandelbaum's approach reflects a binary division: transcendental/pragmatic. Similarly, the Great Tradition/Little
Tradition approach is a binary one. But Gôndôgram, I have argued,
like most Indian villages does not exhibit any simple binary structural
division, as, say, between elite and non-elite. There is a caste structure, a hierarchy if you will, involving in principle more than two
divisions. Any binary division, therefore, must become at times
overly simplistic because it cannot cope with the multiple distinctions
between castes as well as within castes. This will become particularly

apparent when we attempt to construct a village calendar of religious events.

   This book, then, represents an effort to explore and illustrate the complexities of community in West Bengal, India, in terms of economic transactions, social relationships, religious beliefs and practices, and much else. In the course of the presentation certain previously held approaches to the nature of Indian village culture will be examined, and new approaches will be put forth. The ultimate purpose of all this, at least for this book, is to shed some light on the mechanisms, processes, and events of change—as modern industry and the West Bengal rural community come into contact with each other.

Part I

THE VILLAGE AND THE COMMUNITY

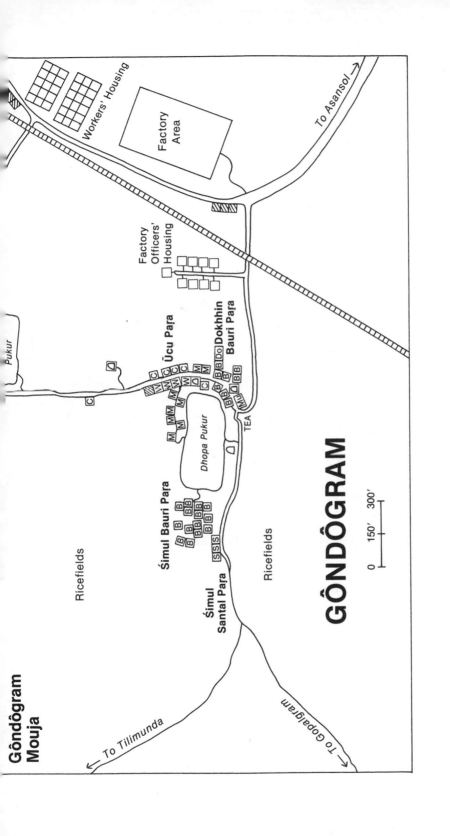

Gôndôgram
Mouja

Workers' Housing

Factory Area

To Asansol →

Factory Officers' Housing

Pukur

Ûcu Paṛa

Dokhhin Bauri Paṛa

Dhopa Pukur

TEA

Śimul Bauri Paṛa

Ricefields

Śimul Santal Paṛa

Ricefields

GÔNDÔGRAM

0   150'   300'

← To Tilimunda

To Gopaïgram →

good year, the ricelands around Asansol grudgingly yield one crop in a year, and that one is rarely bountiful.

The primary attraction of the area was then, as it is today, the possibility of employment in some niche of the industrial sector. Santals from the Santal Parganas to the northwest came or were brought to dig in the collieries that now honeycomb the whole area. Carpenters, members of the Śutrodhôr caste, trekked northward from Bankura District. Other Bengalis and Biharis, along with men from all parts of India (along, indeed, with many from Europe and some from China) drifted into the region during the first half of the nineteenth century as they have continued to do ever since.

Quite obviously, the attraction was not simply the possibility of employment but, for many, the presence of a variety of opportunities: opportunity to follow the ancient trade of one's caste; opportunity to learn a new and more profitable trade; opportunity to offer to those already employed services that would separate them from their wages. Gôndôgram, like many of the villages in the region, has an unusually large number of resident carpenters; there are also many distiller families whose ancestors provided the liquor of fermented palm sap to the laborers. Less than a mile south of Gôndôgram the village of "Haṭ Mônôśa" was established early, and in the *haṭ* (market) there were, among representatives of many other castes, families of Brahmans who provided small loans for needy people. And for some, there can be no doubt, the attraction of the area was land for cultivation—poor land, perhaps, but still attractive to the completely landless.

By the mid-nineteenth century the territory had been mapped and subdivided into *moujas*.[2] We will focus on two moujas, here referred to as "Gôndôgram" mouja and, its neighbor to the north, "Kriśnapur" mouja. In the beginning, the land of Kriśnapur mouja had been acquired by a Hindu temple in Bihar. The priests of the temple, quite apparently, perceived the land as a source of perpetual income. They offered cultivation rights in perpetuity to a number of hitherto landless Brahman families of the Kanauj Brahman group found in eastern Bihar and elsewhere in north India.[3]

2. The word *"mouja"* derives from the Persian *"mouza"* and is translated now as "village"; that is, ideally, a village and its surrounding land.

3. *"Kanauj"* is the contemporary contraction of *"Kanyakubja,"* an ancient kingdom of India from which these Brahmans claim derivation (see Khare, 1970, for an account of contemporary Kanauj Brahman institutions). It might be noted, in passing, that many Brahman groups in India claim Kanauj descent. Scholars may treat some of those claims with skepticism; few of the claims can reflect truly adequate supportive evidence. In any event, the Brahmans of Gôndôgram, and the members of their marriage-circle, claim Kanauj descent, and no one with whom they are in contact has ever seriously challenged the claim.

The offer was of the type know as *Brôhmbottar;* Brahmans were given usufruct (cultivation) rights, but not titles to the land. They might cultivate, administer the affairs of the mouja, and, in return, pay a sum (known as *khajna;* somewhat inadequately translatable as "rent") annually to the owners of the land. In some cases the annual sum fluctuated, or was a proportion of the harvest; in Kriśnapur it was fixed; so many annas per *bigha* (one-third acre) of land. Unspoken, but understood by all, was the right of the landowners at any time to retract the gift and bestow it on others. They could do it for cause—poor productivity, say—or without reason. In Kriśnapur, however, this never happened, and the Brahmans passed the usufruct rights along the generations until land laws changed and their descendants became owners in their own rights.

The Brahmans of Kriśnapur established not one but three settlements in the mouja: Kriśnapur in the north, in some ways the most prosperous; Śivapur, a small cluster of homes on the western border of the mouja; and one on the south, bordering Gôndôgram mouja.

The founder of the southernmost settlement we shall call Achuttananda (*ôchuttônôndô*) Dube. There are no records of Achuttananda, founder of the Dube lineage of Gôndôgram, and only the most shadowy of legends. We know that his *gotrô* (Skt.: *gotra;*-sib) was Goutam and that his *gramer nam* (name deriving from the village of putative ancestral origin in the ancient kingdom of Kanyakubja) was alo Goutam. He was, therefore, a Kanauj Brahman like the others of Kriśnapur mouja, not a Bengali Brahman like the Chattopadhyays, Mukhopadhyays, and others to be found near Asansol and elsewhere in Bengal. He belonged to a marriage-circle that included the Brahmans of Kriśnapur mouja and the other Kanauj Brahmans of nearby villages.

There is no record or memory of Achuttananda's wife; we do not know her name or her gotrô or her village of supposed ancestral origin. Yet Achuttananda must have had a wife, for we know he had descendants. The next Dubes of whom the villagers speak were three brothers. Some say they were the sons of Achuttananda, some that they were grandsons or even great-grandsons. Of these three, the names of two have been forgotten. These three descendants of Achuttananda, then, were the ancestors of the three *ghôrs*[4] of Gôndôgram Dubes: the *bôṛôr ghôr* (senior line) descended from the eldest brother, Guiram, and the *mejhôr* and *chôṭôr ghôrs* (middle and junior lines) descended from the two younger brothers. In Gôndôgram, at the time of this study, there were eight distinct Dube households, all

4. "*Ghôr*" usually glosses as "house" or "household," but in this context "patri-line" would be a better definition.

descended from Guiram Dube and his two brothers, and before them from Achuttananda Dube. The oldest living Dube of the village, the source of all Dube genealogical information, can name all the generations, and almost all descendants, of Guiram and his brothers, and counts himself as a member of the sixth generation from Guiram.

The names that are remembered are of course for the most part those of male ancestors; the names of ancestors' wives or daughters are lost more quickly. It would seem, however, that a daughter, or perhaps a granddaughter, of Guiram or one of his brothers was married to a young man we shall call Khettramahan Upadhyay (*khettrômôhôn upadhhe*). The young man, who was landless, apparently found favor in the eyes of his father-in-law and was brought to Kriśnapur mouja and given land. He built his house near his wife's family, and eight Upadhyay households of Gôndôgram are descended from Khettramahan. The gotrô of Khettramahan (and therefore of all his descendants) was Batśô and his gramer nam was Piaśi.

Sometime after Achuttananda (and possibly after Guiram) but before the coming of Khettramahan Upadhyay, the ancestor of another Kanauj Brahman lineage made his appearance on the scene. His ties, however, were with the mouja of Gôndôgram, to the south of Kriśnapur.

The land of the mouja of Gôndôgram was not as desirable as that of its neighbor to the north. Gôndôgram land is drier and less fertile. It is more undulating and contains more rocks. But rice may be grown on it by those who will make the effort.

Early in the nineteenth century this mouja had come under the control of a man who styled himself (or was called by others) the "Maharaja of Kaśipur." He was, apparently, an old-style zemindar, or tax-farmer, with much land in the area north of Asansol under his control. It would appear that at first he gave little attention to the Gôndôgram mouja, for the land lay fallow, occupied only by a family of washermen (that is, of the Dhopa jati of Bengal), attracted at first, no doubt, by the hope of plying their ancestral occupation among the wage earners around Asansol. There was unoccupied land in the mouja of Gôndôgram, however, and in India even Dhopas dream of becoming *bhôdrôlok*—admirable people, gentlefolk, whose primary defining characteristic in the countryside is the control over land.

Bhoirab (*bhôirôb*) the Washerman, with his family, had settled in Gôndôgram and had put his hand to farming. There are no records of the period, but much dispute. The descendants of Bhoirab in modern Gôndôgram—Dhopa families who all carry the surname Rajak—claim that Bhoirab was a zemindar in his own right, that he had servants and laborers to plow his fields, and that he paid khajna (rent) to the Maharaja of Kaśipur just as the Brahmans to the north paid khajna to the Hindu temple in Bihar. After Bhoirab came his son, Naran, and in the days of Naran the Dhopas lost everything they had. Today, not one Rajak owns even one bigha in Gôndôgram, or anywhere.

The living Dhopas cannot explain the loss; they only know that it happened sometime in the past to some unknown ancestor, for they themselves have even forgotten the names of Bhoirab and Naran! None of them can read or write, and when pressed for an explanation the best they can come up with is this very deficiency; their ancestors were illiterate, while the Brahmans could write. Probably, they say, the ancestors of the Brahmans falsified documents, corresponded with officials . . . who can know the dark and secret ways of the literate, and particularly of the literate Brahman? There are more specific explanations current in the village, particularly among Carpenters and Distillers, the immediate neighbors of the Washermen. It is said that, in the days when Bhoirab flourished, there lived in the market village of Hat Mônôśa to the south a Brahman moneylender named Jagannath (*jagannôth*) Pande. The legend is that he lent money at exorbitant rates and that one of his clients (or victims) was an ancestral Dhopa of Gôndôgram.

The Pandes of Gôndôgram tell it differently, as might be expected. As they relate it, in those days Bhoirab (and they are the only ones in Gôndôgram who remember his name and the name of his son) lived near a pond in the center of Gôndôgram mouja, some distance south of the Dube homes of southern Kriśnapur. Bhoirab, they say, was a pious Hindu, grateful for the prosperity that had come his way. Every morning, therefore, before beginning his day's work, he would trek to the Dube quarter and wait outside the gate of the senior inhabitant, for it gladdened his heart if he could begin each day by gazing upon the face of a Brahman.

Unhappily, however, that meant that the Dube had to begin each of *his* days by gazing on the face of a Washerman. It got to be too much of a burden, and according to Pande legend one day the Dube cried out: "First thing in the morning, and I had to see the face of a Dhopa!"

Offended, Bhoirab went off to Hat Mônôśa and to the home of Jagannath Pande. The Pandes who tell this story profess to have no knowledge of Jagannath's occupation in Hat Mônôśa; they know only that he was a pious man of the Kanauj Brahman jati, proud if landless, of the *Śandillô* gotrô and with the gramer nam Dhutra.

The Pandes say that Bhoirab the Washerman-zemindar made *pronam* (obeisance) to Jagannath and said, "Please come to my

village to live. I will give you land. In return, you need only give me
the dust of your feet every morning."

Jagannath replied, according to his descendants, "Yes, I will
come to your village. But I cannot accept land from you as a gift;
offer me land to live on, but at a reasonable price, and I will pay."
Bhoirab agreed, and so the first Pande came to the village, settling on
the northern border of Gôndôgram, near the Dubes, in what was
eventually to become Brahman *puṛa* (neighborhood).

There are questionable elements to the Pande narrative, not least
of all the assertion that Bhoirab had any land he could actually sell.
This would seem to be in direct contradiction with the other Pande
claim, that Bhoirab occupied the land at the pleasure of the Maharaja
of Kaśipur.

In any case, the Pandes go on to relate how all was well in the
days of Bhoirab, but that Naran, his son, managed the land poorly,
and the Maharaja of Kaśipur came to Jagannath (or perhaps to the
eldest of his three sons, if he had died in the interim) and asked the
Pandes to take over the mouja from the Washermen. The Pandes
agreed, and paid an annual khajna, at first, of 59 rupees and two
annas.

Over time, as more land was cultivated, and as the value of that
land increased, the khajna too was increased (amid some litigation) to
one rupee per bigha (one-third acre) of land per year. The arable land
surrounding what was developing into Gôndôgram village consisted of
more than two thousand bighas in the two moujas. Eventually, by the
twentieth century, the Brahmans of both Gôndôgram and Kriśnapur
moujas had gained title to the lands they cultivated, and the khajna of
one rupee per bigha became a tax of the same amount. After Independence, the villagers say, taxes began to rise again.

Though they were comparative latecomers, the Pandes of Gôndôgram flourished. When it became possible to buy and sell plots of
land, they made inroads into the southern portions of Kriśnapur,
though most of the Pande lands are still to the south, in Gôndôgram.
The ownership picture has become quite complex: Dubes and Upadhyays own plots in Gôndôgram mouja, many of the Brahmans of Gôndôgram own land in distant moujas, and there are plots around Gôndôgram belonging to men of distant villages.

At the time of study, there were sixteen Pande households in
Gôndôgram, divided into three patrilines descended from the three
sons of Jagannath. The oldest Pande in Gôndôgram at the time of the
study, a member of the chôṭôr ghôr (junior line), counted himself as a
member of the fifth generation of Pandes to live in the village since
the coming of Jagannath. He was seventy-five years old.

If the Brahman accounts of the beginnings of Gôndôgram exhibit inconsistencies or lacunae, still they are the only accounts there are. Washermen were present in the early days, but as we have seen the present-day Washermen know only, and dimly, that their ancestors were among the first inhabitants; they have no idea of when that was or what happened.

Another group whose ancestors were presumably present in the village at an early date have even less knowledge or awareness than do Washermen. It seems likely that there were Bauris (a caste of agricultural laborers) in Gôndôgram as soon as there were Brahmans, for the Brahmans of Gôndôgram are forbidden by their jati rules to engage in agricultural activities, such as plowing or harvesting. Present-day Brahmans believe that their ancestors always utilized Bauri labor in the field, and they are convinced that all the present Bauris of Gôndôgram (with the exception of a very few newcomers) are descended from laborers brought in by Brahmans in the earliest days of the village. No one can provide any evidence for this supposition, however, and the Bauris themselves simply shake their heads bewilderedly. At the time of the study there were thirty-one Bauri households in Gôndôgram. None of the Bauris can reckon ancestors beyond grandparents, or is aware of kinsmen more distant than first cousins.

It is certain, however, that all jatis other than Washermen and Bauris arrived after the Brahmans and in fact settled in Gôndôgram only with the permission of that group.

The Carpenters of Gôndôgram still remember their place of origin; they are of the Śutrodhôr (Carpenter) jati of Bankura District to the south, and their ancestors migrated to the Asansol area in search of opportunity. There are many Carpenters in the surrounding region, the greatest single cluster in the nearby village of "Gopalgram" to the southwest, the only village in the district inhabited solely by Carpenters.

The oldest man in Gôndôgram at the time of my arrival (he died during that year) was Śośibośun Śutrodhôr; he was at least ninety years old, it was said. His father's father, Śośibośun claimed, one Kaśinath Śutrodhôr, had been born in Gôndôgram and had been dead these hundred years. The father of Kaśinath, whose name was no longer remembered, had come from Bankura and settled in Gôndôgram. If the account is at all accurate, it would indicate that a Carpenter family was resident in Gôndôgram, across the road from the Washermen, by the middle of the nineteenth century.

Kaśinath had two grandsons; from the elder are descended two households of Gôndôgram Carpenters, and the younger was Śośibośun, himself. Sometime in the early childhood of Śośibośun, another Carpenter moved his family from Gopalgram to Gôndôgram. His first name was Rammohan and, though a Carpenter by jati, he carried the surname, or title, Deyasi (worshiper, religious officiant, priest other than Brahman). Some distant, unknown ancestor of Rammohan had been visited in a dream by the god Dharmôraj, and ever since that dream the male descendants of that Carpenter ancestor have served Dharmôraj as priests and attendants. Rammohan had two grandsons, and the younger—in his late fifties in 1963—lives in Gôndôgram in a large household with the sons of his deceased elder brother and all their children.

After Rammohan came Śrinath Śutrodhôr from parts unknown, and his grandson, a man in his fifties, resides with his family in Gôndôgram. They are related by marriage to the descendants of Kaśinath and Rammohan now (for all the Carpenter families have intermarried), but otherwise they are loners.

Finally, in the 1940s, came Śoilen Śutrodhôr, a poor man of Gopalgram who had married a great-granddaughter of Rammohan Deyasi, to set up the sixth of the present Carpenter households of Gôndôgram.

Sometime after the middle of the nineteenth century, a member of another caste arrived in Gôndôgram. His name has been forgotten, but he was of the Śūri (Distiller) jati, a caste of *tari* ("toddy," or fermented palm sap) makers. He was allowed to settle, although his services were not desired by Brahmans or Carpenters of Gôndôgram; it is speculated that he and his descendants provided liquor for low-caste laborers in the surrounding mines and ricefields. the Śūri, or one of his descendants, took the surname Môndôl, a title of good repute carried by men of many different castes, and it is as Môndôl that the Distillers of Gôndôgram now prefer to be known, though to all others in the village they are still Śūris.

The ancestral Śūri had two sons, and from them are descended five of the eight Môndôl households of Gôndôgram. During the 1940s two Śūri brothers, also calling themselves Môndôl but unrelated to the others, moved to Gôndôgram and established separate households. A decade later came a last Môndôl, also unrelated to the others.

The Asansol area, as has been noted, was once inhabited by Santals, shifting agriculturalists speaking a language of the Munda-Kol subdivision of the great Austro-Asiatic linguistic family. It would seem that few of the original inhabitants survived the European industrial invasion of the nineteenth century, but there were other Santals, particularly in nearby Bihar. As collieries and iron mines began to dot the region, new Santals began to drift in, some coming from as far away as Santal Parganas of Bihar. There was a place for them; Santals took up the occupation of coal miner early in the nineteenth century, and their descendants are still to be found in mines all over Bengal and Bihar.

But coal miners must live somewhere, and so Santal coal miners are to be found, in small clusters, in villages throughout the area. Sometime around the beginning of the present century, a group of Santals asked for and were granted permission by the Brahmans of Gôndôgram to settle in the fields surrounding this village.

In Gôndôgram, the Napit (Barber) is viewed as of the Śudra *varna,* (caste-category) but clean Śudra, with whom a Brahman may associate without fear of pollution. Haripada (*hôripôdô*) Bhandari, the aged and now retired Napit of Gôndôgram, had been born in the village some seventy years before my visit. His father, too, had been born in the village. There was, in addition to Haripada Bhandari's household, another young Napit, Magaram Bhandari, recently brought to the village, occupying a room in a Pande house though not sharing the Pande kitchen.

One household of Doms has been present in the village since about 1950 in a Bauri neighborhood. The eldest woman of the household serves all the women of Gôndôgram as a midwife. The men of the household, along with Doms of other villages, provide music at weddings and religious events in Gôndôgram. There had been an earlier Dom family in Gôndôgram, but they had died without issue, and so Bôndhu Dom and his wife, resident at the time in Chittaranjan, a town to the west of Asansol, had been invited to settle in Gôndôgram by Brahmans.

Since Independence, a family of Muslims has resided in Gôndôgram. They are involved in no way in the social, economic, or ritual life of Gôndôgram, but relations between the one Muslim household and their Hindu neighbors are friendly, if minimal. During the tense days of January 1964, when communal rioting occurred in Calcutta, and when Muslim shopkeepers in Asansol closed their doors and stayed out of sight for a few days, nothing at all untoward happened in Gôndôgram. Rafi the Muslim said that no one threatened or insulted him, and even the most anti-Muslim men of Gôndôgram insisted they had no ill feelings toward the family of Rafi, who were, after all, people of their own village.

In Gôndôgram, at the time of the study, then, there were ninety-six distinct households, with a total population of over six hundred people, representing nine jatis (see Table 1). The thirty-two Kanauj Brahman households were all in Brahman para, the neighborhood, or

TABLE 1   *Composition of Gôndôgram*

	Households	Number of People
Brahman Paṛa		
Brahmans		
Dube	8	56
Pande	16	109
Upadhyay	8	60
Napits (Barbers)	2	7
Ūcu Paṛa		
Śutrodhôrs (Carpenters)	6	75
Śūṛis (Distillers)	8	90
Dhopas (Washermen)	4	25
Gadhapaṭhôr Paṛa		
Bauris	9	47
Santals	8	57
Śimul Paṛa		
Bauris	14	80
Santals	3	14
Dôkkhin Paṛa		
Bauris	8	44
Doms	1	5
Muslims	1	4
Totals:	*96*	*673*

village subdivision, of greatest prestige. The two Napit (Barber) households were also located in Brahman paṛa. Next in prestige as a residential area was Ūcu[5] paṛa, the locus of the eighteen households of
Śutrodhôrs (Carpenters), Śūṛis (Distillers), and Dhopas (Washermen).
The thirty-one households of the Bauri jati (a caste of field laborers)
were divided among three Bauri paṛas, one of which also contained
the Dom and the Muslim household. Eleven households of Santals
resided in two Santal paṛas.

The village has two streets; "Main Street" (north–south) and
"Brahman Street" (east–west). One can enter the village at either
end of Brahman Street or at the southern end of Main Street. Neither
of the streets is paved, nor are any of the roads immediately leading
into them. Narrow footpaths connect outlying Bauri and Santal paṛas
to the main streets of the village.

Villagers claim there are more than twenty *pukurs* (ponds, sometimes referred to in British or Indian literature as "tanks") in Gôndó-

5. The adjective "*ūcu*" means "high" or "elevated" and reflects, according to
villagers, the high embankment of the main village pond, the Dhopa Pukur, found in
this paṛa.

gram, but most of them are small, ephemeral, and inconsequential. Three major pukurs—one in Ūcu para, one in Brahman para, and one shared by a Bauri and a Santal para—provide most of the village's water needs. In a particularly dry year, only the one in Ūcu para is likely to remain filled with water.

North of Dôkkhin Bauri para, on the west side of Main Street, is the eastern embankment of "Dhopa Pukur"—the largest and most important of the ponds of Gôndôgram. This marks the beginning of Ūcu para. The Dhopa Pukur is roughly rectangular in shape. Its contours and depth are obviously the result of human effort, but it does have a strong natural underground spring as its source, unlike the other pukurs, which are formed for the most part by the run-off of rainwater. On the southern side of the Dhopa Pukur is the shrine of the *gram debi/deb'ta* (village guardian spirit).

It is said in Ūcu para that the pukur, in its original unimproved form, goes back before the founding of the village; that its presence, indeed, was what first attracted the ancestral Washerman to the site, for in rural Bengal how can you be a washerman, have you ever so many customers, without a pond? Today, the pond, still known as Dhopa Pukur, belongs to a combine of Pande households, who give exclusive fishing rights to a non-resident Jele (Fisherman) for half the profits. Anyone, however, may bathe in the pukur or draw water for the house from it, and Washermen still wash their clothes in it and pound them clean on the rocks of the pukur's embankments.

Once, earlier in this century, the houses of Dôkkhin Bauri para did not extend up Main Street beyond the beginning of the pukur, and one had to traverse the eastern embankment of the pukur before coming to the first house of Ūcu para. By the 1960s, however, the houses of the Bauri para had crept northward along the eastern side of Main Street, and the houses of Ūcu para had crept southward, until they have almost met. The heart of Ūcu para, however, is at the northeast corner of the pukur where, surrounded on all sides by homes of Carpenters, Washermen, and Distillers, stands the courtyard of the Dharmôraj *mondir,* the temple of the "king of the right way"—in the forgotten past, the Buddha, now identified as Jam (Yama, ruler of the underworld in the Hindu pantheon).

North of the temple, a path leads to a cluster of Distiller homes near the northern embankment of the pukur, and beyond the path, on Main Street, is the one small shop of Gôndôgram, owned by a Distiller. Here, too, are the Washerman homes, probably the oldest residential locations in Gôndôgram, for some boast "Bôrgi wells"—holes where wealth was hidden from the Bôrgi (Mahratta) raiders. Carpenter homes are for the most part on the eastern side of Main Street,

from the end of the Bauri paṛa northward to parallel to the Washerman homes. Ūcu paṛa ends here, and apart from two edifices Main
Street passes no more buildings until it reaches Brahman paṛa.

The first of these two buildings is the unfinished Durga mondir,
temple to the goddess Durga, on the eastern side, in a large open
field. On the western side of the road, farther north, is the walled
compound of the grandson of Śrinath Śutrodhôr and his family; they
are on poor terms both with Brahmans to the north and with Ūcu paṛa
to the south, and associate minimally with anyone but close relatives
residing in other villages.

Main Street ends, and Brahman paṛa begins, with a crumbling,
unused well set in the middle of the street. A few of the Brahman
homes have wells of their own, but people claim to prefer the water of
the pukurs. Some of the Brahmans go to Dhopa Pukur, but most
utilize a smaller pukur, referred to here as ''Brahman Pukur,'' on the
east side of Main Street at its northern terminus. Here, screened
partially by bushes and trees, Brahman men and women come to
bathe, wash their intimate clothing, and draw water for home use.
Across Main Street from the pukur, just before the well, are a few
Upadhyay houses, creeping southward from the crowded settlement.

The thirty-two Brahman households were all in Brahman paṛa at
the time of the study, but the three family clusters— lineages, really—
were noticeably separated within the paṛa. The section north of the
well at the end of Main Street was inhabited mostly by Pandes, and
Pandes were also to be found along the eastern arm of Brahman
Street. Most of the Dubes lived along the western arm of Brahman
Street, with Upadhyays filling up the interstices between Dube and
Pande sections. The two Napit (Barber) households and the old one-
room schoolhouse were on the western, or Dube, side of Brahman
Street, along with a shrine dedicated to Rôkkhô-Kali, the goddess
Kali in a special manifestation as protectress of the village.

West of the last Dube house the road narrows abruptly, becoming hardly more than a wide footpath through ricefields. Crumbling
remains of ancient housesites do indicate that in earlier years the
Dubes lived much farther than they do now from the other Brahmans,
only gradually and perhaps reluctantly moving their homes nearer to
what was developing into Brahman paṛa, the neighborhood of highest
prestige of the emerging village. The path continues, winding westward through field and wasteland, until it ends on the banks of a
small, seemingly deserted pond. This is the site of the *Śôśan* (cremation site), where the dead of Gôndôgram and of a number of surrounding villages are cremated.

Back in Brahman paṛa there is a path threading northward past the Pande homes. It goes on for perhaps half a mile, over fields and sometimes over embankments between fields, until it reaches a slab-like stone known as the *gadhapaṭhôr* (donkey stone). No one presently alive in Gôndôgram remembers why the stone was so named. In any event, there is a pukur (known as Gadhapaṭhôr Pukur) just north of the stone, and the path splits here, one branch going northeast to Gadhapaṭhôr Bauri paṛa and the other northwest to Gadhapaṭhôr Santal paṛa. This latter path continues northward to the two settlements of Kriśnapur mouja.

2

Separation, Interaction, Hierarchy

The inhabitants of Gôndôgram can perhaps best be perceived as members of distinctive and separate ethnic groups (known to them as jatis and to the Western reader as castes). Circumstance has brought them all together (and by no means completely together) in one village. As common residents, even as "sons of the village," they inevitably share certain experiences and interests, and yet the implications of those shared experiences may be widely divergent. Even their sense of common identity ("sons of the village") is usually shallow, for in many situations their identity with "jat-brothers" will easily take precedence.

Economically, and in a number of political and religious contexts, the lives of the villagers are intertwined. In the contexts usually thought of as "social"—the patterned relationships having to do with the life crises (birth, marriage, and death), with eating together and playing together, and with forms of what we tend to think of as friendly association— interaction between people of different jatis, even if they have lived side by side all their lives, is minimal to the point of nonexistence.

But to say that the villagers of different jatis do not associate with each other, in both formal and informal ways, is equally false. The relationship between people of the same village, but of different jatis, is complex. There are, of course, reciprocal economic obligations. But there are other reciprocal relationships as well, quite important in the village, if not as well known outside of it: the "godparent" relationship of elder Carpenter to young Brahman; the Brahman feast at which *all* in the village must be fed; and so on.

"Hierarchy" is manifested in inter-caste relationships in Gôndôgram, as elsewhere in India. It is agreed, for example, that Brahmans are at the apex; anyone may take water and food from them and they will accept water and (cooked) food from no one. All other jatis arrange themselves below the Brahman, expressing their putative position in the jati hierarchy in terms of *jôl-côl* exchange: from whom will they accept water (higher than, or equal to, themselves), and from whom will they not accept water (lower than themselves)? There is much dispute over these matters in almost any village, and an absence of absolute consensus. Bauris and Santals in Gôndôgram, for example, dispute the other's claim to higher position in the hierarchy.

Still, the principle of hierarchy is recognized by all (with the possible exception of the Santals). The varna system is known, and is referred to, at least by villagers of the higher-ranked jatis. Under this approach to hierarchy, the Kanauj Brahmans of Gôndôgram, as the representatives of the Brahman varna, have the highest rank in the village. There are no Kśatriya or Vaisya jatis in the village, though there are some in neighboring settlements. In Gôndôgram next in rank would be the two "clean Śudra" jatis: Napits and then Carpenters.

In the village, Washerman and Distiller are also viewed as Śudra, but as "unclean Śudra." In Bengal at large, however, the Śuṛi (Distiller) caste is considered "unclean" or "untouchable" and is, therefore, one of the "scheduled" castes for which special provisions are made in education and in government employment. Since the Distillers and Carpenters of Gôndôgram live in the same paṛa and are approximately equal in wealth and property, the Distiller prerogatives are a source of irritation to some Carpenters, who have been heard to complain: "We must compete with Brahmans on an equal level!"

In western Bengal, the most ubiquitous caste of field laborers is that of the Bauri. Though they are "unclean," or, in local parlance, "*namaśudrô*,"[1] they are by no means at the bottom of the social hierarchy. It is universally agreed that they are "cleaner" than such castes as *muci* (Leatherworker) or *mæthôr* ("Sweeper" or cleaner of latrines). None of these particular castes, however, is represented in Gôndôgram. Of the castes of Gôndôgram itself, Bauris will accept food and water from all except Doms and Santals, but none—including Doms and Santals—will accept food or water from the Bauris.

The issue is actually a somewhat hypothetical one, since in every caste water is procured for each household by the women of that

1. "*Namaśudra*" is, and has been, defined in many ways in Bengal. For some, it is only a synonym for "Chandāl," a low-ranked caste of what was formerly East Bengal. The villagers of Gôndôgram, and their neighbors, translate it as "below the Śudra varna," which would be in accord with one of the definitions noted by Risley (1892: 183).

household and by nobody else, and since no one offers food to anyone else, apart from those few wealthy people (mostly Brahmans and
a few Carpenters) who feed their servants (mostly Bauris plus an
occasional Dom or Washerman). A few of the very wealthy of the
village (which again means the Brahmans) conduct religious events at
which "everyone in the village" is fed, but otherwise feasts, when
they do occur, are in every caste for one's caste-brothers at rites of
passage.

The Gôndôgram Bauris make a point of their high position in
another hierarchy, that within the Bauri jati as a whole. The jati, they
claim, has four major subdivisions, based upon ancient practices for
cleaning the ground upon which one has just eaten. Their ancestors,
they say, cleansed the eating area with *gobara* (cow dung), and so
they are Gobara Bauris, the highest of the four subdivisions, and will
not marry with any of the other three. On the other hand, they admit,
all the Bauris of all the surrounding villages are also Gobara Bauris;
they have never seen any others. But somewhere to the east in Bengal are representatives of the other, lower, subdivisions.

Bauris associate almost exclusively with Bauris, within the
village. One young Bauri man, who has an excellent singing voice,
may be seen occasionally sitting and singing with a small group of
Brahman youths, all in their late teens and early twenties, who gather
together of an evening in a Brahman "drawing room" for a music
session. Otherwise, the relationships between Brahman and Bauri
appear to be exclusively those of master or servant, or perhaps, employer and employee. A few Carpenters employ Bauri laborers, and
so have a similar relationship with their employees, but for the most
part Bauris have less interaction with the people of Ūcu paṛa than
they do with the people of Brahman paṛa. There is, in fact, considerable hostility between the inhabitants of the Bauri paṛa adjoining Ūcu
paṛa and their nearest neighbors (one incident growing out of this
hostility will be discussed in a later section), and there is similar
hostility between the inhabitants of Gadhapaṭhôr Bauri paṛa and the
neighboring Santals.

In the fields surrounding the village, one sees clusters of small
boys playing, mostly six to eight years of age and a half-dozen or so
in number for each cluster. Brahman boys play only with boys of
their own jati, as do Bauri and Santal boys, though the boys of Ūcu
paṛa playing together may be of any of the three jatis represented
there. Very occasionally, Brahman and Ūcu paṛa boys will get together for a game, but never any of these with Bauri or Santal boys.

"Our mothers say they are dirty and to stay away from them,"
Brahman and Ūcu paṛa boys relate when asked why they are not

playing with the Bauri boys hardly fifty feet away. "They think we are dirty," Bauri boys say, when asked the same question, and shrug.

When questioned about gotrô (sib), Gôndôgram Bauris insist emphatically that Bauris, like other respectable castes, have "gotrô." What they call gotrô, however, seems structurally very different from the exogamous patrisibs of Brahmans and others. "Our gotrô," say the Bauris proudly, "is Kukur (dog). We are Kukur Bauris." All Bauris, in fact, are "Kukur" as far as they know. This means that no Bauri, on pain of punishment by other Bauris (possibly even expulsion from the caste), may touch the carcass of a dead dog; "We and the dog are one." It would appear, therefore, that what the Bauris call "gotrô" represents their totem, which serves for the entire endogamous group.

A few of the Bauris claim an additional gotrô for themselves, again for "all Bauris": *Kaśbôk* (the heron, a bird that no Bauri residing in Gôndôgram has ever seen). It is tempting to consider this a residue of some ancient totemic division when the Bauris were an independent tribe, if indeed they ever were. Another possible explanation, however, is that the Kaśbôk appelation has been borrowed in recent times from their Santal neighbors, among whom it has clear meaning and structural significance.

In English the Santals are usually called (by everyone, including the Bengalis) a "tribe." In the Bengali language, however, the only word used for them is *"jati."* Brahmans consider them about as ritually unclean as they do the Bauris. They do note, however, that Bauris are Hindus, while Santals are not. Santals look down on Bauris as unclean, physically and ritually, but as a matter of fact Santals are not eager to share food and water with anyone, not even Brahmans.

The Santal paras of Gôndôgram are strikingly different from the other paras of the village. Though the people are for the most part as poor as the Bauris, and are considered by the bhôdrôlok (gentlefolk) to be of about the same low social level, the Santals are self-contained and sure of themselves. Santal houses, all of them mud-walled and thatched, are kept in excellent condition, with seemingly never a scratch on the walls or a section of thatch out of place. Unlike almost all the other paras of Gôndôgram, houses in both Santal paras are arranged side by side in straight lines; obviously the location of houses, their positions, and the directions they face are all matters of general consensus.

Most striking, however, is the difference in the condition of the lanes outside the houses; at almost any hour of the day Santal women may be seen sweeping the streets. When they clean their own yards

In Santal paṛa a man stands in front of his home. Santals take great pride in the cleanliness of their streets and in the appearance of their homes.

they simply continue through their doorways and verandas (for Santal houses face the street; besides the veranda and the usually open doorways, there are windows opening on the street) out into the roadway. Housewives in other paras may appear in their doorways momentarily in order to sweep refuse out into the street; Santal housewives sweep both interior and exterior refuse together into a neat refuse heap, jointly shared, off to one side and away from all homes.

Santal paras, furthermore, are alive with laughter and communal visiting. Women and children are in and out of one another's homes; if a man has an item of household furniture or agricultural equipment to repair he will drag it into the street outside his house to work on it, and other men will gather to watch him. Biting comments on skill or clumsiness will pass back and forth. It may be stated unequivocally that all the families in the para are on good terms, for if they were not, somebody would soon move away to another para or another village. Santals shift residence much more casually than do the other villagers.

Not only is there a strong sense of communal interaction in a Santal para, but there are also structured relationships that are missing in other paras. In the other paras there are leaders (though invariably they have enemies and there are factional disputes). These leaders may be wealthy men or simply wise ones. They have no titles and their positions are informal and often challenged. In a Santal para, however, there are invariably three formal officials, chosen by the para and accepted as such by all. There must be a *majhi môrôl* (headman, or judge), a *naiki* (religious officiant), and a *gurit* (town crier) in every para; in the smaller Śimul Santal para, where there are only three households, each household head holds one of the three offices.

The question of evaluating the separatist attitudes of a pariah group is always a tricky one. A Bauri child may say resentfully, for example, "Brahmans won't let us in their kitchens, but my mother says that if a Brahman came into *her* kitchen she'd throw her food away, too!" It sounds like mere bravado, and probably is. But the Santals seem genuinely unconcerned about the low rank assigned to them by the Bengalis around them. They know they keep their houses and streets cleaner than do Bengalis of any jati, and they know they themselves are Santals—and what could possibly be better than that? They have, in other words, an élan, and a pride in themselves and a sureness of worth, completely missing in the Bauri and remarkably similar to that of the Brahman.

Doms, who live with Bauris, consider themselves a cut above the latter, who disagree. To everyone else in the village, however, both

Dom and Bauri are unclean, or namaśudrô. The Santals, we have
seen, are considered equally unclean and, in addition, "not Hindu."
The same holds for the Muslim family residing in a Bauri paṛa. The
Santals reject the Hindu hierarchy; the Muslim keeps his opinions to
himself.

And, given the operative principle of "separation," the differences of opinion about position in the hierarchy hardly matter very
much. The disagreements about hierarchy or precedence have little
impact on commensality, for example; the rule in Gôndôgram is that,
apart from certain specific exceptions, no men of different jatis eat or
drink together. One dines customarily with the members of one's own
jati, and indeed for the most part with members of one's own household. To go further, even in one's household one avoids dining with
people of the other sex or of different age. Most of any individual's
meals, therefore, are eaten in solitude: in a corner, facing a wall, perhaps with a mother (or wife, if one is an adult male) hovering nearby
with more food, but no one sitting alongside, eating in company.

That is, for most of the meals an individual eats during the year.
There are exceptions and special cases, of course; a young child will
eat with his or her mother, possibly out of the same plate. At special
feasts—at such times as marriage and death—one eats *poŋkti-bhojôn*
in public, that is, sitting in a row made up of caste-mates of the same
sex. All begin eating together and try to finish together. At certain
village feasts, sponsored for the most part by wealthy Brahmans, all
the castes of the village will be fed, but separately: first Brahmans will
eat, then clean Śudras, then unclean Śudras (always caste-mates of
the same sex together, sitting apart from any other caste being fed at
the same time), and finally the Bauris, who wait outside the compound for the final scrapings of the pots. Last of all are the beggars
(not of the village, but drawn from all over the district), who receive
the leavings on the plates. Santals, who would be likely to be classed
with Bauris, stay away from such feasts.

There are other exceptions. Brahmans and the wealthier folk of
Ūcu paṛa will press a cup of tea on any guest. In practice, this means
for the most part visiting officials, the rather occasional anthropologist or other foreigner, and, almost as rarely, a villager of another
caste who happens to drop in on a business matter. This means, in
essence, that a bhôdrôlok of any caste will offer a cup of tea to
another bhôdrôlok of any caste, for a Bauri or a Dom will not come
"to visit"—and is not likely to be offered a cup of tea by anyone. The
poorer folk, having no business, usually visit neither the wealthier nor
each other.

Another exception to the rule applies to the rare occasion when a villager dines or drinks outside the community structure; in town, in the factory canteen, or in a tea shop somewhere along the road. In theory, and according to law, such public establishments serve men of any caste; discrimination is forbidden. In practice, certain hotels or restaurants attract a clientele of one range of castes, while other eating places cater to a different range. Still, the rules of commensality are abrogated under such conditions—but the villager hardly ever visits such places anyway.

And, finally, the only actual circumstance of "accepting cooked food from another caste" that occurs in Gôndôgram (apart from special ceremonial feasts) has to do with wealthy Brahmans and their Bauri servants. A Bauri woman who works for a Brahman as a household servant receives, as part of her wages, a heaping plate of cooked rice every evening at the end of her day's work. This rice, plus some portions of curried fish or vegetables (or whatever the Brahmans are having for dinner), constitutes the evening meal for her family.

The disagreements about position in the hierarchy have absolutely nothing to do with marriage; every marriage in every jati—on penalty of expulsion from the jati—takes place invariably within the jati and within a known and usually delineated marriage-circle. Nobody may marry out of the jati, whether up, down, or sideways. From the perspective of *marriage,* therefore, it can be said that the jatis are in fact not arranged in a "hierarchy"; there are only absolutely separated groups.

On the other hand, within the jati "hierarchy" is often to be noted. Gobara Bauris, we have seen, profess to look down on other Bauris, and we shall find similar phenomena in other jatis. The point is that the three structural principles—separation, interaction, hierarchy—are always present and always operative in different combinations and permutations.

3

Household and Family

"When I was a child in my grandfather's house . . . " is invariably
the way an old Brahman man will begin an account of what life was
like in Gôndôgram in the early years of the century. Some elderly
Carpenters might begin an account that way, too, but no Bauri or
Santal elders would, for they grew up, almost invariably, in their
father's homes. How, then, shall we describe family structure in Gôndôgram? Dare we say that people in the village live customarily in
joint families? No, because only a minority (though a substantial minority) of households are joint-family. But can we not say that joint-
family is the ideal form, preferred even by those whose present households do not conform to the ideal? No again, because only for the
bhôdrôlok, the landholding gentlefolk, is joint-family the ideal. The
Brahmans, the few wealthy Carpenters and Distillers, prefer to live—
do their best to live—brothers and their families together in the home
of their father. Poorer men, however, and particularly Bauris, live
typically in nuclear-family households and indicate no desire to share
quarters with brothers and parents.

The typical Brahman residence, in Gôndôgram, is a walled compound. At the entrance in the wall there is usually a small anteroom,
customarily referred to by an English term: the "drawing room."
Here visitors are received and welcomed. If they are not Brahmans
(or servants of the household), they rarely penetrate farther. Beyond
the "drawing room" is the *uthan,* or courtyard, containing the
tulsi-môncô, or family shrine, incorporating the sacred tulsi (basil)
plant. There are also pieces of farm equipment and much else. Much
of the men's work of the household takes place in the courtyard; rice
is threshed here and, if there is room enough, stored here. At one side

A street in Brahman para. The windowless houses seem to turn their backs to the street, for the interior courtyard is the focus of houshold activities.

is the cattle byre. Surrounding the uṭhan are the dwelling quarters, and few other than the family may penetrate these. Here are the bedrooms, shrines, storerooms, and—most of all—the kitchen, in which the cooking is done. Near the kitchen is the room in which the family eats.

The walls of the Brahman compounds are usually too high to see over; most are of packed mud but a few are constructed of brick. Within the walls, the houses themselves are mostly of mud with thatched roofs, but about one third of the Brahman homes (thirteen, to be exact) are of the type known as *pôkkô*,[1] built of brick, cement, and plaster, often two or three stories tall. There are few pôkkô houses in Gôndôgram outside of Brahman paṛa.

Though Brahman compounds adjoin one another, often sharing walls in common, the living quarters—set variously at different points in different compounds—are separated from those of other compounds. Despite the proximity of other compounds, the average Brahman compound seems to ignore its neighbors; there is little sense of consensus about alignment of houses, direction in which to face, or even neighborhood center of focus. The uṭhan and the living quarters are usually kept clean; a fresh application of cow dung and mud is smeared on the kitchen floor every morning, but the condition of the street just outside the compound wall is of no concern to the householder.

Although most Brahmans of Gôndôgram will insist, when asked, that the ideal household arrangement is that of brothers living together under one roof with their respective wives and children, sharing their father's property (even more ideally, with the old father and mother still alive and in the household), not every household reflects this ideal (see Table 2). Of the thirty-two separate Brahman households, fifteen exhibit one form or another of joint-family composition (two or more married brothers, two marital units or more of different generations, or both). Fourteen Brahman households contained no more than a nuclear family (husband, wife, and unmarried children), and three households were made up of various fragmented clusters (a mother and her adult unmarried son, two unmarried men—uncle and nephew—living together, and so on).

Some of the nuclear households are clearly potentially "joint," as where the younger brothers of the household head are still in school but are likely to continue living with him after their marriages. In a few cases, however, brothers have separated, divided their inheritance, and established independent households. Most such men

1. "*Pakka*" is from a term meaning "cooked" or "ripe" and thus by extension implying "fulfilled" or "proper" or "of good quality."

TABLE 2   *Household Types*

	Joint-Family				
Jati	Fraternal Only	Filial Only	Both	Nuclear-Family	Fragmented
Brahman	3	6	6	14	3
Barber		1			1
Carpenter	1	3	1	1	
Distiller	2	2	1	3	
Washerman		1		3	
Bauri	2	7	2	19	1
Santal	1	4	1	5	
Dom				1	
Muslim		1			
Totals:	*9*	*25*	*11*	*46*	*5*
	(Total Joint-Family: 45)				

still indicate a preference for joint household as an ideal arrangement, blaming their contentious brothers for their family's inability to conform to the ideal.

It is understandable that they should regret the break-up; life in a joint-family compound has many advantages from the point of view of a Gôndôgram Brahman. Most important, unquestionably, is the economic advantage. A man who is part of a joint family shares in the wealth of the entire family: the harvest of the undivided land and whatever income the working members of the household bring in. His personal needs and those of his children (for marriage and educational expenses) are more likely to be met by the purse of the joint family than by his private purse when he lives separately.

Division of inherited land among a group of brothers who have decided to go their separate ways is unpleasant and unrewarding at best; at worst, it can degenerate into protracted and ugly legal battles. The Bengal landholding villager will insist that all sons must inherit and must inherit equally.[2] This principle does *not* mean simply that if, say, four brothers inherit four acres of land from their father each must receive one acre of land. Rather, each must receive one quarter of all the *kinds* of land in the total property; the fertile bottom land, the sandy soil, the rocky patches, and so on. Each will emerge from the division, therefore, with a set of scattered parcels and fragments, some too small to be economically worth working. Break-up of a joint family, it can be seen, must diminish everyone.

2. Indian law, since Independence, has required that sisters also be included in the equal division, but this rarely if ever happens in Gôndôgram and its neighbors.

But there are other advantages to living together. Work and pleasure are shared, the latter no small point when it is remembered that
one rarely socializes outside one's own household. As for work, it is
under the supervision of the male head of the household, and of his
counterpart, the female head of the household.

In a joint-family Brahman household, the day begins early, before 6 A.M., as it does in any village household. There are no latrines
or other sanitary facilities in Gôndôgram, and so the women arise at
dawn or before to make their separate ways to the open fields, each
carrying a container of water. Returning home, the women put together a hurried breakfast for the men and children who are now
awakening and going about their own ablutions.

All of this is much the same in every household, but in joint-
family households there are significant differences in procedure after
the morning meal, and after the older children have gone off to school
or play. Where, in the nuclear household, there is only one adult
woman, she must see to all the woman's work of the day. Where
there is only one adult man, he can either go to a job, supervise his
crop, or do other necessary work about his property. He cannot do
all. After the morning meal in a joint-family household, however, the
malik, the household head, assembles his brothers and the older boys
and distributes assignments. Those with jobs in factory and town will,
of course, go off to work. One or two men will go out to the scattered
fields and supervise the laborers. Another will be told to see to the
improvement or extension of irrigation ditches, and still another may
be sent off to the market.

And when the men and children have gone off about their business, the women bathe and eat and then assemble before the eldest
female. She assigns their tasks: one to see to the day's meals and
another to clean or supervise the cleaning of the house and compound; one to see to the laundry and sewing and another to mind all
the babies and small children; and so on. If the eldest female wishes,
tasks may be changed the next day, or the assignments may hold until
further notice.

When the daughters of the household grow up, it is the duty of
the eldest male and female to decide which of the girls is to be married next and to seek a husband for her. In the event of an inquiry
from the family of a marriageable girl, they must decide which of the
boys of their household is ready for marriage (see Klass 1966). They
decide, too, which if any of the children are to be sent to receive
advanced education. In brief, together they make all the important
decisions for the members of the household; that is, those involving
any outlay of money.

A street scene in a Bauri para. The roofs are poorly thatched and the walls this is a depressed neighborhood of very poor

The rule is that the malik (household head) has the authority to make all decisions. There is nothing to prevent him from consulting with other adults in the household, or even outside it, before making a decision. A sensible malik will want to discuss things with his female counterpart (wife or mother), and in the arrangement of the marriage of a child not his own (of a younger brother, say, or of his son) the parents of the child are certainly likely to enter into the discussions. The point is, however, that he doesn't have to discuss his decisions with anyone if he doesn't want to; in the end, he is the malik, and, therefore, the guardian of every person in his house, and his decision cannot and will not be challenged.

One man, malik of a household that included the families of three younger brothers, was asked how he would react to an objection to a decision he might make. Suppose, for example (he was asked), he had decided that one particular girl of the household was next to be married, or one among the older boys was to be sent to secondary school, and suppose one or more of his brothers questioned the malik's judgment and advanced an argument for a different child? "My brothers know," he replied quietly, "that I am ready to divide up the family property at any time they ask me to." The options available to an adult member of a joint family are either to accept the decision of the malik or break up the household.

We note, therefore, that the joint-family household exhibits a hierarchical structure, reflecting seniority in age modified by sexual ascription. All juniors treat with respect, and obey without argument (in principle), all senior members of the household of the same sex. Seniors of the opposite sex within the family are also afforded respect, but lines of authority may be obscured by varieties of avoidance and joking relationships between men and women.

If an old man, then, begins an account of his boyhood with the words, "When I was a child in my grandfather's house . . . ," he is being very accurate. "Father" may well have been present in the house, probably even sharing the same bedroom with the mother and the other children. The small boy owed his father respect and obedience, but he owed them, too, to any male in the household older than himself: his older brothers and his father's brothers. All decisions affecting the boy's life (and the lives of all in the house) were made by the malik. If "Father" is not the malik (and he is not if his own father is alive or if he has an older brother), then he has no more authority, no more power to make decisions, than his son or any other non-malik male in the household. There is a hierarchy of respect within the family, but for each sex the person at the top has all the *authority*, unless he or she is senile. The household has only one officer; all the rest are merely spear-carriers. Thus, a youth respects and obeys his older brothers and his father, but he knows that all decisions are really made by, and flow from, the malik.

The people who live in Ūcu paṛa (the Carpenters, Distillers, and Washermen) also prefer when possible to live in joint-family households. And, interestingly, while there is more discussion in this paṛa about the difficulties and problems of such households, joint-family households are more common here than in Brahman paṛa. Of the eighteen households of Ūcu paṛa, eleven exhibit joint-family composition (eight of them primarily filial, however, rather than fraternal) and only seven are nuclear. Among the Carpenters, furthermore, all but one household reflects joint-family composition. Of the four Washerman households, on the other hand, only one is joint-family, while three are nuclear.

The homes of Ūcu paṛa are for the most part set closely together, lined up along Main Street. There are only two pôkkô (brick and plaster) houses in Ūcu paṛa, one of a Carpenter and one of a Distiller. The living quarters are usually entered directly from the street, with a wall—when there is one—in the rear, enclosing a small uthan (court-yard) and cooking area. If the houses are on the street, however, it would not be accurate to say they "face" the street; they seem rather to turn their backs on it. What faces the street in most cases is a high, windowless adobe wall, a continuation often of the adjoining house-wall, broken only by a doorway. In some cases the wall exhibits a ledge, or steplike projection, some two or three feet from the ground. This serves to buttress the wall and also as a sitting area for the men of the household and for occasional visitors. It is the functional equivalent of the Brahman's "drawing room."

As is the case for the Brahmans, life in an Ūcu paṛa household focuses inwardly, upon the uthan and the cooking area. Life in these households is much the same as in Brahman paṛa; the malik of the joint-family household is equally authoritarian, controlling and super-vising all income and expenditures. The proximity of other house-holds, however, and the fact that they are often of a different caste, does make for slight differences in experience.

Women of Ūcu paṛa, like their counterparts in Brahman paṛa, spend most of their time within their own uthans, but here the neigh-boring uthan is very close (one's own uthan may be no more than twenty feet wide) and may be separated only by a waist-high wall. Women of Ūcu paṛa, therefore, seem more in communication with their neighbors, particularly when the latter are of the same caste. Among the men, too, one sees a greater sense of neighborliness; when they are not working, men lounge in front of their houses, visiting back

and forth, joking and smoking
this kind is still caste-segregat
terms with the Washermen,
gatherings. Even when inter
more of it than in Brahman
members of one's own hous

Only in Ūcu paṛa, in fac
close friendships cutting ac
dren, too, in this paṛa mor
other than their caste-mat
exclusively with Brahman
dren; Santal children with
paṛa play with the children

Of the thirty-one Bau
nuclear-family in compos
brothers or sisters in the
parents of some, too, are
twelve, one is a househo
completely separate from
their own. Eleven of the
entitled to the appellatio
essentially nuclear-famil
one or the other spouse.
Santal paṛas, five are nu
family plus an aged par
family composition: one
two of a brother and sis

The aged Napit liv
them a married son. T
clear-family household
together with his wife,

All three Bauri pa
and dejection. Thatche
of general disrepair. L
with rubbish, much m
paṛas even the small
and uncared for. Th
about a Bauri paṛa d
rently unemployed)
houses or against the
course, that no one la
and discouragement,
ety is very much par

4

Kinship and Caste

All the inhabitants of Gôndôgram with the exception of the Santals (who use the Santal language at home) speak the language of Bengal and exhibit the kinship terminological system of northern India characteristic of Bengal (cf. Karve 1968: 150–57). The Santal kinship system, like the language, is quite different.

But just as the assertion that the Bengali-speakers of the village "speak the language of Bengal" is something of an oversimplification, so is any notion that Bengali kinship is identical throughout the strata of the village. Wealthy, educated villagers—which for the most part means the Brahmans—speak and read Standard Bengali, the language of Calcutta, if with a touch of regional accent. They know the local dialect, but tend to use it primarily when speaking to villagers of lower caste, particularly the Bauris and Santals. People of Ūcu para speak the local dialect; it is their language and they use it without affectation or embarrassment. Bauris know only the local dialect, but in a rougher, less acceptable form; the Bauri pronunciation and grammatical construction are often confusing to a visitor from another part of Bengal, and so, too, is the Bauri habit of sprinkling their speech with mispronounced and misunderstood words of Standard Bengali and even Sanskrit derivation. Santal women rarely speak anything but Santal, but most of the men can manage to communicate in a variant of the local dialect.

And so with kinship; there are variations and differences between all the Bengali castes, despite the basic similarity of pattern that they all share. It must surely be understandable that there would be such differences. We have noted that an inhabitant of Gôndôgram has little informal interaction with people of castes other than his or her own.

The pleasures of simple friendship—such as eating, drinking, and visiting together—are largely restricted to members of one's own caste. Marriage, of course, and the complex of relationships associated with marriage (as between in-laws, for example), may only be within one's own caste.

It would seem, therefore, that the relationships of kinship constitute the major arena of the third organizing principle of Indian life, that of "interaction." And this is largely true, but just as "interaction" occurs between men of totally different castes, so "separation" and "hierarchy" occur within a caste, and between kinfolk. Furthermore, since the position of each caste in the total socioeconomic system is different, the manifestations of intra-caste as well as inter-caste "separation" and "hierarchy" are likely to be different, and they are.

For the villagers of Gôndôgram, kinfolk are primarily those to whom one is bonded by either an assumption of common ancestry or a marriage tie. There are in addition, as we shall see, certain other special bases for kinship ties, but blood and marriage are the most common. People of Brahman and Ūcu paṛas (that is, all the Bengali castes apart from Bauri) perceive "blood and marriage kinfolk" as comprising three rather than two categories. With some slight individual variation, they all use the same three terms to encompass these categories: śôŋśar, āttiôra, and kuṭumbô.

Śôŋśar, a term said to derive from the Sanskrit saṃsāra, or "universe," now applies to the domain of worldly or mundane concerns: the home and the people who make it up. The villager actually uses the word "ghôr" for "household," the compound or building in which he lives. He uses pôribar to encompass his own wife and children. Śôŋśar encompasses the compound and everyone in it. It can be, however, more than just the members of one's immediate household; in principle, the category termed śôŋśar encompasses all the adult men (and their households) with whom a man has demonstrable common patrilineal descent. In practice, it is likely to be restricted to those in the village descended from the same ancestor—or, even more specifically, those households of that group with which one's own household is still on intimate and cooperative terms, most often the households of men with a common father or grandfather.

It could be asserted, therefore, that all the Pandes of Gôndôgram constitute one śôŋśar, and some will piously make just such a claim. Others, however, will dispute it, noting that the Pandes are divided into three patrilines and that even within a patriline there is often hostility and factionalism. Since śôŋśar, they say, implies affection and cooperation, it would be a distortion of the term to apply it to any group larger than small clusters of closely related households within a patriline.

Carpenters and other inhabitants of Ūcu para use the term śôŋśar much as do the Brahmans, although they have no patrilines to complicate matters. A Bauri does not use the term in ordinary discourse; he speaks only of his ghôr.

The term *"āttiô"* (pl. *āttiôra*) is related, ultimately, to the Sanskrit *ātmā* (self, or soul) and is defined in the dictionary as "relation, kinsman, friend." In the village it may be used in this way, somewhat poetically, for any relative or friend with whom one has a warm and close relationship. More exactly, however, it is used to encompass all those to whom one is related through a marriage tie. In principle, again, this would include all one's in-laws: a man's wife's family and a woman's husband's family, the family of one's brother's wife and sister's husband, and so on. In practice, the term "āttiô" seems to be used primarily by a man for those in-laws, such as his daughter's husband's parents, to whom he must be careful to give special attention at any feast he sponsors—and also for those male in-laws, such as, say, a sister's husband, he is likely to consult for aid in finding a husband for a daughter.

The other term the villagers of Gôndôgram use—*kuṭumbô*—is also defined by the dictionary as a kind of kinsman: "relation; relative; one matrimonially related." In the village, for all castes, it encompasses in principle all the members of one's own jati. Since, like the two preceding terms, the word is used primarily by men for men, it has been translated in this text as "jat-brothers." In practice, it is used to encompass all the men (and their households) of one's operative caste group: the *sômaj,* or marriage-circle. The dictionary says that a kuṭumbô is "one matrimonially related"; in Gôndôgram it is anyone with whom a man is, *or can potentially be,* matrimonially related. Furthermore, only kuṭumbô may be invited into one's home to dine.

Kuṭumbô, then, encompasses the other two terms; it is the largest set of kinsmen the villager knows—the circle of in-laws and potential in-laws. It is, in other words, the rural Bengali word for what Nur Yalman has called "an endogamous kindred" (1962). Among this endogamous kindred there are two separate smaller sets: the āttiôra, with whom the household has already contracted marriages; and the śôŋśar, those households which are so close (patrilineally) as to be extensions of, or even almost identical with, one's own household.

Put another way, for the Bengali castes of Gôndôgram, śôŋśar refers to the set of people, including one's own household, whom one can call upon in time of emergency or need. They are your "family"; you need not pose or pretend in their presence, and they will not fail you or desert you. Such a group is of particular importance to the wealthier households; Brahmans in Gôndôgram exclude from śôŋśar any related household heads who have failed them (or whom they have failed) in time of need, and with whom they are therefore usually feuding. Bauris, on the other hand, expect nothing—and get nothing—from anyone outside the actual ghôr.

An ãttiô, on the other hand, is a kinsman who cannot be expected to provide any material help or even to stand at your side in a crisis; but he has provided a member of your household with a wife or husband. Therefore, he deserves special treatment within the jati brotherhood, and he is likely to be turned to for assistance in another marriage arrangement.

Beyond a śôŋśar and ãttiôra are the rest of the kuṭumbô: potential sources of spouses for members of the household. But they are more than that; they are also kinsmen. True, they are not close, and a relationship with a non-śôŋśar, non-ãttiô kuṭumbô is usually formal. Not only have you no expectation that such a man will side with you in a dispute, but he may very well be the source of the dispute! He oversees the morals and behavior of your household (as you do his) and can bring you up on charges, as we shall see, or vote for your expulsion, if he learns of any irregularities. Nevertheless, he is still a kinsman, a jat-brother. You may eat and drink freely in his home even if the two of you have never met before. And, under special conditions—in a distant city, say, where both of you are far from other relatives—you can turn to him for aid and shelter and advice, and from "jat-brother" he may become like your own brother.

The foregoing are operative categories, affecting the broad-spectrum interaction. There are other subdivisions of kuṭumbô, however, among certain castes, which appear to be of significance (today, whatever they may have been in the past) only at the time of marriage arrangement.

All the Brahmans of Gôndôgram, for example, belong to gotrôs. Membership in a gotrô is inherited patrilineally, but no effort is made to trace out ties. Brahmans assume that, within their jati, all members of a gotrô are descended from an eponymous ancestral holy man, or *muni*. They are, in other words, members of a patrisib,[1] one of eight (some claim ten) known to the Kanauj Brahmans. As I have pointed out elsewhere (Klass 1966), gotrô membership is an issue for the malik of a household only, and only when he is in the process of arranging a marriage for a member of his household. One of the first questions he asks of another malik, guardian of a potential spouse, is

1. A descent group in which—if we follow George P. Murdock's definition (1949)—membership is by stipulated (*not* demonstrated) common descent through the male line.

his gotrô identification. If both men have the same gotrô, they can proceed no further, for the gotrô is an exogamous unit. Among Gôndôgram Brahmans, it is worth noting, gotrôs are exogamous, but they are equal; there is no hierarchy among gotrôs, and marriage may be arranged between two children of any two different gotrôs.

There is another kin category among the Kanauj Brahmans of Gôndôgram, however, which does exhibit hierarchy. This is the *gramer nam* mentioned earlier, the "village name" supposedly reflecting the village in ancient Kanyakubja territory from which the first exiled ancestor migrated. According to local Brahman legend, there were exactly sixty-four villages of origin, and the Kanauj Brahmans of Gôndôgram and their marriage-circle still keep the memory of their patrilineal ancestral homes.

When, in the initiation of a marriage, two Brahman guardians have satisfied themselves that they represent different gotrôs, they will inquire—if either is a traditionalist—into each other's gramer nam. Now, gramer nam and gotrô have nothing to do with one another; one cannot predict one after learning the other. As may be noted, they are nowhere near equivalent in number. Two men may belong to different gotrôs but carry the same gramer nam; they may belong to the same gotrô but carry different gramer nams; and so on. If, therefore, the two guardians, of different gotrôs, discover they have the same gramer nam, it will be no impediment to the marriage, since gramer nam is not an exogamous (or endogamous) category. If, however, their gramer nams are different (which is most likely to be the case), the traditionalist will want to determine the relative rank of the two gramer nams before proceeding further.

The sixty-four gramer nams are arranged on a series of rank steps, each step occupied by a number of gramer nams. Of the highest rank (but equal to each other) are four gramer nams: Gorgô, Goutam, Pindi, and Piaśi. On the next, and lower, rank step are eight gramer nams, and so on in clusters of two, four, or eight. On the bottommost step are two gramer nams: Bhôrśi and Biraśi.

The marriage rule about gramer nam is straightforward enough, even if it is not always observed in modern times: a malik should give a daughter of the household to a boy of a household of equal or higher gramer-nam rank; he should take a daughter-in-law from a household of equal or lower rank. In other words, wife-giver may not rank higher than wife-taker. In principle, therefore, men of the highest gramer-nam rank can only marry their daughters to households with one of the four top names, although they can take daughters-in-law from any household in the marriage-circle. On the other hand, Bhôrśi and Biraśi men—on the lowest rank step—will have comparatively little difficulty finding husbands for their daughters (anyone may marry them) but may have difficulty finding wives for their sons, for they may only look, if they follow the rule, among Bhôrśi and Biraśi households.

With sixty-four names, there will be very few men, it is likely, who will know the rank order of all. Brahmans in Gôndôgram admitted to an ignorance of all but a few names and their ranks, explaining that at time of marriage they would consult a *murubbi,* a wise old man of the jati. I was directed to such murubbis for further information, only to find that these themselves had incomplete knowledge; at best, the average murubbi could name no more than twenty-five or so gramer nams in proper rank. Murubbis tend to know the gramer nams of their own vicinity and relatives; if an unknown one should be encountered in a marriage negotiation, a number of murubbis from the concerned villages will get together and work out relative rank.

All this, of course, if the Brahman maliks are traditionalists and concern themselves with gramer-nam rank. It would seem, from an examination of Gôndôgram Brahman genealogies, that for the last two or three generations the rule has been broken a number of times, without the application of any sanctions. It is widely admitted that the social and economic status of the household counts for more in the scales than gramer-nam rank, and Gôndôgram Brahmans know of wealthy Bhôrśi and Biraśi men, in other villages, who experienced no difficulty in finding wives for their sons, even from households of the highest gramer-nam rank.

One might well ask why, with all the other problems to contend with in arranging a marriage (jati endogamy, gotrô exogamy, and so on), this issue developed as an additional factor to plague the marriage-bent guardian. Village Brahmans are vague about the origins of the hierarchy. Some say the villages of origin were ranked before their ancestors departed from them; others deny this, claiming that the rank-order reflects the vicissitudes of the early exiles, some rising and others falling in social and economic position. Neither explanation is completely satisfying, for each poses problems.[2] It is easier to assume, therefore, that the development of gramer-nam ranking reflects a felt need, at some point in the past, for hierarchy within the jati. Without further facts, this assumption leads only to tempting speculations, such as the notion, for example, that the ancestors of these Brahmans adopted, for reasons of prestige, a variant of the

2. For example, if gramer nams really reflect villages of origin in north-central India, why are they not exogamous categories? If Bhôrśi and Biraśi were real villages at one time, it is hard to imagine as a viable situation one in which the Brahman households of those villages were drawing wives only among themselves. And if the gramer nams acquired rank order after exile, this would imply that, in every case, all the Brahman families deriving from a particular village were able to maintain exactly the same social and economic level.

Bengali Brahman *kulin* structure, in which four lines reflecting presumed village of origin (Chattopadhyay, Bandopadhyay, Mukhopadhyay, and Gangopadhyay) were considered too pure, or too high, to marry their daughters to any lower line, though the men of the four could take wives from any lower line. Another possibility, perhaps even more likely, is that the Bengali Brahman kulin system and the Gôndôgram Kanauj Brahman gramer-nam hierarchy both reflect similar structural impetus to hierarchy and hypergamy. For the purposes of this work, however, let us simply note the presence of hierarchy within the Brahman jati, and the form it takes.

Carpenters also manifest a degree of internal hierarchy, though it takes a form different from that of the Brahmans. Carpenters know nothing of "gramer nam" but they do have "gotrô" just as the Brahmans do. In fact, they even share certain gotrô names with the Brahmans, such as Śandillô. Brahmans and Carpenters, however, offer different explanations for the occurrence of the same gotrô name in different and presumably unrelated jatis.

Brahmans claim that they alone are descended from the eponymous ancestral muni (holy man), but they point out that he must have had servants of various occupations. Lower-caste people with the same gotrô name, therefore, must—in the opinion of Brahmans—be descended from the servants of the ancestral holy man. As Carpenters see it, however, they are as much descended from the ancestral holy man as any Brahman. They reason that, like any man who leaves many descendants, the gotrô-founding muni must have had many sons. And, as is often the case today, the fortunes of the individual sons would be different. As they see it, therefore, Brahmans with a particular gotrô name are descended from the most fortunate son, while Carpenters of the same gotrô are descended from a less fortunate son—one who was forced by circumstance to become an artisan.

Some Carpenters, if not all, claim that their gotrôs are ranked. In Gôndôgram, and among the villages surrounding it, the Môdhukullô Carpenter gotrô is considered the highest in that the men of that gotrô may take wives from the lower-ranked gotrôs but—if they follow the rule—may not give their daughters to the men of the other gotrôs. Since gotrôs are exogamous, and since none of the Carpenters who vouchsafed this information utilized the concept of rank-steps (with two or more gotrôs of equal rank on each step, as in the case of Brahman gramer nams), none could explain where Môdhukullô Carpenters who observed the rule would find husbands for their daughters. The reply to my query was the explanation that no one observed the rule anymore, in any case. Other Carpenter informants, in fact, vehemently denied the existence of any kind of gotrô hierarchy in their jati.

Such informants insisted (and the others agreed that from a practical point of view they were correct) that what mattered today, in the arrangement of a Carpenter marriage, was the *bôŋśô* status of the family. After determining that they represented two different gotrôs, two Carpenter guardians contemplating a marital union of their children would then inquire into the *cal-côlôn* of the other household. The dictionary defines "cal-côlôn" sweepingly: "Ways or mode of living; movement; conduct; behavior; habits; customs; practice; fashion." The definition, sweeping as it is, appears to reflect quite accurately the way the Gôndôgram villager uses the term; and so he looks into the cal-côlôn of the other household and on the basis of his investigations decides the household is either *uccubôŋśô* (high bôŋśô) or *nicubôŋśô* (low, or inferior, bôŋśô).

"Bôŋśô" is another one of the many words defined as "lineage" by the dictionary, and also as "family; race; pedigree; parentage; bamboo." For Gôndôgram, the definition "pedigree" comes closest, perhaps, but still not close enough. Perhaps the closest gloss would be "stock" as it would be used in the special Anglo-American formulation "Mr. Smith is of good stock; the Smiths have been hardworking, God-fearing law-abiding folk for generations."

As it was explained to me, therefore, a Carpenter guardian who marries a girl of his household to a boy of a household with a poorer reputation for piety than his own, or one with less land or income, or, in short, one considered in any way of inferior cal-côlôn, can expect to hear others remark disapprovingly: "*Nicubôŋśô meyeṭir biye dile!*" (You've given the girl in marriage to someone of inferior stock!).

It is perfectly all right for a Carpenter to find a *wife* for his *son* in such a family; the hypergamous principle is exactly homologous to that of the Brahman gramer nam—he may take a bride for his son from a household equal to or *lower* than his own, but must give his daughter to one equal to or *higher* than his own. The Gôndôgram Carpenter puts the rule succinctly: "*Ami jôkhôn jamata korbô, tôkhôn uccubôŋśô jamata korbô*" (When I make a son-in-law, then I make a son-in-law [only] of good stock).

Distillers and Washermen, like Carpenters (and for that matter like Brahmans) are equally concerned that daughters marry into equivalent or better households, while sons take wives from equivalent or inferior households. The determination of bôŋśô is entirely relative to that of the questing household, since neither caste has gramer nam or ranked gotrôs, although both practice gotrô exogamy.[3]

3. None of the Bengali jatis of Gôndôgram exhibits any stated rule of village exogamy. For further discussion of this and other practices, see my essay "Marriage Rules in Bengal" (1966).

Bauris in Gôndôgram, on the other hand, have minimal concerns in these areas. A man will give his daughter only to a man of the same jati, born or properly naturalized. He will not give his child to the child of his sibling or to any Bauri who is not Kukur (dog) and Gobara (cow dung), though of course he is unlikely to meet any other kind. Bôŋsô and cal-côlôn are not meaningful terms to the Bauri, at least in terms of marriage-arrangement, since a Bauri is in principle destitute and without prospects. It is interesting, however, that there is a trace of hierarchy to be noted even among the Bauris; we have seen that there are four ranked Bauri divisions and that the one found in Gôndôgram is claimed to be the highest.

The Santals of Gôndôgram exhibit no signs whatever of hierarchical structure in their social relationships. They consider each Santal to be the social equal of every other Santal, and the Santal people as a body the social equals of anyone; the Santals may be considered socially inferior by all others, but the Santals profess to find this an amusing aberration, without reasonable basis.

There is equality even in the para; we have seen that there are certain officials, but these have circumscribed duties apart from which they are in no way different from any other Santal. A Santal neighborhood must have a *naiki,* a man competent to perform the necessary rituals at birth, marriage, and death, and on religious ceremonial occasions. There must be, too, a *majhi-môrôl,* an impartial judge who can arbitrate and mediate in conflicts between Santals. He is likely to be a respected man, obviously, and may even represent the group to non-Santals, although the occasions for such representation are few and every Santal feels free to speak for himself. Someone there must be, too, to remember the proper order of yearly events and to inform the rest. This is the *gurit;* he informs all households of a coming festival and collects contributions for feast and ceremony. He announces deaths and other sad tidings, and it is his job to alert the majhi-môrôl to conflict between the households. These three officials must be present for it to be a Santal neighborhood, but sometimes there is a fourth, the *ojha,* or medical practitioner. These men are respected by all if they perform their duties properly, but they are not otherwise obeyed or followed, for they have no special or higher rank.

Each Santal in Gôndôgram belongs to an exogamous patrisib, called a *pariś,* of which some eight are known to them. Each pariś is exactly equal to every other one, but each contains a number of subdivisions (*khuts*) which are totemic. Thus, the Hãśda pariś is made up of some ten to fifteen khuts; one is the Raj-Hãśda, from which the pariś takes its name. The men of this khut consider themselves associated with the *hāśda* (a variety of wild duck), which they may not eat; they may not even drink the water in which it swims. Another khuṭ is the Hôr-Hāśda; men of this khuṭ are forbidden to eat the tortoise. Women share the food taboos of their husbands in homes of the latter, and those of their fathers when visiting their natal homes.

Santals, in Gôndôgram, unlike their Bengali neighbors, express no sense of the superiority of wife-taker to wife-giver.

It may be seen, then, that for all the inhabitants of Gôndôgram the greatest number of social relationships, and by far the greatest amount of social interaction, takes place within the jati. This should not be interpreted to mean, however, that interaction occurs on any equal or even indiscriminate basis with all those who claim to be, or are even recognized as, members of the same jati as oneself. Brahmans of Gôndôgram, for example, call themselves Kanauj Brahmans and thereby claim and admit kinship with all those of that jati, from Bengal to Uttar Pradesh and beyond. Carpenters of Gôndôgram see themselves as one with all Śutrodhôrs of Bengal and Orissa, and so on. Actual interaction and formal association, however, is in practice restricted; marriage, commensality, and other forms of social interaction characteristic of jat-brothers all occur within a subgroup of the total jati—the individual's marriage-circle.

Every inhabitant of Gôndôgram belongs to a specifiable *śômaj* (marriage-circle) of his or her jati. The marriage-circle consists of a number of villages, including Gôndôgram, containing households of the individual's jati. These households contain either kinsmen or potentially marriageable persons. At the time of a marriage or death in the family, the household is expected to invite many guests and to provide a feast for them; it is to members of the marriage-circle that invitations go, never indiscriminately throughout the jati. Moreover, the marriage-circle in the West Bengal countryside is a corporate body, in Weber's formulation (1961: 223) with the power to control the behavior of its membership on pain of expulsion. Further, it is autocephalous, for its leadership (the śômaj malik, and the marriage-circle assembly) recognizes no higher authority.

All formal interaction may be limited to the single marriage-circle, or it may, in particular cases, be extended to one or more neighboring, usually contiguous, marriage-circles of the same jati. Beyond the boundary of association, whether it is limited to one śômaj or two or three, lie the other marriage-circles of the jati. Members of those marriage-circles are full members in every way of one's own jati, but they are as separated—as closed off from commensal, mari-

tal, and other interaction—as people of another jati, or another varna.[4]

Each marriage-circle makes its own rules, interpreting in its own way the behavior expected of members of the jati as to dietary rules, widow remarriage, permissible occupations, circumstances leading to expulsion, possibilities and conditions of recruitment, conditions of leadership, and so on. Information that, in another śômaj of the same jati, there is a different rule in operation is invariably interpreted as confirmation of the need to avoid (or punish) association with the other śômaj. "We do not know them," people say; it is obvious their ways are inferior or at least suspect.

Furthermore, the circle of villages comprising the śômaj of one villager need not contain any other village found in a śômaj of a fellow villager of different jati. There may be overlap or congruence; such factors as the presence of natural or political boundaries, or a similar pattern of migration for two castes may conspire to bring about astonishingly similar circles for different castes in the same village. The point is that there appears to be no structural factor, however long people of different castes reside in the same village, to impel congruence in the marriage-circles; in principle, they have nothing at all to do with one another. And in Gôndôgram, in fact, the marriage-circle for each jati represented is different from those of all the others.

The Brahmans of Gôndôgram all belong to a śômaj of the Kanauj Brahman jati known as the Śergôr śômaj. The origin of the name "Śergôr" is uncertain; some believe it refers to a certain ditch once marking the boundary of the marriage-circle. It is one of the eight such marriage-circles within the Kanauj Brahman jati known to people of Gôndôgram (who suspect, correctly, that there are more, unknown to them). The Śergôr śômaj is made up of all the Kanauj Brahmans living in villages between the Ajay and Damodar rivers. Those are the northern and southern boundaries of the śômaj; the western boundary is in the neighborhood of the Barakar River and the eastern boundary is undefined, since the Śergôr śômaj is the easternmost śômaj of the jati. North of the Ajay lies the Śattopa śômaj; south of the Damodar is the Khaśpôl śômaj; west of the Barakar is the Pâtra śômaj—and then farther westward lie the other marriage-circles known to them.

4. The phenomenon of "marriage-circle" is of course not restricted to West Bengal. Srinivas (1952), Ghurye (1950), and Mayer (1970) use the term "subcaste" while Mandelbaum prefers "jati" (1970) for what I am calling "marriage-circle." The Bengali will use the terms "*śômaj*" or "*mojliś*" where his counterpart in central India may use the term "*biradari,*" and in other parts of India still other terms are in use. It is not clear from the literature, however, whether or not the marriage-circle is in each case a corporate body, a *verband,* to use Weber's word.

The hereditary malik of the Śergôr śômaj lives in the village of Kriśnapur, just to the north of Gôndôgram. His father before him was malik, and before that his father's father. According to the present malik, his job—with the aid of the older and wiser men of the śômaj—is to supervise the behavior of the membership. Particularly, he says, he must be ever vigilant to prevent the marriage of any member of his śômaj with someone of any other śômaj—of his own or any other jati. Exceptions may be made in the case of Śattopa and Pātra śômaj members, but that is all. He must also ensure that no member of his śômaj eats or drinks with anyone not of the śômaj, a much more difficult matter to supervise.

Accusations of violations are brought to him by members of the śômaj, who reside in some twelve villages and comprise some three to four hundred households. The malik listens to the complaint, but defers further action until the next large gathering of the marriage-circle. This will be at the next marriage or obsequial feast of some śômaj household, for a man is obligated at such times to invite and feed as many households of his śômaj as he can afford to, or even more than he can afford to. In principle, he should invite the entire śômaj; indeed, in practice, many men do, thereby impoverishing themselves. Wealthy men of the śômaj will even invite more; households of Śattopa and Pātra marriage-circles are also invited. At such occasions, the immediate household and their close kinsmen (śôŋśar) are occupied with the minutiae of hospitality. The rest of the men of the śômaj gather, when they are not eating or observing the ceremonies, and conduct the business of the śômaj.

At one such marriage-circle assembly of almost all the men of Śergôr śômaj, a debate was conducted on a proposal to discontinue the practice of paying a dowry for marriage of a girl. Some argued that the payment of dowry was a Bengali custom, not native to Kanauj Brahmans, acquired in recent centuries. Others contested this. Still others objected that ending the payment of dowry would be unfair to men like themselves who had given dowries on the marriage of daughters and were now expecting to receive back equivalents at the marriage of sons. One hinted darkly that the proposal to end dowries emanated from men who found themselves in the reverse position. No decision was reached, and the matter was tabled for future discussion.

Once, some twenty-three years before my visit, an accusation was made to the father of the present malik that a man of the marriage-circle had taken a wife of unknown origin. At a gathering of some one hundred household heads, the matter was investigated. The accused man confessed that his wife was not of Śergôr śômaj, nor of any known, acceptable, neighboring ŝômaj, but he swore that she was a Kanauj Brahman from a distant ŝômaj in Bihar. The Ŝergôr marriage-circle assembly refused to countenance the marriage and voted the expulsion of her husband. Before the assembled ŝômaj, therefore, the malik rose and pronounced the formula of separation. To the culprit he said: *"Tomake pôritæg korlum"* (We have abandoned you—we have cast you out).

From then on, no Ŝergôr Brahman (and no other Kanauj Brahman acquainted with the case) would eat or drink with him. They might greet him on the path if they so wished, as they could any man of any caste. No one made any effort to drive him from his home, his land, his village, or his job (if he had one). Members of his household, such as brothers and their children, shared in his expulsion, however, if they continued to reside with him. The true impact of the expulsion, it was explained to me, came as the children of the household sought spouses, for they could no longer seek them in the Ŝergôr ŝômaj. The children of the expelled Brahman have therefore wandered away from the neighborhood, and there was no one left of the household. Some speculated that they have found spouses in the wife's ŝômaj; others doubted that. No one really cared.

Carpenters in Gôndôgram and surrounding villages belong to a far-flung marriage-circle made up of villages from the Asansol neighborhood to the Damodar River and then southward for many miles almost to Bankura District. Carpenters were able to name nineteen villages in which their kuṭumbô resided, and insisted there were still more whose names they could not immediately bring to mind. Once, they said, all these villages had comprised a single Carpenter ŝômaj, but a few generations ago it had split, by friendly arrangement, into two marriage-circles.

The position of Carpenter malik is hereditary, and the Carpenter ŝômaj is in fact named after the malik. Thus, until just before my arrival, the two Carpenter marriage-circles had been known as Kalipôdô ŝômaj and Ŝôtiŝ ŝômaj. Four months before, however, the malik Kalipôdô had died and his son Nimai had assumed the office; henceforth the ŝômaj would be known as Nimai ŝômaj.

Apparently, though no one now knew for sure, when the ŝômaj division had first been made, each Carpenter household was free to choose the ŝômaj to which it would adhere, and in some villages there are households of both marriage-circles. In Gôndôgram, however, all Carpenter households belong to Nimai ŝômaj and thus acknowledge Nimai, son of Kalipôdô, of Salanpur, as their hereditary leader.

In any case, the division appears for the moment to be purely one of administrative convenience, since there is no restriction whatever on marriage or association between members of the two bodies. At most large gatherings, men of both are invited, and the two maliks sit side by side. They even hear disputes together, and an expulsion from one is automatically an expulsion from the other.

Once, about the year 1952, I was told, a young man of the nearby village of Gopalgram took himself a wife in Asansol. The Carpenters of Gopalgram and Gôndôgram began to mutter among themselves, and sometime later the marriage was challenged at a gathering of the two marriage-circles. The young man was unable to name the śômaj of his wife's father, and the pronouncement of expulsion was made.

As in the Brahman case, no action was taken against the young man's property or employment, and Carpenters said they felt free to greet him and ask after his family; expulsion meant only that he was not to be invited to Carpenter gatherings (at times of marriage and death) and that the children of his household could not contract marriages within either Carpenter śômaj. It was even possible for him to be invited to a feast sponsored by a Carpenter family, if they wished to do so, but he could not be seated and fed alongside other Carpenters; he must be fed separately and to one side.

Some five years after the expulsion, the young man appeared at a great gathering of the two marriage-circles and petitioned the maliks for a reconsideration of his case. The petition was granted, but since he was still unable to provide the necessary information about his wife's antecedents and unwilling to send her—and his children by her—away from his home, the original verdict was upheld. The maliks informed him they had set up a special committee of five men to investigate the question. Any time, he was told, he could bring evidence to this committee that his wife was of a Carpenter household the question would be reopened, but not until then.

It would never in fact be reopened, my Gôndôgram informants insisted, because the wife had not been of Carpenter origin. Most said they had no knowledge of (or interest in) the wife's caste, but one man of Gôndôgram said he had investigated privately and was satisfied that the wife's father had been a Kôiyasthô (Kayasth), one of the highest-ranked castes in all Bengal. Whether she was or not, no one really cared. It didn't matter whether she was of a jati ranked higher or lower; what mattered very much was that she came from a different jati, or even from an unknown śômaj.

Distillers, Washermen, and Barbers—like Brahmans and Carpenters—belong to marriage-circles within their own jatis. Each marriage-circle has a hereditary leader, and—in the case of these three—each marriage-circle is a completely endogamous unit. The Barber śômaj, stretching far down into Bankura District to the south, has the greatest areal coverage.[5]

With the exception of the Bauris, all the Bengali castes of the village use the words "*pôtit kora*" (to be degraded) to express the act of expulsion from the śômaj (and therefore from the jati). The adjective "*pôtit*" is used not only to convey the sense of "degraded," "fallen," "outcaste," and so on, but also as a modifier for the word "land": pôtit land is fallow land, once under cultivation but now neglected and unused. Wasteland—land, that is, which has never known the plow or human care—is called *daŋa*.

Bauris, however, perhaps because there is no lower level to which the expelled man can fall, use for expulsion the words "*bahir kora*" (to expel or drive away, to put outside). As they themselves point out, this rarely happens; violators of the rules are more often punished with severe beatings by the men of their para. Expulsion, however, can occur, and there is at least one legend of it having in fact occurred in the case of a Bauri who dragged the carcass of a dead dog from the home of a Brahman, thereby violating the Kukur Bauri prohibition of such an act.

Bauris are vague and occasionally confused about the organization of their jati. Few men are wealthy enough to afford, at marriage or death, a feast for more than their own para plus a few nearby kinsmen. Gatherings of large numbers of Bauris occur very rarely, although there was one some three or four years before my visit. The term "*malik*" can be used to refer to the political leader of the para (it is hardly ever used for head of household, since Bauri households are usually nuclear-family) or to some leader within the marriage-circle. The marriage-circle is not clearly defined and it contains more than one malik; the office is not hereditary, but is assumed by any man with special aptitude for leadership. Some maliks are wealthier than the average, some more educated, some are just wise old men. Bauris of Gôndôgram know they may seek spouses for their children among Bauris living in any of the villages around Gôndôgram and eastward for perhaps some twenty miles—and who would want to walk farther than that? The malik living in the town of Jamuria, a few miles to the east, is considered by some to be the chief malik of the śômaj. Others dispute the authority of the malik of Jamuria, naming other maliks they would consider of greater importance.

For most of the Bauris of Gôndôgram, the assemblage of Bauris that took place some three years prior to my visit was the most

5. Gould has noted that a Barber marriage-circle is likely to be a widely scattered unit, for there is rarely more than one Barber household to a village, and many villages have no resident Barbers (1960).

important political event of their lives. It was summoned at the insti-
gation of some fourteen maliks, many from villages far to the east.
Hundreds of Bauri men trekked to the meeting, they say, following
the leaders of their respective paras.

They were addressed by one of the maliks, a schoolteacher and
perhaps the most distinguished member of their jati. He proposed
that they take steps to elevate the social position of their jati by
eschewing practices that brought upon them the contempt of other
Bengalis.

After considerable debate, the Bauri assemblage voted to
change or give up a number of traditional practices. No longer
would Bauri women go with their men on the wedding party that
carried a young man off to his marriage, but they would wait respect-
ably at home for the coming of the new daughter-in-law, as do
women of higher-ranked castes. Though Bauris would continue to
remove the carcasses of dead animals (all except dogs) from streets
and byres and deposit them in the fields away from the village, no
longer would they eat carrion meat. This meant, in effect, that they
agreed to give up the eating of beef, since the meat of cattle is
accessible to Bauris only in the form of carrion. Finally. and perhaps
most impressively, the Bauris agreed to give up the raising of pigs
and the eating of pork.

Though Bauris in Gôndôgram insist they all now obey all these
rules, there is some question about whether the prohibition against
the eating of carrion beef is observed by all. One thing is sure: a dead
ox left in a field at nightfall will be reduced to a small heap of bones
by morning. Bauris say the dogs of the village are hungry, but it is
hard to imagine how the dogs manage to remove and devour the very
femurs of the ox. In any case, the prohibition against pigs and pork is
unquestionably in effect in Gôndôgram; there are pigs in the Santal
paras but not in any Bauri para. Bauris say firmly that any man
caught raising a pig or eating pork would be severely beaten.

Brahmans in Gôndôgram profess to know nothing of these prohibitions and doubt the capacity of Bauris to organize and pass such
regulations, let alone observe them. When pressed with the argument
that there are, in fact, no pigs to be seen in any Gôndôgram Bauri
para, a Brahman will attribute the absence to some disease which
must have decimated the pig population ("pigs are dirty animals"),
insisting again that Bauris lack the discipline and organization to
maintain such a prohibition. Besides, it is pointed out by Brahmans,
raising pigs and eating pork are intrinsic attributes of Bauris; one gets
the impression that, even after decades of Bauri denial, Brahmans

would still view them, unchanged, as a pig-raising, pork-eating and therefore unclean caste.

The Bauris constitute the only caste represented in Gôndôgram that admits members through a mechanism other than birth. Individuals originally born as members of other jatis may apply to Bauri para maliks or murubbis (wise elders) for admission to the Bauri jati. If they are not of certain unacceptable jatis (Santal, Muci, Mæthôr, and a few others) they are likely to be admitted. Almost invariably such an applicant has been expelled by his own jati and is seeking a new marriage-circle.

Some thirty years earlier, for example, a man wandered into Gôndôgram claiming to be a Bengali Brahman from a distant village who had been expelled from his sômaj. He asked to be accepted into the Bauri jati. After interviewing him, the Bauri elders were apparently satisfied that he had been a Brahman.[6] The Bauris appear not to have been interested in the reasons for his expulsion. It could not have been for making an improper marriage, since he came without wife or family. Some Bauris suggested to me, half in jest, that it might have been for habitual drunkenness, for the man today is one of the mightiest drinkers of tari (palm liquor) among all the Bauris. But no one knows and no one cares; it was a Brahman violation, and therefore not of any concern to Bauris.

The elders assembled a small group of Bauris as witnesses, and before them the Brahman recruit was asked to recite, *"Aj theke amake ghena na; ek thalate bhat khabo"* (From this day forward do not disdain me; we will eat rice from the same dish).

Taking "Bauri" as his surname and a Bauri girl as his wife, he settled down in a Bauri para, where he still lives with her, their married son, and two grandsons. He and his son work as laborers; all in the household are called Bauris.

Santals, scattered in tiny clusters all around Asansol, consider themselves free to marry among all Santals; there is no sense of circumscribed marriage-circle. Authority, such as it is among Santals, is limited to that of each majhi môrôl (impartial judge) and the other para officers. Together, the men of a Santal para oversee the behavior of the households of the para. Never in the memory of any Santals interviewed has there been a large gathering of the Santal jati. At a

---

6. When I inquired of Gôndôgram Brahmans whether they believed the man had been born a Brahman, they said they neither knew nor cared; even if he had claimed to be a member of his sômaj in good standing and could have proved it, no Gôndôgram Brahman would have eaten with him or given him a daughter in marriage since he claimed to be of a jati other than Kanauj Brahman.

wedding, the household of the girl, with the assistance of the other households of the para, prepares the feast, and to it come the men of the groom's para. Unlike the other—Bengali—jatis of Gôndôgram, Santals have a strict rule of "village" (gram) exogamy, but they apply it only to a para (which they tend to call a "gram" in any case); a man of Gadhapathor Santal para may seek a wife for his son, or a husband for his daughter, in Śimul Santal para (even though the latter is a fairly recent colony of the latter) in a household of any pariś but his own.

5

Life Cycles and Rites of Passage

Almost all the present male inhabitants of Gôndôgram have been born there; few come in and few move away. Most girls go off at marriage to their husbands' homes, and so almost all of the married women come from elsewhere. But although the men of Gôndôgram are born, grow up, and die only a short distance from one another, the patterned life experiences of men can be very different if they are not of the same caste.

For the eight years prior to my study, all babies born in Gôndôgram—from Brahman through Santal—were delivered by the same *dai* (midwife), Basmôti Dom. Before Basmôti, there was a Bauri midwife in the village, but she herself had no surviving children, and so after her death the Dom woman and her husband were invited to settle.

Basmôti is called once the contractions of labor begin, and the men and children are immediately sent out of the house. In the case of a difficult birth, Basmôti will summon other women for assistance; in extreme cases, she says, she will advise the family to rush the woman to the nearest hospital. Otherwise she works alone. With a knife that has been plunged in boiling water and then washed with antiseptic, she cuts the umbilical cord. The cord is burned and the ashes are buried secretly in the uthan; should anyone steal the cord, or any animal eat it, it is believed that harm would come to the child.

The midwife bathes and feeds the mother, cleans the room in which she lies with the baby, and sees to it that the necessary piece of iron chain is placed across the doorway of the mother's room. In the mother's bed she places an iron *kaśte* (sickle) for further protection against malevolent beings or forces. For five days (six, in the case of

77

the Brahmans), the midwife comes to the home in the morning, bathes and feeds the mother, and sees to the baby. At night she returns to her own home to eat and sleep, and other women of the household (or some nearby female relatives) watch over the mother. On the fifth day, known as *pāceta,* the mother is bathed by the midwife, and all other members of the household also take baths. The napit (barber) comes (to all who live in Ūcu or Brahman paṟas) and for the first time since the birth, hair, nails, and beards of the members of the household are cut. Ceremonial gifts are given to friends and neighbors, and there is rejoicing in the house. The midwife puts a small amount of *dhan* (unthreshed rice) by the side of the baby and receives her payment of ten rupees. Once, in the past, she would be paid less for a girl than a boy, but no longer. Brahmans celebrate on the sixth day (*chôtti*) and on the seventh day (*śośthi*) the Brahmans invite kinsmen and make a feast.

The mother has now been cleansed of the birth pollution, but she is still considered ritually impure, much as she would be during the time of menstruation. She must avoid touching certain objects and foods and does not sleep with her husband. On the twenty-first day after birth, the midwife comes again and bathes the mother. The midwife receives food and (from the wealthiest) the gift of a sari. After that, all pollution is considered to be removed from the mother. Naming the baby is done privately when the child is around six months of age, in consultation with the family's religious advisor.

Stillborn babies, like all children who die before the age of twelve, are buried without ceremony in some wasteland. Those who die after having attained puberty are cremated.

Boys of jatis other than Brahman and Bauri experience no other ceremonies until marriage, nor is the girl's first menstruation greeted in any jati in any public way.

Childhood, and particularly early childhood, is usually a pleasant time, at least for the children born in Brahman and Ūcu paṟas. Children under the age of five are never beaten (or at least no one would ever admit to such a thing or even accuse a neighbor of doing it). Weaning takes place as soon as another child is born, perhaps one to two years after the birth of the preceding baby. If no new baby is born the mother is likely to continue nursing, but it is rare to see a mother nursing a child of three or four even if she has no more children.

Toddlers are usually naked (or wear only a shirt) and urinate and defecate anywhere the urge strikes them, in house or uṭhan. No one punishes the infant or even comments on the event; some female of the household comes forward and cleans up the mess and, if necessary, the child. If she notices in time, a mother may try to move the child out into the yard and away from the cooking and eating areas, but that depends on the fastidiousness of the household; in one Bauri house during my visit, a small boy defecated on the spice grindstone without precipitating any comment or notice. By the age of three or four the child has taken to tagging along with the household members of the same sex when they go to the fields to eliminate.

From about five until their early teens (for girls, this means until marriage) children will be disciplined, particularly for noisy, raucous behavior and for disobedience. People of Brahman and Ūcu para disapprove of corporal punishment and claim that most of what little does occur is done by elder brothers, but children insist that parents slap or beat them about as frequently. The ideal punishment for misbehavior, people claim, is to make the child feel *lôjja* (shame), either by lecturing him or by making him stand in a corner, arms crossed, fingers holding earlobes.

At about six or seven most Brahman children, many children of Ūcu para, and a very few Bauri boys, begin to attend the village school in Brahman para. A new one was under construction at the time of my study, but the old one-room thatched building was still in use. All classes were taught by one teacher, a poor relation of one of the wealthier Brahman families, with whom he resides. The curriculum concentrates on reading and writing Bengali, and arithmetic, all learned by communal chanting. The teacher has only a slight knowledge of the English language, but he imparts whatever he has, for a knowledge of English is desperately desired as a passport to economic advancement.

A decade or so ago, girls were usually withdrawn from school by the age of ten, if indeed not earlier; people feared that after that age coeducation would lead to a friendship between a boy and a girl and then to a desire to marry. Older and more conservative people still fear that this will happen, but there is increasing pressure from teachers and progressive elements to keep the girls in school. Even so, there are few girls over the age of twelve in the Gôndôgram school. Boys continue until their early teens, after which a few (so far, invariably Brahmans) go on to secondary school outside the village and the rest move into the occupations and employments of adulthood. For Brahman adolescents (those who did not continue their schooling) this meant, until the coming of the factory, supervision of the family crops and cattle. For the boys of Ūcu para, this meant training in the traditional occupations of their castes. For Bauri boys, most of whom never saw the school, childhood ended when they were eight or nine and began to herd Brahman cattle. No Santals have had any schooling whatever; at an early age boys began to help their fathers in agricultural work and in their early teens sought work in the collieries.

In the past, before Independence, a girl was married before she reached puberty, although among Brahmans and other high-ranked castes she returned to her natal home and continued to live with her parents, taking up residence with her husband's family only after her first menstruation. Boys, too, were young when they were married—perhaps thirteen or fourteen—and therefore marriage and puberty were in many ways fused. Even today, boys are considered children until marriage; even in his late teens, an unmarried male is assumed to have no interest in sex and to be without the capacity to offer up proper prayers. Only after the boy's marriage will the Ūcu para father summon the family *gurudeb* (spiritual adviser) to teach the young man the mantras he is expected to know.

Brahman boys, however, do traditionally undergo a ceremony, before marriage, marking their coming of age. This is the *upônôyôn,* the ceremony at the first donning of the sacred thread. There is no specific age at which this must take place; it can occur any time between the ages of eight and fourteen, and usually takes place when the boy is eleven or twelve.

In brief, the boy undergoes a number of days of fasting, prayer, and seclusion within his own home. His head is shaved and he enters upon the stage of life known as *brôhmôcari*—a time supposedly of learning and religious devotion preceding marriage—by becoming for those few days a mendicant holy man. During this time, a feast is made and the household invites and feeds many guests from the Brahman śômaj. The average cost of the affair is 300 to 500 rupees, but the rich men spend more. Even a poor Brahman cannot hope to spend much under 100 rupees on his son's upônôyôn.

On the last morning, at the climax of the ceremony, a Brahman couple from among the guests, unrelated to the boy, volunteers to lead him forth, eyes closed, to greet the sun. Childless Brahman women cluster before his bedroom door as the man and woman, each holding a hand of the boy, come forth; it is said that gazing upon such a boy at such time will cure barrenness. The boy is led out into the uthan as all the guests watch, and is instructed by his guides to open his eyes and gaze upon the red, rising sun.

A few moments later, the boy goes to the outer door of the compound, leading to the street. He opens it and gazes upon the faces of a man and woman standing there, waiting for him. They too are husband and wife, and volunteers, but of some caste other than Brahman though not as low as Bauri or Santal.

From this day forward, the Brahman youth refers to and calls both Brahman and non-Brahman man and woman his kinsmen. He calls both men "*bhikku-baba*" and both women "*bhikku-ma.*" The terms mean "alms-father" and "alms-mother" (for he is still a mendicant this day, seeking alms) but the English words "godfather" and "godmother" probably convey the sense of the terms more exactly.

He will visit his Brahman godparents frequently over the years, as he would any close and loved kinsmen, and he may not marry their daughter, for all their children are his brothers and sisters. He will visit his non-Brahman godparents frequently, too, though he cannot eat with them or sleep in their house. Their relationship is with him, not with his parents. He can have a cup of tea with them and talk with them intimately about his problems and theirs. Indeed, they may be the only adults he knows with whom he can speak freely and from whom he can ask advice. On important holidays they will give him gifts. And, when he is a grown man and they perhaps have come upon hard times, they know they can turn to him for aid and comfort.

Brahmans are happy to have such non-Brahman godparents, and Carpenters, Distillers, Washermen, and men of other such castes in other villages express deep joy and pleasure at being godparents. None will say they do it for any advantage, but for the pleasure and the honor only. Nor is a non-Brahman ever pressured or even asked to perform the function of bhikku-baba; he must volunteer, and if he is the first to make the request of the boy's father, he must be accepted.

Bauris and Santals, as has been noted, do not participate in this ceremony. But Bauris have a ceremony of their own which takes place when a Bauri boy is about of the same age as the Brahman at his upônôyôn, although not every Bauri male undergoes it.

At the age of eight or nine, the Bauri boy begins to herd cattle for a Brahman household, customarily the one for which his father works as plowman. The cattle are grazed in the wastelands between villages and in the stubble of harvested fields. The boys wander in the interstices of the villages, seeking grazing for their herds, and so the Bauri *bagals* (herdboys) of different villages join and herd their cattle together. While the cattle graze the boys play and talk. It happens often that an abiding friendship develops between two Bauri boys of different villages.

When this happens, the boys go to their respective fathers and announce that they wish to become *bôndhu-bhai* (the expression may be translated as "bonded-brothers" but the gloss "blood-brothers" conveys the relationship). A Bauri man is invariably pleased to hear that his son has found a bôndhu-bhai, and the two fathers will make a small feast at the home of one of them for friends and relatives of both. At the feast, the two boys will sit side by side and profess their eternal brotherhood; they will cut their wrists slightly and press the wounds together.

After this ceremony, a Bauri man is often closer to his bôndhu-bhai than he is to his uterine brother. They will visit each other regularly as they grow older, and help each other in every way they can. Most particularly, a Bauri man seeking a spouse for his child is likely to consult his bôndhu-bhai before anyone else, for the latter is the person on whose advice, discretion, and concern he can most depend. He cannot marry his child to the child of the bôndhu-bhai, however, for the two children are brother and sister to each other.

Marriage is an essentially similar experience for all the castes of Gôndôgram, despite the small differences in detail. Marriage is initiated almost invariably by the guardian of a marriageable girl (Klass 1966). Bauri girls are the youngest in the village to be married, often nine or ten years of age, and Brahman girls tend to be the oldest at marriage, sometimes as old as seventeen or eighteen. In all jatis it is customary but not invariable for the girl to go off to the boy's home. In all jatis but the Santal it is possible (but rare) for the girl to be married to a boy of the same village; in all Bengali jatis but the Bauri she could not be married to anyone of the same gotrô or otherwise patrilineally related, or to anyone with whom there is any known bond of kinship by blood. Among Bauris, the only two restrictions to an intra-village marriage are that the boy and girl not be the children of siblings and that they not be the children of men who consider themselves *gāer sômporkô*: neither blood kinsmen nor yet formal bôndhu-bhai, but still close enough friends to be "village-kin."

For all jatis it is customary that bride and groom do not see each other until the groom arrives in the bride's village for the wedding—the Brahman groom in a taxi followed by a procession of cars, the Santal groom carried in a wicker basket by the men of his village from the fields near the bride's household. Only after the ceremonies have been completed does the time come that men and women of all jatis remember with fondness and sentiment: the days succeeding the marriage when the bride and groom are left to walk together and to talk alone, and so to build, if they are fortunate, the deep bond of affection that should exist, as all believe, between husband and wife.

If his wife dies, a man may marry again; if she is barren, and gives her consent, he may even take a second wife. But if the husband dies, no woman of the bhôdrôlok will or can have a second husband. However brief the marriage may have been, she must go into perpetual mourning, in a white sari, without jewelry of any kind, forever giving up the eating of meat and spices. If she has had children before her husband died, she continues to live in her husband's household and can expect her sons to care for her in her old age. If she has had no children, her future is likely to be bleak; she may be sent back to her father's house where she is likely to live unwanted and alone as a kind of servant to her brothers and their families.

Among the Bauris, where marriage can be brittle in any case, a widow can, like any other woman, take a new spouse. The form of marriage is called *saŋa,* and in discussing it, Bauris express a degree of embarrassment, at least with non-Bauris, but still there are a half-dozen or more women among them, widowed or divorced, living in saŋa unions.

The solemnity, and expense, of death and the attendant ceremonies depends upon the age and sex of the deceased and the wealth of the houschold. As soon as possible after death—often within an hour or two—the body, cleaned and wrapped and carried on a litter, is brought to the banks of the śôśan, the place of cremation. Anyone may follow the procession, but for the most part it is made up of members of the mourning household, plus a few close relatives and friends. Brahmans do not permit anyone but Brahmans to touch the body of the deceased, and in all castes the intimate handling is done primarily by jat-brothers. Male relatives, preferably the sons, light the pyre and perform the rituals before the mourners return home. The next day, members of the household sift the ashes, lovingly collecting all bone fragments. Ideally, these should be carried one day to the Ganges, and thrown into it, but few can afford such a trip. There are, however, nearer rivers where the ashes of the dead may be thrown.

The length of the mourning period depends upon the caste. Bauris and Santals observe a relatively brief period, usually ending it without ceremony. Brahmans observe a nine-day mourning period, during which hair and nails may not be cut in the household and people eat only boiled rice with a little ghee. Carpenters, and others in Ûcu paṛa, observe a thirty-day mourning period similar to the Brahmans, though with somewhat less repressive food restrictions. Cutting a finger during this period is considered very bad luck, which makes for problems for those employed in the factory.

At the end of the mourning period (on the tenth day after death for the Brahmans, the thirty-first for Carpenters and others) comes the *śaddhô* (Skt.: *śrāddha*), the obsequial feast and attendant ceremonies. After the final mourning rites, the members of the household bathe and, on the banks of the pond, have their nails and hair cut. Men are shaved and sons of the deceased have their heads shaved as well. Then all return home to feed the guests: as many members of the śômaj as they can afford to feed, and probably more besides.

It is difficult for even a poor man of Brahman paṟa or Ūcu paṟa to conduct a proper śaddhô for his father (at whose death the greatest outlay is expected) for less than 1,000 rupees. A wealthy Carpenter, during my stay, spent about 2,000 rupees for his father's śaddhô, and most Brahmans spend about that, too. The wealthiest spend even more.

Households go into serious debt to raise the money; land may be sold and even the *Kabuliwala,* the dreaded Afghan moneylender, may have to be approached. In Ūcu paṟa the effort is made to avoid borrowing at prohibitive interest rates by lending to one another without interest. A neighbor, of any caste, will approach a mourner and offer anything from 50 to 200 rupees, depending on his resources. Then, in his time of need, he can expect a similar assistance from the other. Meanwhile, payment can be in the borrower's own good time.

The wealthiest of Brahmans (to date, no one of Gôndôgram) perform an additional and expensive ceremony at the śaddhô of their fathers, the *briśôt-śôrgô,* or bull-dedication. A fine healthy bull is purchased at the cattle market, along with a heifer. The latter is a gift for the *purohit* (Brahman priest) performing the ceremony. The bull is branded on both rumps with the *triśul,* the trident of Viśnu, and then is released to wander at will in the fields. Such bulls are chased away from growing crops, but otherwise they are welcomed as they wander, for they fertilize the herds of cows.

6

Producing a Crop

From its founding early in the nineteenth century, Gôndôgram has been primarily an agricultural village; over the generations the overwhelming majority of its inhabitants have depended for their sustenance upon the crops grown in the fields of the village. This does not mean, however, that the villagers of Gôndôgram all labor—or have ever labored—side by side, each in his own field. Rather, they draw their sustenance from the fields and crops, but men of each jati in a different way.

Originally glorified sharecroppers, or exalted tenants, as you will, of absentee landowners, the Brahmans today own most of the productive land of the village, as they have for about a century. That broad statement is in many ways more satisfactory, more useful, than a detailed analysis. What is the total land area of the village? What proportion or quantity of it is owned by which Brahman families, what by non-Brahmans? Unhappily, such information is not only difficult to come by, but it can also be, even when accurate, very misleading.

It is difficult to come by, because land-ownership records for the area are often not easily accessible and sometimes incomplete or out-of-date. And, even when seemingly complete and up-to-date, they may still reflect only the legalities of ownership and not the realities of control and cultivation. Faced, for example, with recent laws severely limiting the number of acres that may be owned by any one person, families have legally divided up their property among the various members, whose names now appear in the records as owners. Effective control over the property, however, usually remains in the hands of one man, the malik of the joint family, who is, according to the records, the legal owner of only a portion. Some of the legal owners, moreover, may be sisters or daughters of the malik, residing with their husbands in distant villages. In turn, in Gôndôgram there are women who "own" land in other villages, though in practice neither they nor their husbands work, control, or derive income from such property.

The issues raised by the ambiguities of "control" versus "ownership" are many and complex. Tattered deeds and other records are tucked away in many homes throughout the countryside, to be put forth as claims—as the bicycle factory officials discovered to their sorrow—whenever a parcel of land anywhere goes up for sale. Boundaries between any two parcels can be the subject of unending litigation, since survey records are also often inadequate and incomplete. In Gôndôgram as in most other villages in the area, substantial portions of land are owned and controlled by residents of other villages. These may be worked by the original owners, but they are more likely to be cultivated by tenants who have come over the generations to think of the property as their own, and who not infrequently discover that they do indeed have some legal right to claim ownership. And, of course, many Gôndôgram landholders own property in other villages and may depend upon such land for more of their income than they receive from their Gôndôgram lands. Fearing the laws limiting landownership, they are reluctant to discuss the extent of their possessions with anyone, and an investigator would have to examine the records for every mouja within a radius of perhaps fifty miles to amass any reasonably reliable statistics on the land owned by the landholders of Gôndôgram.

Gôndôgram, we have seen, perceived as a village surrounded by the land owned and cultivated by its inhabitants, actually occupies parts of two moujas, that of Gôndôgram and Kriśnapur. The best available estimate is that the village is surrounded by approximately two thousand bighas of land that can be considered "village land."[1]

Of these two thousand bighas of village land, only about twelve hundred were actually being cultivated in rice at the time of my study.[2] And of the twelve hundred, some two hundred bighas were

1. A bigha in rural Bengal is approximately one third of an acre. While farmers are familiar with the term *"acre"* from their dealings with British officials and their records, and while they know of other ways of dividing land (e.g., one bigha equals twenty *kathas* or thirty-three *sôtôk*; seven bighas constitute one "plough"), the bigha is the most commonly used unit of land measurement among the farmers themselves.

2. In addition to land under cultivation in rice, there is land occupied by houseplots, by ponds, or by crops other than rice. Some land is owned by the factory and kept out of cultivation. Finally there is *daṇa* (wasteland). This latter constitutes a small proportion of the land, but it is a shifting category and difficult to estimate with any accuracy. All of it is owned, and any of it may be put into cultivation, or removed from cultivation, at any time. The quantity of *daṇa* maintained by a given family will depend upon such factors as the amount of labor available, the price of rice in the market, the

owned and cultivated by men of other villages, primarily but not exclusively from Kriśnapur. Together, Gôndôgram men—mostly Brahmans—owned more than five hundred bighas (some non-Brahmans said as much as a thousand) in other villages, in many scattered and often small plots. Approximately three fourths of Gôndôgram land actually owned by Gôndôgram residents belonged to Brahman families. The rest, mostly small plots, was owned by a few Carpenter and Distiller families. Washermen, Bauris, and Santals of Gôndôgram owned no land whatever.

A joint family controlling as much as forty bighas of land is considered well off. Most Brahman families have at least that much land; a few have much more. One Brahman family, considered the poorest in the Brahman para, has less than twenty bighas of land. Only two Carpenter families have more (but not much more) than forty bighas, and are therefore considered by their fellow villagers to be prosperous. At least one Carpenter of Gôndôgram owns only a single bigha—and works when he must for wealthier men as a day laborer to earn his bread. Two of the Distiller families are on approximately the same level of landownership as the two wealthy Carpenter families, but the rest depend upon other sources for their primary income.

In sum, the thirty-two Brahman households of Gôndôgram control most of the land in that village and are responsible for most of the rice cultivation. Most of these households own or control some forty bighas of land, with a few owning considerably more, and a few less. Between them, they own and control about fifteen hundred bighas (five hundred acres) of land, about half surrounding Gôndôgram and the rest scattered in other moujas.

In Gôndôgram, as in its neighbors, agriculture means almost exclusively the production of a rice crop. According to the old men of the village, there was a time in the past—or at least there were times—when the village produced two full crops of rice a year. Such times were rare and distant; today the Gôndôgram farmer counts himself fortunate if his land bears one good crop of rice in a year. He counts himself fortunate, too, if his land is good enough to produce as much as twenty to twenty-five "maunds" (from *môn,* a measurement of approximately eighty-two pounds) of rice in a good year, per bigha. There are a few locations in the village land where as much as thirty

success of last year's harvest, or the need for grazing land for the family's cattle. The cohesiveness of the household is also an important factor, for the decision on the part of a group of brothers to break up the joint-family holdings and go their separate ways may lead to the cultivation of all the daṇa available to them.

maunds of rice have been harvested per bigha, but most people are satisfied if they harvest ten to fifteen maunds per bigha.

Plowing and preparation of the ricefields usually begins sometime in May; seeding must take place in the Bengali month of Jôiśthô (between May and June) and some farmers say, in fact, on the twelfth of Jôiśthô specifically. As is customary in wet rice cultivation, there are two steps to the implantation of the rice crop. First comes the seeding, during which the cultivator's seeds are sown in a relatively small and constricted part of his fields. This is the "nursery plot" or, in Bengali, the *aphôr bari*. Here, the rice seeds germinate and produce seedlings (*aphôr*). One month after planting, between June and July, in the middle of the Bengali month of Aśarh (again, some say exactly on the twelfth of Aśarh), the seedlings must be transplanted throughout the cultivator's fields. This activity, one of the most delicate and laborious of all those associated with rice cultivation, is performed in Gôndôgram—as indeed almost everywhere—entirely by hand. All personnel available to the cultivator—laborers, family, friends—are pressed into the work of removing the tender seedlings from the nursery one by one and then replanting them in the mud of their new beds. Any wrench or bruise is likely to destroy the young plant. Generally, men remove the seedlings from the nursery, but women customarily perform the transplantation, for it is considered by far the more delicate task.

Until harvesting time the fields require a certain amount of steady care. Animals must be kept out, weeds removed, and most of all the embankments around each field must be maintained in good order, for the growing rice requires as much water as possible. A cultivator whose ricefields are beginning to dry up is in serious trouble and seeks water desperately from any source available—including, occasionally, his neighbors' fields.

Rice that is ready for harvesting is called *dhan* (or, occasionally, "paddy"). Two basic types of rice are planted, as is customary elsewere in eastern India: an early-maturing rice, locally called *jhulu* and corresponding to what is elsewhere in Bengal called *aus*; and a late-maturing variety, locally called *bôrôn* and corresponding to *amôn* rice. The early-maturing variety will be harvested in the middle of the month of Kartik (approximately October–November) and the late-maturing variety about a month later, in Ôgrahayôn.

The cut rice plants are stacked and then transported on carts to the uthans (courtyards) of the cultivators. In the yard, on a wide flat slab of stone set obliquely in the ground, the rice is threshed. The rice straw (*khôr*) is saved; it will be used for thatching and as cattle feed. The cattle feed, too, on the rice stubble.

Harvesting the rice crop. Bullocks, waiting for the carts to be loaded, graze on the stubble in the fields.

The threshed dhan is heated (not boiled) in water, then put out to dry in the sun for two days. It can be stored now for great lengths of time, usually in thatch-protected shelters in the uthan. Husking usually takes place not too many days before the rice is to be cooked.

Traditionally, village rice was husked in a *dhēki,* a simple see-saw shaped instrument. The crosspiece, some six or eight feet long, is weighted at one end with a heavy stone. One operator pushes the unweighted end down, then releases it, causing the stone to come down on a small pile of dhan. The second operator squats near the dhan, brushing out the husked rice and the husks and feeding more dhan onto the pile. The work is slow and requires effort on the part of the first operator and considerable dexterity on the part of the second; fingers caught under the descending stone can be crushed badly. In Gôndôgram, both operators are almost invariably women of the Bauri caste.

Rice-husk is called *khośa* and has a number of uses, including that of cattle feed. Husked rice is called *cal* until it is cooked, after which it receives its final name: *bhat*—rice as food, ready to be eaten. A small portion of a household's rice may be husked without going through the heating and drying process. Such rice, known as *atap-cal,* may be eaten, but is usually reserved for offerings and special *pujas* (religious ceremonies).

The main occupation of the village—the "business" of Gôndôgram—is the raising of the crop of rice. Almost everyone is affected by the success or failure, each year, of the enterprise. Most of the adult men, and a large number of the adult women, participate in the production of the crop, but in sharply different ways that are in large measure determined by their caste identification.

Brahmans in Gôndôgram, for example, are in principle barred from engaging in most of the productive activities. A Brahman who cuts any living plant, even the most undesirable weed, has compromised his Brahmanical purity, as far as the Kanauj Śergôr śômaj is concerned. In theory, he could be brought up on charges and expelled from the jati. It must be noted, however, that (a) no one has ever been expelled from the śômaj on such grounds, according to anyone's memory or records; and (b) only the poorest Brahman men in the village ever engage in manual labor in the fields, and then only rarely—in times of true desperation.

During the period of my study, I never saw or knew of a village Brahman plowing, seeding, weeding, or harvesting. I have seen two of the poorer Brahman men working on embankments and digging ditches to lead irrigation water to their fields. I have heard that Brahmans might, in some cases, participate in the transplanting process, but that was all.

Basically, then, Brahman men of Gôndôgram *supervise*. During any phase of the agricultural cycle, when men are at work one is certain to see, among those present, a member of the Brahman household that owns the land. He (and the household representative is almost invariably a man) stands a little to one side, hands clasped behind his back—a stance characteristic of superiors, for it is considered insolent in a subordinate. He is in the field early, and he stays late, for he is convinced that his inattention to any activity, however simple or routine, will mean that it will be done improperly (cf. Swartzberg 1970).

Among Brahmans, therefore, who constituted a third of the village households, the pattern of activity was uniform and predictable until the coming of the factory: children went to school; women maintained the house under the ultimate authority of the eldest female; men supervised all activities relating to the production of a crop on their household farmland under the ultimate authority of the eldest male. At crucial times in the agricultural cycle, and at all emergencies, the eldest male would be present himself, if his health at all permitted it. Otherwise, other males, from graybeards to teenagers, would represent him, with authority vested in the eldest male present, as the malik's representative. Since a family's holdings are almost invariably scattered, and sometimes indeed in different villages, and since there are many different tasks to be done in any day—from weeding to embankment-mending, to digging and repairing irrigation ditches, to repair work in the home—the men of even a large household were all likely to be kept quite busy, each attentively supervising some activity in some place.

This is another reason for keeping the joint family from breaking up; when brothers have separated, dividing their holdings into small scattered parcels, a single man, with infant sons, cannot be everywhere at once. And where he is not, work will go slowly and poorly, if at all. At such times, and of course nowadays when men are away in the factory, Brahman women will go to the fields to help in the supervision of the work. But women tend not to be familiar with all the details of the work, nor can they—for the most part—give orders with masculinelike authority. Brahmans say that where there is not a large contingent of Brahman men to supervise production on the household farmland, production must and will suffer.

Most of the actual agricultural labor of Gôndôgram, before the coming of the factory, was performed by members of the Bauri jati of the village and specifically by adult Bauri men (that is, over the age of fourteen), although Bauri women contributed at times to the field labor, particularly during transplanting. Bauri boys (from about nine to fourteen) herded Brahman cattle, while Bauri girls and women performed the more menial tasks, such as sweeping and dishwashing, in the Brahman households—and, of course, also took care of their own homes.

In Gôndôgram agricultural labor is performed in one of three modes—apart, that is, from actual landholders working their own land. The laborer may be a *mahindôr* (Standard Bengali: *mainadar*), a regular and permanent employee of the household, paid regular wages and contracted to work for at least a year or until further notice. The laborer may be a *din môjur*, a day laborer paid only for the day he works. Or, finally, the laborer may be doing the work of agricultural production not for wages but for a share of the crop. This mode of agricultural activity is called *kirśani*. Let us translate the categories as: "agricultural servant" (mahindôr), "day laborer" (din môjur), and "sharecropper" (kirśani).

Before the coming of the factory, agricultural production on Brahman land was overwhelmingly (perhaps 80 to 90 percent) derived from the labor of agricultural servants (mahindôrs). Almost all Bauri men of the village were employed as such agricultural servants for Brahman households. Though this is the way villagers put it, it might be more accurate to say that the entire Bauri household was in fact in service to the Brahman household. In such cases, the Bauri man is the pivot; he is called the mahindôr, but his wife and daughter are expected to work for the women of the Brahman household and his young son as bagal (cowherd) for the same household.

In the old days, before the factory, a male agricultural servant would have received about fifty rupees per year, usually paid on a monthly basis or on some other agreed-on intervals. For the bagal-labor of his son, perhaps another ten rupees a year would be paid, perhaps less. His wife would receive no cash payment, but at the end of the day's work she would receive a heaping plate of rice and whatever curried vegetables were in the Brahman family's dinner. She received enough food, usually, for the evening meal (the major and sometimes the only meal) of her entire family.

There were, in addition, certain more indeterminate forms of payment. At two or three important religious occasions during the year, the Bauri family could expect gifts of new clothing from the Brahmans who employed them; worn and cast-off clothing would come their way throughout the year. In times of illness, the Bauris could turn to their employers for help with some of their medical expenses. Some employers even paid the tonsorial expenses of their male servants.

In return, as can be seen, the Bauri household was at the disposal of the Brahman employers. All Bauri men, women, and children could be ordered into the fields at the times of seeding, harvesting, and transplanting, or at any emergency. Bauri male servants were expected to work in the house as well as the field, repairing walls, roofs, and so on. And so the web of reciprocal obligation went back and forth between Brahman and Bauri.

In the old days, a Bauri family could expect (and would want) to be in servitude to a particular Brahman household not only throughout the lives of its members but over generations. The Brahman household usually provided the homesite for the Bauri household in some otherwise undesirable corner of the Brahman's lands. The Bauri homesite usually included a small parcel of land, enough for a tiny kitchen garden. The Brahmans exacted no rent for homesite or garden, but the Bauris expressed (and were expected to express) gratitude for home and garden by making the Brahmans a gift of a substantial share of the produce of the garden, usually eggplants. Brahmans in Gôndôgram normally do no gardening whatever, and while they could never accept cooked food from anyone of another jati (and Bauris among the least of all) a raw vegetable in its natural state cannot be contaminated by the impurity of its donor. And Bauris, as we have noted, were perfectly willing to receive cooked food from Brahmans.

Much has happened to the texture and substance of this Bauri-Brahman mahindôr relationship, as we shall see in a later section. For now, let us note one more time that some ten or twelve years before the study, most of the Bauri households of Gôndôgram were engaged in such regular service relationships with landholding (mostly Brahman) households of the village.

Some of the Brahman households had more than one Bauri mahindôr; a few had as many as five or six, but even the poorest had one Bauri family in regular service. Two of the Carpenter families have traditionally had regular Bauri agricultural servants, but the rest of the Carpenters and Distillers who own land either work the soil themselves or hire day laborers.

Years ago, landholders say, day laborers could be hired for as little as one anna (one-sixteenth of a rupee) per day. Bauris remember having received as much as one rupee a day for din môjur in the early 1950s. The truth, undoubtedly, lies somewhere inbetween. Part of the problem is that, even when there is a more or less standard going rate, individual employers may pay considerably more or considerably less, depending upon the availability, desirability, and gullibility of particular laborers. Once, we have seen, a landholder could acquire the services of an entire family for 50 or 60 rupees a year; in the mid-sixties he had to pay from 200 to 250 rupees a year for the same services. At the time of the study, he had to pay day laborers 1.50 to 2.50 rupees for a day's work; it is therefore unlikely that he had to pay as much as a rupee in the old days.

And, in the past, there was comparatively little day labor, anyway. Most Bauris were in regular agricultural service, as we have seen. There were a few Bauri men—old, mentally or physically feeble, newcomers to the village, or whatever—who had no regular jobs, and these would hire out as day laborers wherever opportunity offered. Women who were not involved in the regular service of their husbands (widows, deserted wives, and so on) also became day laborers. The Washermen and Doms of Gôndôgram, and one or two poor Carpenter men, occasionally worked as day laborers in the fields when all other sources of employment failed. Even more commonly, Santal men worked as day laborers whenever there was unemployment in the collieries. Of all of these, only one, a Dom, was willing to accept employment as a regular agricultural servant. None of the others—not Santal nor Carpenter nor Washerman—would take a position as a mahindôr. To be a day laborer is unfortunate, these men say, but to become an agricultural servant is to degrade oneself.

It was difficult to acquire information about sharecropping in the decade before the coming of the factory. Kirśani was unquestionably known, for the rules are old but the mode of production was apparently of little importance in Gôndôgram before the coming of the factory. It is likely that in the early 1950s no more than one or two Carpenter families, and perhaps one Bauri and one Santal family, were engaged in sharecropping. In recent years, however, sharecropping has become much more common.

Two sharecropping arrangements are known and followed in Gôndôgram. In one form (known simply as kirśani, for it is the most common of the two) the landholder supplies not only land to the sharecropper, but seed, plow, carts, bullocks, and whatever else is needed. The sharecropper supplies all necessary labor. If he must hire day laborers he must pay for them himself, so for the most part he and his family provide all the labor. The harvest is divided so that two thirds goes to the owner of the land and one third to the sharecropper. The other form, more likely to be in effect in the rare cases where the parcel of land to be sharecropped exceeds ten bighas, is called *bhag-kirśani* (the word *bhag* means division or share). Here, the owner of the land supplies only the land, the sharecropper supplies everything else, and they divide the harvest equally between them.

Some attitudes toward agricultural activities and modes of production are shared by all villagers; some attitudes are sharply different depending upon one's position in the system. All villagers, for example, make the same sharp distinction between the man who owns the land and the man who works it (where, as is usually the case, they are not the same person). The owner of the land is called the *munib,* and the man who cultivates someone else's land is called the *muniś,* whether he is a sharecropper, an agricultural servant, or a day laborer.

Villagers differ sharply, however, on preferences. The land-holder—the munib—invariably prefers to have his muniś be a regular agricultural servant. The munib is very willing to devote all the time necessary to supervising such servants in the fields. Only in emergencies, or when regular servants are not available, will the munib turn, reluctantly, to day laborers. The munib considers sharecropping the least desirable mode of production, even though it means he will acquire a portion of a rice crop with no work on his part whatever; he feels that he is likely to receive much less from the same land than he would if he employed laborers and supervised them. The munib, therefore, will accept the sharecropping mode only when he has no other alternative: when labor becomes scarce, expensive, and/or undependable, and when he cannot give the necessary time to supervision, either because he is otherwise employed or because the munib is a female or a minor.

However, the muniś—the man who owns no land but who must cultivate the land of someone else—considers agricultural service (mahindôr) to be degrading and undesirable. Bauris feel this way just as strongly as do men of other castes; even when a Bauri admits with resignation that to be a mahindôr is his lot in life and that he neither looks nor hopes for anything else, he would be unlikely to indicate that he takes any pride or pleasure in his work. Daily labor in the fields is considered equally unpleasant by the muniś of any caste in the village, but is not quite as degrading as being an agricultural servant; at least one is a paid employee for a specified task and a specified time, not a permanent and general servant. Sharecropping, however, is seen by all as neither degrading nor unpleasant; it is the next best thing to owning the land yourself. Men without land, of any caste ranked below that of Brahman (for whom sharecropping is unacceptable because the economics of it require the sharecropper to do his own agricultural labor), without some valuable non-agricultural source of livelihood, would accept an offer to become a sharecropper without hesitation. Bauris, in fact, in their humility rarely dream so high.

There is so much individual variation from household to household throughout Gôndôgram that it is difficult to perceive patterns of rice production and income. For any given landholding household, the pattern of production—the amount of the land worked by agricultural servant, daily laborer, or sharecropper—is likely to be unique, not repeated in any comparable household. Even among sharecroppers patterns vary, depending upon the type of sharecropping practiced, the amount of land available to the family, the availability of labor, and—most significant—whether or not any member of the family has an outside source of income.

With this caution in mind, some illustrations may still be of help. Let us look briefly, therefore, at one sharecropping family and one landholding family.

Sôilen Bauri of Gadhapathôr Bauri para was about forty years of age at the time of the interview. For about five years he had been sharecropping some four bighas of land belonging to one "Kalipôdô" Pande, a Brahman of Gôndôgram who works in the bicycle factory in a supervisory position. The mode of production is bhag-kirśani. Sôilen has a total household of twelve people, but considers himself responsible for feeding only ten; his eldest son and the son's wife were in the process, during the interview period, of building a separate home for themselves. The son was employed, by the same Brahman, as a mahindôr. Sôilen, his wife, and their eight younger children provide all the necessary labor for their fields; he cannot afford to pay for labor (and would be reluctant even if he had the money) and there is no pattern in Gôndôgram of cooperative work groups or other forms of neighborly labor exchange.

For their efforts this Bauri family can expect to retain from their harvest, in a reasonably good year, about three *kucuri* (storage baskets) of rice. A kucuri holds about six to seven maunds of rice, so this works out to about twenty maunds of rice in all, or about sixteen hundred pounds of rice. The ten people of Sôilen feeds require about eight pounds of rice a day (actually, he estimates one pound per day per adult, and six for the eight children). If they actually received that much every day for an entire year, they would consume almost three thousand pounds of rice, so it is understandable that Sôilen's eldest son must provide for himself. Sôilen has a kitchen garden and does occasional day labor, and so they piece out their larder, but obviously there is no surplus to take to market.

Sôŋkar Śutrodhôr, a Carpenter, is malik of a household of twenty-six persons. He controls some fifty bighas of land, all in rice cultivation, and his life-style, problems, and outlook are all closer in most ways to that of the Brahmans than to that the Carpenters. He now works full time in the factory, as do other adult males in his household, and so there is no one competent to supervise agriculture.

In addition, mahindôrs are expensive and difficult to come by. Most of the household land, therefore, has been turned over to some eight Santals who sharecrop it according to the bhag-kirŝani mode.

The Carpenter malik hires two Bauri laborers on a daily basis, as needed, at a wage of 1.50 rupees per day plus a morning meal to work the less than ten bighas the family keeps for themselves. Ŝôŋkar puts together all his rice—from his own fields and those of his sharecroppers. He subtracts the family's needs and sells the rest. In a good year, after all expenses have been met, he nets about 1,000 rupees. For its basic monetary income, therefore, the household depends upon the regular wages of the three men employed in the bicycle factory, plus the contributions of the member who operates a small *pan* (betel) shop near the factory.

7

Livestock in Gôndôgram

The English word "cattle," according to the *Oxford English Dictionary,* is "a collective name for the bovine genus . . . for live animals held as property, or reared to serve as food, or for their milk, skin, wool, etc. . . . Extended to vermin, insects . . . also to men and women . . . ." The use of such an all-encompassing term in an examination of animal husbandry in India, even when resolutely restricted to "the bovine genus," can precipitate more confusion than clarity. The Bengali countryman, wisely I think, tends to avoid such a term, except when he speaks English.

In Gôndôgram, the "bovine genus" includes representatives of the domestic cow (*Bos taurus*) and the domestic water buffalo, sometimes called bison (*Bubalus bubalis*). The villager uses the term "*môhiś*" (water buffalo) in casual conversation for the water buffalo in general, sex not specified, much as many use the word "cow" in English. More accurately, however, môhiś refers to the adult female water buffalo, while the male water buffalo is called *kaṛa,* whether he is a bull or a castrate. A water buffalo calf, of either sex, is called *môhiś-cha.*

Much more attention is paid in the Bengal countryside to differences in sex and maturity among representatives of *B. taurus,* however, and no one word is used casually for all. The mature female cow, who has borne young and has given milk, is called *gai.* Before that, she is known as *bôkôn,* or heifer. The male of the species, the bull, is called *eṛe,* unless he is one of the special, magnificent bulls consecrated occasionally at Brahman funerals; such a bull is known as a *śar.* And finally the castrate—the ox or bullock—on whom rest most of the burdens of Indian agriculture, is called *bôlôd* in Gôndôgram.

It is difficult to overemphasize the importance of cattle (both cow and buffalo) to the bhôdrôlok (the village elite) of Gôndôgram. An elderly Brahman enumerated not only the number of cattle owned by his family in his childhood ("four buffalo-oxen, six bos-oxen, twenty-five buffalo-cows, ten bos-cows . . .") but even the cattle of other families of the village, from Brahman through Carpenter, to one cow owned by a Bauri!

At the time of the study, there were some three hundred head of cattle in Gôndôgram. Of these, about fifty were owned by Santals and another fifty by other non-Brahmans (five by Bauris, twenty-four by Carpenters, twenty by Distillers); all the rest belonged to Brahmans. Ten years before, the cattle population of Gôndôgram was well above four hundred, again owned for the most part by the Brahmans. The decrease in Brahman-owned cattle, and the increase in Santal-owned, have both been particularly marked.

If a household owns any cattle at all, it is likely to possess, at minimum, one pair of oxen. These may be buffalo, but bos-oxen are more common (for example, of the five pairs owned by Carpenters, only two pair are buffalo-oxen). In the case of the only one-animal-owning household in the village, where the livestock consists of a cow but no oxen, one elderly Bauri woman lives alone and sells the milk of her cow in order to buy cheaper food for her own subsistence. The two other Bauri owners of cattle, incidentally—who own a pair of bos-oxen each—own no land but rent out the services of their animals, along with themselves, during the agricultural year. After the necessary minimum pair of work-oxen, a household may have cows (almost invariably bos), from one to as many as nine or ten. Only two households, the wealthiest of the Brahmans, have as many as twenty-five.

Milk production is estimated in *ṡers* (one ṡer is approximately equivalent to two pounds) and the cows of Gôndôgram are said to fall into two varieties: one variety can be expected to produce only one and a half ṡers (three pounds) of milk per day; the other variety can give as much as three ṡers (six pounds) of milk per day. This is a great amount for Gôndôgram. A cow producing as much as four ṡers a day is considered by villagers equivalent to a "Western" cow. Unfortunately, this variety has a short milk-producing span, for only four months after the birth of a calf. A buffalo-cow can give upwards of eight ṡers of milk a day for eight months after the birth of its calf.

Since a buffalo-ox has greater strength and a longer life span than his bos counterpart, one might wonder at the greater representation of bos cows and oxen in the village. Villagers note the advantages of the buffalo, but claim that the bos is easier to keep under present conditions. The buffalo requires more food, a serious problem in a village such as Gôndôgram, where public grazing land has been reduced to hardly more than three hundred and fifty bighas. Even more of a problem, according to some, is the extra work involved in the care of a water buffalo; it must be bathed, if it is to stay healthy, at least once a day. Mahindôr labor and the concomitant bagal has become more expensive and harder to acquire, year by year, and livestock owners who work in the factory have little time of their own to spend on the bathing of water buffaloes.

A family with rice of its own and milk to the quantity of one ser per adult per day need spend little in the marketplace for food. A heifer, therefore, is the most desired of calves, though a bhôdrôlok—good Hindu that he is—will insist that he is pleased, too, when a bull-calf is born to his cow. True, of course, this means the cow will give milk, but the bull-calf is an addition neither to the larder nor to the work force.[1] It cannot contribute to the labor of Gôndôgram because no Hindu of the village may castrate a bull-calf or even hire someone to do the job. As one Carpenter responded piously when asked whether he would consider having his young bull castrated: "If I struck the bull I would be expected to make a feast for as many Brahmans as I had damaged hairs on the hide of the bull! How, then, could I castrate it?"

And so, when the bull-calf is about two years of age the owner takes it to the nearby cattle market and sells it there for some thirty rupees. To whom does he sell it? The villager shrugs; he does not know those people, nor would he care to associate with them. Few if any who make a living in a cattle market are Hindus, or at least of high-ranked castes; they are, he believes, Christians and Muslims, and other such who have no respect for the cow. He does not know what they will do with his bull-calf; if they harm it in any way, he says, the sin will be on their heads. And when the village cultivator needs an ox for his plow, he goes to the same cattle market and buys one—a healthy, strong young ox selling for as much as seventy-five rupees. One such cultivator, providing me with this information, paused suddenly and glanced at me, adding: "But I never buy back my own bull-calf!"

Apart from the religious prohibition, there is an economic advantage to the arrangements outlined above for the cultivator. The bull may die of the operation, and the cultivator avoids that risk. Even if the ox lives he must be nursed back to health and strength and he cannot be expected to labor for many months. The burdens,

---

1. No one in Gôndôgram, apart from the Bauris and the Muslims, would eat beef, and even for them it is not a common food. No one in the village would kill a calf.

financial and otherwise, of maintaining an ox when he is not working are substantial, and many landholders in the village find it advantageous, in fact, to buy a team of oxen only when needed, selling the team again at a loss of twenty to thirty rupees, or more, right after harvest.

A calf—of either sex or species—born into a cattle byre in Gôndôgram is likely to be well treated. At first it will be kept in the byre and allowed to nurse. As quickly as possible it is weaned to milk substitutes and introduced to grazing. At that point it can join the family herd, under the care of a bagal, as it leaves for the fields in the morning. The herd grazes alongside other herds, of the village and of nearby ones, for bagals merge their charges and graze them together in terms of their own patterns of friendship and association. The large, amalgamated herds graze in wasteland, fallow land, and on the stubble in recently cut ricefields. Should a cow stray into a field in which a crop is growing, it will be chased out swiftly by its bagal, who curses it and strikes it with his stick. He is a Bauri, it must be remembered, and is not subject to the restrictions on striking cattle imposed on bhôdrôlok. And, should he be slow about driving the animal out of the field, he can expect blows from the owner of the field or of the animal; for a bhôdrôlok is forbidden only to strike a cow, not the Bauri bagal who tends her.

Since no one in the village (or in any neighboring village) maintains a stud bull, and little or nothing is known about artificial insemination, it will be perceived that the *śar*—the noble bull dedicated to Śiva at the death of a wealthy Brahman—is of considerable economic importance. There are two such bulls wandering regularly in the neighborhood of Gôndôgram, and there are others, with cometlike orbits, who appear in the neighborhood much more infrequently. These sacred, free-wandering bulls are the sole sources of fertilization for the cows of Gôndôgram and the neighboring villages.

It is worth noting, too, that the villagers of Gôndôgram are perfectly aware of the vital role of these dedicated bulls in the economy of the village; it would be fair to say that this awareness contributes to the veneration in which they hold these animals, and the villagers' willingness to suffer the bulls' occasional depredations in planted fields. On the other hand, no one thinks of these bulls as simply communally supported studs. The external observer may so conclude, as I have done, but the thought is a somewhat disturbing and unpleasant one for the villager, who prefers to think of the bull solely as a living memorial to some departed Brahman and as a visible possession of Śiva.

One might shrug aside the perceptions of the villager as naive and

irrelevant; my own feeling is that they are not. The villager's perceptions, apart from any other significance, have certain economic and
political consequences of no little moment. First of all, since he thinks
of the bull as a memorial, and not at all as a stud, he chooses a bull—
if it is given to him to make such a ceremony—solely on the basis of
its memorial-enhancing qualities (nobility of mien, say, or magnitude
of hump), and not at all on the basis of such issues as its likely
fertility, or ancestral milk-productivity. And since these latter issues
are faintly distasteful as well as irrelevant, he is likely to resist or
ignore any efforts to bring them to his attention in order to improve
the breed; the ceremony is, after all, a holy and ancient one, expressive of the highest degree of filial piety—it has *nothing* to do with
"improving the breed"!

Possibly the area of greatest reluctance to perceive process and
consequence is that having to do with the disposal of dead cattle. The
bhôdrôlok has genuine affection for all his cattle, and most of all for
his cow. It is of course overly simplistic to say that he "worships" his
cow; true, it is a holy animal—even its emissions (milk, urine, feces)
have purificatory qualities—but it is still an animal. He may well say,
in a transport of piety, that he considers the cow to be a member of
his family, even "another mother," but in actuality he treats the animal as a beloved pet, not as a human. He remembers the animal in
later years with affection, but mostly for having given much milk or
having had many heifers. He calls her by an affectionate name, but
not one that would be used for humans (cf. Lévi-Strauss 1968: 181–
182); he calls her by a name reflecting some quality of her appearance, such as color or size (for example, *bôṛô gai*, "big cow"), or her
history, such as the day of the week on which she was born. And
when at last she comes to die, he and his family will mourn her
passing sincerely. It is, they say, in voices filled with grief, as if a
member of the family has died. The assertion, while honestly put
forth, expresses values and not the behavioral reality.

In February of 1964, for example, a Brahman of Gôndôgram sent
an ox cart laden with rice to the rice mill of the nearby village of
"Tilimunda." Though the load was heavy, only one ox (bos) was
hitched to the cart; the household at that time in fact possessing only
one working ox. In Tilimunda the ox slipped and fell, dislocating its
left rear hip. Friends in Tilimunda came to the aid of the Brahman;
another ox was hitched to the cart to bring the milled rice home, and
the dislocated bone was reset and the animal returned to Gôndôgram.
The ox was rested for a few weeks and then returned to harness. On
April 25 the hip again became dislocated, this time as the ox was
pulling the cart in Brahman paṛa of Gôndôgram. The animal was

dragged to the owner's compound. After an examination of the animal by the owner and his friends, it was decided that the injury was irreparable and that the animal would never be fit for labor again. The ox, in pain, unable to use its left hind leg and therefore unable to stand, was left dying outside the entrance to the compound.

For two days the animal lay there. No one gave it food or water or any other attention. The Brahman malik went off to the nearby cattle market and purchased a pair of young oxen. On the morning of the third day the ox was missing from in front of the Brahman home. Its owner explained sadly that it had died in the late evening, the day before.

When they became aware that the ox was dead, he reported, the men of his household trooped out to it and performed, tenderly, a puja (ceremony) commemorating its death. They burned *durba* grass and a few grains of dhan (paddy rice) and offered prayers. Had the animal died inside the compound, the Brahman men of the house-hold—aided perhaps by relatives and Brahman friends but not by servants—would themselves have dragged the carcass outside the compound wall before performing the puja of farewell.

The Brahman was truly sad. He never mentioned the financial loss he had sustained, but only the affection in which his household had held the ox. But when queried about what had happened to the carcass *after* the puja, he seemed surprised. He had sent a servant to the village *coukidar* (official), as is the custom. This official, a Bauri, had arrived with some other Bauri men, and, at the completion of the puja, had dragged the carcass away.

And what had the Bauris done with the carcass? The Brahman seemed to find this question confusing. He had not gone with them, he explained, and so he didn't know for certain. He had told the coukidar to bury the animal, he added, and hoped that it had been done, but did not know. It was very clear that he felt that his relation-ship with the ox ended with that final puja.

The Bauri coukidar, when interviewed, was happy to report on his role in the proceedings. It is an important part of his job, he explained, to see to the removal of dead cattle from the village. He had had his men drag the carcass from the Brahman house to a fallow field a considerable distance from any habitation, and he offered to take me there. As we walked, he replied to a query by saying that he didn't see any need to actually bury the animal. He would do that, of course, if the remains began to rot and gave off an unpleasant odor of corruption, but that was unlikely because dogs and crows and other carrion-eaters would swiftly dispose of the carcass.

At this point we arrived at the field and he pointed triumphantly to the remains, noting that already most of the dead ox was gone and concluding that the rest would be gone before nightfall. When asked whether he thought any humans had taken parts of the animal, he replied that he himself had not heard of any people doing that. Perhaps Santals had taken some of the meat; Bauris were Hindus, he said, though many were of course poor and very hungry. Still, as far as he knew, only animals had been at the carcass.

As the coukidar went about his business, I examined what remained of the ox. There was no trace of the hide, or of either hind quarter. For the most part, in fact, the remains consisted of the head, vertebrae, some of the ribs, the forelegs, and most of the intestines, at which dogs were worrying.

A Bauri bagal, about ten years of age, left his cattle grazing nearby and joined me. I asked about the missing parts of the ox. The hide, he explained, had been taken by some men of the Camar (Leatherworker) caste from the village of "Kônnôgram"; the Bauri who had called them would receive a pair of sandals in payment. The missing meat, he said, had disappeared during the night into various homes in Bauri and Santal paṛa.[2]

Bauri reluctance to admit to the eating of carrion beef reflected, as we have seen, efforts on the part of Bauri sômaj leaders to do away with the raising of pigs and the eating of pork and carrion beef. The raising of pigs and the eating of pork had in fact both been discontinued among Gôndôgram Bauris. Bauris continued, however, to dispose of dead animals, and though they had apparently become secretive about the eating of beef, the practice itself continued.

It would appear reasonable to assume, therefore, that Brahmans know that Bauris eat carrion beef. They summon Bauris to remove the dead animals, but they disclaim all responsibility for what the Bauris do with the carcasses. As one bhôdrôlok put it: *"Amader prôtha ache pūte deoar. Kintu caridike kôlkarkhana loker bas—e sôber jônnô baire phele dilei—coukidar aro dure niye giye: ora abar maṇsôṭa khae* (ugh!)*—choṭolok baurira!"* (Our custom is to bury [dead cattle]. But many people live in the area around the factories [implying a shortage of space for cattle burial]—for this reason the dead [cattle] are thrown outside—and then the coukidar drags them still farther away: And then *they* eat the meat [ugh!]—Bauris are low people!)

If the cow is the animal favored by, and mostly owned by, the Brahmans of Gôndôgram, the goat represents the more common livestock of the castes of Ūcu paṛa. And, with the pig gone, the chicken

2. See Berreman (1962) for an illuminating discussion of secrecy with regard to meat-eating.

is the most common and characteristic livestock of the Bauris. None of these is a totally exclusive category, but the pattern is clear enough. Brahmans own most of the cattle of Gôndôgram, but only three or four Brahman households have goats, and only a few each. Some of the Dube families, recognized as particularly conservative, eat no goat meat (and indeed no meat at all). The rest of the Brahmans, though claiming Kanauj and therefore vegetarian ancestry, have given way to the custom in Bengal, even among Brahmans, of meat-eating. They eat fish and mutton, that is, plus eggs, but a few will admit to the eating of chicken. One Brahman family keeps a few ducks, for the eggs, they say; most of their neighbors express disapproval. Brahmans will drink goat's milk when cow's milk is not available, but leave no doubt as to their preference for the latter.

Carpenters, like others in Ūcu para, consider the cow the queen of animals and her milk preferable to most other foods. Few of them, however, own cows, and even fewer can depend upon having much cow's milk in their steady diets. There are at least two or three goats in every house in Ūcu para; a few households can boast a half-dozen or more, and in at least one there were sixteen goats for a while, a few years before the study. Most of the goats are female, kept for milk, but there are castrated males raised for meat and a number of rams may also be noted in the village.

And while Carpenters, Distillers, and Washermen prefer cow's milk to goat's milk, they note the greater availability of the latter and admit to being perfectly content with it. Those who have more than they need sell goat's milk to neighbors, and the meat of a slaughtered kid may also be sold, but since the latter is frequently dead as the result of some religious ceremony, much of the meat eaten in Ūcu para is actually distributed as gifts to friends and relatives. The people of the para are fond of eggs, particularly duck eggs, and most will eat fowl. At least one Carpenter woman observed cooking chicken, however, claimed she had never before cooked it; she was doing it now only because a doctor had recommended it for her ill husband, and she was using special utensils for the unpleasant task, she said.

As was noted earlier, there are some half-dozen head of cattle (mostly oxen) owned by Bauris. Goats may be noted in about one out of three Bauri households, but there appeared to be none without at least a few chickens in the yard, and two or three of the Bauri households had ducks. At the time of the study, there were no pigs in any Bauri household in Gôndôgram. For most Bauris, therefore, such protein as may be found in the regular diet comes, for the most part, from eggs and chicken. Milk, from either cow or goat, is not a regular item in the diet, and goat meat is likely to be eaten only after a religious sacrifice. In the most prosperous of Bauri homes, however, protein is in short supply, and the practice of some Bauris—particularly the poorest—of retrieving secretly the meat of dead cattle must be evaluated in these terms.

The broad pattern of animal husbandry noted for Gôndôgram— cattle in Brahman paṛa, goats in Ūcu paṛa, and chickens (and once pigs) in the Bauri paṛas—does not appear to extend to the Santal paṛas. Chickens are ubiquitous and are the preferred animal for Santal religious sacrifice, but cows and goats are also present. The number of cattle appears to be increasing because of greater Santal participation in kirśani (sharecropping), and most of the cattle observed in the paṛa were oxen. It may well be that the number of cattle present (two or three in almost every household) is in fact due to this alone; Santals still drink little cow's milk, indicating a preference for goat's milk, and there is a goat or two to be found in every household. It is likely that, until the coming of the factory and the movement of Santals into sharecropping with (for them) increasing prosperity, cows and goats were as rare in a Santal paṛa as they still are in Bauri paṛas.

In Gôndôgram there are few specialists in animal husbandry. Chickens scratch about the uṭhan of the households in which they are present, seeking spilled grains of rice, or other such. Goats, too, tend to be kept near the house, for those that stray too far away have a tendency to disappear, people say, looking darkly in the direction of the home of some hated neighbor. Ducks must be allowed to swim on the ponds, and so they, too, have a tendency to disappear. A son of the household may be detailed to watch the goats or ducks, but such boys are usually busy with their schoolwork. The family rarely considers it worth the expense to hire someone to herd goats, though this is the common practice for cows. As we have seen, most Bauri boys spend their years between nine and thirteen years of age as bagals, herding the cattle of, for the most part, the Brahmans. Presumably, therefore, these boys could be considered specialists in animal husbandry. They, however, tend to consider this only the occupation of childhood, and when a Bauri bagal is asked about his hopes and plans for the future, he is most likely to reply: "*Ami hal dharbo!*" (I shall hold the plow!).

If a fisherman can be conceived of as a specialist in animal husbandry—and it would seem fair to do so for rural Bengal—then Gôndôgram can boast one such specialist, though not as a resident, at least at the time of study. This man, a member of the jati known locally as Jele (Fisherman), raises fish in one village pond, catches them, and markets them himself.

Pukurs (ponds) are, we have seen, the main source of water for irrigation, drinking, cooking, bathing, and washing of clothing and household utensils. Water from a pukur is freely available, in principle, to anyone in the village for any of the aforementioned purposes, with the exception of irrigation. The owner of a pukur (and every pukur is owned) reserves its water for his own irrigation needs first, and only when these have been satisfied will he allow others to draw upon it for irrigation.

No one in the village will acknowledge that any formal segregation exists. Brahmans admit to a discomfort at the thought of using a pukur otherwise exclusively used by Bauris and Santals; the latter suspect, probably correctly, that a series of visits by one of their number to the Brahman pukur would probably give rise to irritation on the part of Brahmans. Most people claim, nevertheless, that all the pukurs are open to all; it is merely, they say, that people tend to use the pukur nearest home. Furthermore, it is certainly true that Dhopa Pukur is used by people of every jati in the village; even Brahmans come there to bathe, particularly on ceremonial occasions.

But if the water of the pukurs is in principle available to all without charge, the same is definitely not true of any fish in the pukurs; these may be taken only by the owner of the pukur or his delegate. The analogy between a pukur and a plot of cropland is apparent to all. Anyone may walk across another's field or perform a religious ceremony within it. If the field is not in cultivation, a stranger may even defecate in it. But he may never, without permission, take anything growing in it. The pukur is very much like a ricefield. It is not a natural pond—it is a "tank," a man-made, or at least man-improved, cachement. Usually it has straight, raised banks, reminiscent of the embankments of the ricefield, and like the latter it is usually rectilinear. And, perhaps most significantly, every pukur (like every ricefield) is *owned* by someone. In Gôndôgram, as has been noted, the pukurs are owned by Brahmans.

While the pukurs are important for comfort and indeed for life in many ways, the major economic role of the pukur is seen as that of providing the water necessary for irrigation of the ricefields. In the months of June and July, just before the coming of the monsoon, the owners of each pukur see to its condition. The water is low in the pukur at this time (indeed, except for Dhopa Pukur, the pukurs are often dry) and dredging, cleaning, and deepening operations are comparatively easy. As in the ricefield, the Brahman owner supervises the work, which is done by the laborers (mostly Bauris) who work for his household. The embankments are built up where necessary to prevent undesired run-offs, and the channels leading out to the ricefields are cleaned and put in readiness.

   Government assistance is available in the form of loans for the costs of "tank" (pukur) improvement; one must be able to demonstrate that a substantial amount of land will be irrigated by the improved tank. The Brahman family that controls Dhopa Pukur inquired into this possibility the year before this study was made. They could have had a loan, the head of the household informed me, but they decided not to pursue the matter; they would be exposing themselves, they began to suspect, to all manner of unwanted government supervision and regulation. Instead, they spent some two hundred rupees of their own on the improvement of the pukur.

   They then contacted a young man of the Fisherman jati living with his family (wife, children, older brother, father, etc.) in the village of "Charpukuria." The name of the village means "four pukurs," and the pukurs are all stocked with fish under the supervision of three Fisherman households containing some thirty people. The young Fisherman agreed to administer Dhopa Pukur; he would stock the pukur with fish fry, visit the village periodically to check on the condition of the fish, and finally see to the harvesting and marketing of the fish crop. Half the crop would go to the Brahmans, half belonged to him. For this privilege he paid 400 rupees for the first year, as a down payment on a total rent, for three years, of 1,100 rupees.

   When interviewed (midway through the first year, and before the first harvest), the Fisherman indicated his satisfaction with the arrangement; he felt reasonably certain he would show a profit, though not a large one, for the three years. Until the expiration of that time, however, and the final assessment—and the negotiation of a new contract—he said he preferred to keep his domicile in Charpukuria. If the venture proved successful, however, he would move his own nuclear family to Gôndôgram, taking up residence in Ūcu paṛa.

8

Services and Specialists

The inhabitants of Gôndôgram have need of certain specialists; they need artisans to build and repair, and they need certain personal services performed for them, for there are many things which villagers—either because of lack of skill or because of religious restriction—cannot do for themselves.

No man of a caste ranked higher than Bauri and Santal shaves himself in Gôndôgram, and yet every such man feels that he must have a shave at least once a week. No man cuts his own hair,[1] yet he wants a haircut about once a month. Few if any men of the Brahman, Carpenter, Distiller, and Washermen jatis trim their own fingernails or toenails; this too must be done for them at least once a month, and usually more often.

The family of the Napit (Barber) has been resident in Gôndôgram for four generations. In recent years it has become reduced in number by death and defection, but in the decade preceding the coming of the factory, the Bhandari family of Gôndôgram boasted three adult men able to provide the full services of the Barber jati. They cut hair, beards, and nails, but this was only the beginning of their work. For the household that retains him on a regular basis (the Napit refers to the head of such a household as his *jôjman*), he provides many essential services. At all important household ceremonies, from birth through marriage to death, the Napit sees to the grooming of the male members of his jôjman household, and a female member of his family grooms the women. He assists the priests, carrying equipment and assisting in the ceremonies. Finally, he serves the family as a *ghôṭôk*

1. Girls and women normally never cut their hair.

(marriage broker), if requested to. His qualifications for this last role derive from the far-flung client network once enjoyed by Gôndô-gram's Napits. Prior to 1950, the Gôndôgram Barber family provided its services for the four aforementioned jatis of Gôndôgram and for the bhôdrôlok jatis of five other villages in the area. In one or more of these villages they were certain to have jôjmans of a particular jati represented in Gôndôgram, and so could seek potential spouses. Perhaps more important, as neutrals in the proceedings (not of the families concerned, nor even of the jati) their information was considered better and their judgment more to be trusted.

Once, a decade or so ago, a Barber received ten maunds of paddy rice (about 820 lbs.) from each large and reasonably prosperous jôjman household for his yearly services. On special occasions, he could expect additional gifts of food, clothing, and even money. The Barber household kept sufficient rice for its needs and sold the rest. Nowadays, most jôjmans in Gôndôgram pay cash; usually one rupee per month for regular services plus additional amounts for special occasions.

Bauris and Santals visit, at very much irregular intervals, members of their own jatis who have sufficient skill to trim hair. Many men of these jatis trim their own hair and nails. In recent years, those Bauris and Santals with regular employment in or around the factory have taken to patronizing the Bihari barbers who have set up small shops near the factory. More commonly, they patronize the poorest of these, the barbers who conduct their professions by the side of the road, providing customers with a brick or flat stone to sit upon. In Bengali, such a stone or brick is called an *iṭ,* and in schoolboy slang the roadside barber is known as the "Italian barber."

Once, decades ago, a family of the Kamar (Blacksmith) jati resided in Gôndôgram in Ūcu para. Their work it was to repair plowshares, knives, and other metal tools and implements. They were supported by the rice contributions of their jôjmans, in smaller quantities than that received by the Barber, and they, too, had clients in other villages. The family has since died out and has not been replaced. There are Blacksmith families scattered in other villages not too far away, but villagers see little reason to seek them out and to establish jôjmani relations. There are hardware stores in Asansol and Blacksmiths near the factory and the mines. Gôndôgram villagers patronize these establishments when necessary, and pay cash.

A few of the wealthiest Brahman families of the village send garments to the village Washermen to be washed. Even for the wealthiest, the wash they send out consists of special, or ceremonial, garb for the most part; everyday clothing is washed by members of the family or occasionally by Bauri servants. No families in the village have ever established jôjmani relationships with any of the Washermen; those who send laundry to them pay in cash, item by item. Until the coming of the factory, the Dhopas could hope for little business and engaged in their traditional occupation only enough to keep the profession alive from generation to generation. For their livelihood, most of the Gôndôgram Washermen worked in the fields, as day laborers or even mahindôrs.

There are still other services provided by families resident in Gôndôgram. As has been noted earlier, a woman of the Dom jati serves as dai, or midwife, to all the other families of Gôndôgram, a service performed in the past by a now-deceased Bauri woman. The present dai provides her services for families in four villages in addition to Gôndôgram. Dom men of Gôndôgram join their fellow caste-mates of other nearby villages to serve as musicians whenever the occasion presents itself. A Dom band usually consists of three men—two percussion, one woodwind—who play at religious ceremonies (of any caste or village). Some of the payment (five or ten rupees) finds its way back to the family; most is usually consumed by the musicians themselves in the nearest liquor shop.

Gôndôgram has a school of its own, located until 1964 in Brahman para, and the village teacher has traditionally been a Brahman, usually a landless poor relation, as was the one at the time of study. In principle, the school is open to children of all the jatis in the village.

For the older men of the Carpenter jati, the making and repairing of the *gari* (the traditional ox-drawn cart) represents their jati's most basic and most preferred endeavor. Without exception, every Carpenter man over thirty could recite in meticulous detail all the parts of a gari and all the steps in the construction of one. The work is done in Main Street, in the middle of Ūcu para usually, and Carpenter men and boys gather around a caste-mate so employed to watch, to joke, to comment, and to reminisce.

It is said that all *silpis* (artists) are Carpenters—for all artists are in fact, in this area, of this jati—but not all Carpenters are artists. Gôndôgram can boast one resident silpi, a poor Carpenter who has been making *murtis* (religious statuary) since the age of twelve. He learned his techniques from his uncle, who resides in Gopalgram, the village of Carpenters, and who is acknowledged as the finest silpi of the côkrô (circle of villages). The work of the silpi of Gopalgram has appeared in the most distinguished temples of the villages of the region, but there is still work for his less-skilled nephew. The sons of the silpi evinced no signs of artistic skill, and so they remain ordinary

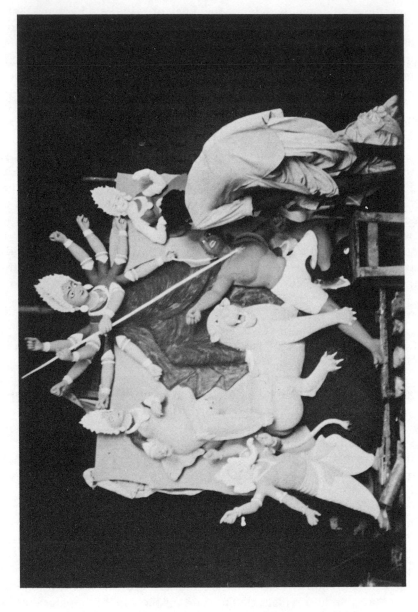

An artist putting the finishing touches on the murti of Durga for the annual village ceremony.

Carpenters. The Gôndôgram śilpi receives from fifteen to fifty rupees for his murtis, representations in clay over rice-straw armatures of such divinities as Kāli, Durga, Saraswatī, and Lakṣmī. His work is bought by schools, for children's ceremonies, and by the humbler temples.

Bauris are laborers and are specifically thought of as without skills. Still, at the time of the study, three young Bauri men (in their late teens and early twenties) had recently purchased musical instruments after months of scrimping and saving. These were the same kind of instruments played by Dom musicians: one large drum, one small drum, and a flute. The men practiced diligently, hoping to be hired occasionally to play at weddings, particularly of Bauris and other impoverished castes for whom Dom musicians might be too much of a luxury.

As we have seen, Gôndôgram, like most villages in Bengal, boasts a coukidar, an official whose title has been variously translated as watchman, constable, village-secretary, records-keeper, and so on. In Gôndôgram it might best be translated as, simply, "official," for the person occupying the position holds the only office in the village. He keeps the forms that must be filled out whenever a birth or death occurs in the village, and he brings the completed forms every month or so to the nearest police station, from whence they find their way to appropriate district, state, and national records. The coukidar has other responsibilities, such as seeing to it that the bodies of dead animals are removed quickly from the village streets. In Gôndôgram, traditionally, only a Bauri may hold the office of coukidar. As villagers of different caste explained the matter, earnestly and humorlessly, the office is looked upon as a somewhat menial one, partly because of the nature of the work—such as removing dead animals—and partly because of the limited emolument (ten rupees per month). It is asserted that only an illiterate man would take on such a job at such a salary. In the collective memory of the villagers, therefore, the position has never been held by anyone who could read and write, and has in fact been held by a succession of Bauris.

Since the primary responsibility of the office of coukidar (occasionally referred to in the village as *ṭhandar,* presumably from *ṭhanadar,* or police officer) is that of keeping records of vital statistics, some might find it amusing that the office is held invariably by an illiterate. The villager sees nothing amusing about it. A member of the household in which a birth or death has occurred, it was explained to me, has the responsibility of notifying the coukidar as soon as possible after the event. The coukidar goes to the shelf on which he keeps blank forms; one pile is for births, the second for deaths, and he knows which is which though he cannot read them. He hands the appropriate form to his informant, who fills it out and hands it back. Once a month or so, the coukidar brings the completed forms to the police station.

But suppose the informant is also illiterate, as are many men in the village? In that case, he—or the coukidar—seeks the aid of a literate villager. Or perhaps, not infrequently, births and deaths among the poorest simply go unrecorded.

Though the coukidar of Gôndôgram is not a watchman, the village does have such guardians, although they are not men of the village. Once, I was told by Brahmans, before the coming of the factory, Gôndôgram was peaceful, law-abiding—and secure. In recent years, however, a number of thefts had occurred in both Brahman and Ūcu paṛas. Religious statuary, often of gold, had been disappearing from household shrines, along with other articles of value. Some men blamed personal enemies within the village, a few Brahmans suspected Bauris no longer under proper Brahmanical control, but most were certain that outsiders—not members of their own village— were responsible. Around the factories and collieries of the area, they claimed, were hundreds of unemployed men from all over India, many of whom were believed to roam at night in predatory fashion through the unprotected villages.

Gôndôgram, therefore, had found it necessary for the first time in its history to employ professional night watchmen. The man chosen by the Brahmans, some two years before, was surnamed Singh; he was elderly and not at all fierce in appearance, but he was of a jati of the Khôtriyô (Kśatriya or Warrior) varna, and he and his people customarily served as watchmen and guards. He lived in the village of "Saldanga" and was recommended by a fellow villager, the mother's brother of a Brahman of Gôndôgram.

Singh arrived in Gôndôgram every evening at about 10 P.M. Until five the next morning, he patrolled the streets and lanes of Brahman para, and the main street as far as the temple of Durga. In his hand he carried a ceremonial spear, and as he patrolled he howled eerily from time to time. The howls, it was hoped, would frighten away thieves, but they also served as evidence for his employers throughout the night that he was awake and doing his duty. He received twenty rupees per month for his work. While it was true that he had never succeeded in catching any thieves—and thefts did continue to take place—it was widely felt that his presence at least served to keep down the number of robberies. The inhabitants of Ūcu para had their own watchman, a man of Nepali origin who, some believed, had seen service in a British Gurkha regiment.

Many other services are provided by specialists from beyond Gôndôgram. All jatis other than Bauri, Santal, and Dom have family priests who perform religious ceremonies for them and who officiate at family life crises. Each such priest (purohit) is a Brahman and of a marriage-circle of landless, relatively poor Brahmans who make their livings primarily as family purohits. But the purohits who visit Gôndôgram do not all belong to the *same* marriage-circle. The Chakrobartis of Ethora village belong to a marriage-circle of purohits-to-Brahmans only and the purohits who provide similar services for Carpenters come from Salanpur, a town to the west, and belong to a different marriage-circle. Neither would care to marry Brahmans who serve as purohits for Distillers or Washermen, each of whom come from different villages and separate marriage-circles.

Santals are excellent house-builders, and the Santals of Gôndôgram are often employed by men of other castes in the erection of mud houses and walls. Thatching, however, is a craft of specialists, and those who can afford to do so summon men for that purpose from the Baroe jati, some of whom may be found in a village about five miles away to the west. Construction of brick and plaster, of course, requires the services of still other specialists. Gôndôgram, however, does produce much of its own brick needs. Many men, particularly Carpenters, Bauris, and Santals, know how to use the material.

The villagers of Gôndôgram are by no means self-sufficient, although they can provide a large part of their needs. Few of any caste need to supplement their rice needs by purchase outside the village, and rice is hardly ever brought into the village to be sold. In other words, the village still produces sufficient rice to feed all the villagers, including those who have no riceland of their own but must provide services in exchange for rice. Rice from the village also goes to people in other villages who perform services for villagers, such as purohits. The protein needs of the villagers, as we have seen, are met to a considerable extent within the village in the various forms of cow's milk, goat's milk, fish, goat meat, chicken, eggs, and carrion beef. Fish, an important item of Brahman diet, is the only protein food purchased in large measure outside the village. Some Bauris, those with steady employment, may occasionally purchase goat meat from a butcher's stall near the factory, but this is still a relatively rare occurrence.

Yet, for all of that, the village is not self-sufficient and probably never was as far back as anyone can trace. Brahmans are not gardeners, as they themselves will tell you, and indeed few among the bhôdrôlok of Gôndôgram grow anything but rice. No one who can afford it, however, considers plain rice a satisfactory or adequate meal; it is served and eaten with sauces, spices, and vegetable side dishes. Bauris and Santals manage to grow, in their kitchen gardens, much of the material that goes into such dishes. Apart from the traditional gift of eggplants to Brahmans, however, the vegetables and spices do not circulate beyond the household growing them, and so the other villagers must bring such food items into the village. Obviously, there are two ways in which this importation can be made; villagers may go individually to the surrounding marketplaces where such items are sold, or a village entrepreneur may buy wholesale and sell retail to his village fellows. Both methods are practiced.

Few Bauris and fewer Santals ever go shopping, but when they do they follow the bhôdrôlok practice and send only men to the distant bazaar, or hat. Men of any caste, who work in or near the factory, make purchases at the shops and stalls surrounding it as they return home from work. Wealthier men, particularly among the Brahmans, try to make at least one visit a week to the town of Asansol, which has a large vegetable market and many shops. A few, particularly if they have special business, make the long trip on occasion to Domahani to shop at the hat held there every Wednesday. Some attend the Tuesday hat held at a nearby village, but most think of this primarily as a market in which to buy or sell animals. Throughout the côkrô there are other hats, held on other days of the week. For the most part, however, men—who do most of the shopping for their families—do their shopping near the factory or in Asansol.

The second approach to supplying the needs of the village is also in evidence. There is one shop and some stalls in Gôndôgram, and those who have neither time nor inclination to do their own shopping can buy most of what they want right in the village, if at slightly higher prices and with somewhat less selection. Distillers run the oldest and seemingly most permanent shop, selling—in small quantities—anything and everything. But anyone who wishes may try his hand at shopkeeping, and many ephemeral shops and stalls operated by Brahmans and Carpenters have opened and closed quickly, over the years.

In March of 1964, for example, a young Brahman man, employed in the bicycle factory, set up a stall in Brahman para near the Dube houses. With an unemployed brother to assist him, he had dreams of establishing a permanent business, ultimately building and opening a store. On the first day, the stock of the two brothers consisted of some fifteen items, including large white potatoes, small white potatoes, onions, ginger, chilis, garlic, squash, tomatoes, a spinachlike vegetable, *pan* (betel), Western-type cigarettes, and Indian cigarettes (*biris*). Business was poor, and in a week the stall had closed down. Within a month, however, another one—similar in every way—had opened and closed, this one set up by a Carpenter family.

9

Gôndôgram's Neighbors

One of the dimensions of *community,* it was earlier asserted, is that of côkrô—the "district," the circle of total resource. For the Asansol countryside, it is easy enough to demonstrate the need, and the presence, of such a dimension, but delimiting it is much more difficult.

This work shall attempt to do no more than block out the côkrô dimension of community; most of all, the places mentioned in this text as visited (in a patterned rather than simply in a personal way) by members of the village, and the places from which patterned visitations are likely to emanate. In addition, a sampling of other villages will be introduced (whether or not they are part of patterned visitations) in order to provide some sense of ethnic variation and settlement appearance in the district.

In the past, it is said, Gôndôgram, like the villages around it, considered itself administratively and in many ways economically subservient to the large village of Eṭhora, some three miles to the northwest. Here, until independence, resided the zemindar successor to the Maharaja of Kaśipur to whom the landholders of the area paid khajna. There were schools and religious centers here, too, and therefore people who could advise and who could help settle disputes. Since Independence, however, and the total abolition of the zemindari system, Eṭhora has lost not only its resident zemindar but also much of its raison d'être. By 1963 it had become a sleepy village of mud houses scattered among the ruins of once much grander buildings. Eṭhora is still a hub of sorts, however; most of the Brahmans who serve as family priests for the higher castes of the surrounding region reside in Eṭhora. There are other specialist castes represented in Eṭhora, and the village, which at first glance seems the only "self-sufficient'' multicaste settlement of the district, turns out to be a locus of special services for the other villages.

Even at the height of its importance, however, Ethora had no hat, or market. For Gôndôgram even a century ago, as has been noted, the village of Hat Mônôśa provided the nearest market. But the hat of Hat Mônôśa has been long since discontinued; the attractions of the *bajar* (bazaar, or marketplace) at Asansol proved irresistible.

There is, we have observed, a small regular market at a village northeast of Gôndôgram. This hat is held once a week and is concerned primarily with the buying and selling of livestock. Asansol, however, has a large and permanent marketplace; there are shops filled with foreign goods; there are tea shops, cinemas, hotels, and other centers of amusement and excitement. Asansol also has a major railroad station, a prison, law courts, and the office of the Assistant District Magistrate, the second highest official in the entire District Burdwan (the District Magistrate is located in the town of Burdwan). The senior Community Development Officer for the entire Asansol subdistrict operates out of Asansol, too. Such records of the past as have not disappeared or been sent to Calcutta or Ranchi are kept in the archives of Asansol.

The countryside is divided into *thanas*. The word "*thana*" is usually defined as "police station" but since it refers, in India, to a large stretch of territory administered by the police and a few other officials, perhaps "prefecture" would be a more accurate definition.

Gôndôgram, like most of the area directly north of Asansol, is within the Baraboni thana. The offices of administration for the thana are located in the market town of Domahani, some eight miles north of Asansol. The roads to Domahani were bad and getting worse, and few of the villagers saw any reason to visit the town. If trouble develops, the police in Domahani could be notified by the nearest telephone (now, at the Das-Walters factory) and they would come as quickly as possible. A Community Development office for the thana is also located in Domahani, but its operations had begun only just prior to my own arrival in the area; none of its Village Level Workers had been to Gôndôgram, and few visited it during my study.

At the time the study was being conducted, in fact, "Community Development" had been largely neglected in the areas contiguous to Asansol. The rationale offered was that this is an industrial region rather than an agricultural one, and the Community Development Program is designed primarily for the improvement of agriculture and of agricultural communities. Attention had been given for some time, however, to rural government; Gôndôgram voters participated in local Union Board elections, but the village was considered too small to have a *panchayat* (village council) of its own and sent representatives to one shared with other small villages.

Religious observance, as we shall see later, can take place in the home, in the village, or with relatives and friends in other villages. Some villages are noted for the annual *melas* (fairs) which they traditionally sponsor at times of certain religious observances. The village of "Marickota," for example, some three miles north of Gôndôgram, is noted for a mela held at its temple of Côndrôcur during the month of Côitrô in honor of the god Śiva. Brahmans of Gôndôgram, most particularly young men and women, make the pilgrimage to Marickota each year. Farther to the north is the village of "Śātaibhil," to which Bauris and others of low-ranked castes make pilgrimage once a year to offer sacrifice to the "seven sisters." These and similar events will be discussed more fully later on.

One last issue remains, then, to be discussed here: Is Gôndôgram unique or even unusual, or is it much like the other villages of the district? To provide a provisional answer, some comparative data is given for nine other villages of the district. Some are close to Gôndôgram, some more distant; they were chosen pretty much at random.

Most of the information provided here on villages of the district is encapsulated, for the sake of brevity, in tables 3 through 12. Essentially, the tables indicate the population breakdown for each village; the jatis, the number of households of each jati, and the total population in that village for each jati. No formal census was taken in most cases, of course, and the figures are approximate.

For each village, finally, the table indicates the position of each jati in the socioeconomic structure. That is, while the order given reflects the precedence assigned by village informants, each jati is further assigned, in terms of the approach to Indian community detailed earlier, to one of three strata:

(a) *Upper stratum*—the landowning "dominant" castes, who live in the neighborhood (or neighborhoods) of greatest prestige and who control village economic and political life.

(b) *Middle stratum*—those jatis providing services of a non-polluting kind, tenant farmers, and others residing in the para or paras of lesser prestige.

(c) *Lower stratum*—castes and tribes providing menial labor in field and house, or services of a polluting nature.

Such is the basic pattern; some villages depart from it. For purposes of comparison, information on Gôndôgram is given in table 3.

TABLE 3   *Village 1: Gôndôgram*

Stratum	Jati Name	Number of Households	Persons
Upper	Kanauj Brahman	32	225
Middle	Napit (Barber)	2	7
	Śutrodhôr (Carpenter)	6	75
	Śūri (Distiller)	8	90
	Dhopa (Washerman)	4	25
Lower	Dom	1	5
	Bauri	31	171
	Santal	11	71
	Muslim	1	4

There are 9 jatis represented in Gôndôgram, 7 of them Hindu. Among them, there are a total of 96 separate households, as of the time of survey, with a total population of 673 persons. Gôndôgram villagers depended in the past upon agriculture, primarily in the form of rice cultivation, but by the time of the study income from work in the bicycle factory was important for almost every household. In the past, too, Santals derived most of their income from work in nearby collieries. Finally, note that while Barbers are ranked by villagers as higher than all jatis but Brahman, and they live among the Brahmans, they own no land and are in general lower than Carpenters and Distillers in most social, economic, and political issues affecting village life.

TABLE 4   *Village 2: Charpukuria*

Stratum	Jati Name	Number of Households	Persons
Upper	Goala (Milkman)	22	200
	Kumor (Potter)	8	50
Middle	Jele (Fisherman)	3	30
	Kamar (Blacksmith)	1	5
	Bene (Shopkeeper)	1	5
Lower	Bauri	25	125
	Kora ("tribal" group)	7	35

Approximately 450 people, divided up into 67 households reflecting 7 jatis (6 of them Hindu) make up the population of Charpukuria, a village on the main Asansol–Domahani road, on the banks of the river Nunia. According to village legend, the village was founded more than a hundred years earlier by the ancestors of the present Goala (Milkman) households. The Goala settlers chose the site because it was unoccupied, because there was good grazing land and running water for their animals. The Milkmen (along with a few of the Potters) have since acquired title to over 600 bighas of land around the village, on which they raise rice. Though they are the bhôdrôlok (gentlefolk) of the village, concerned with rice cultivation, Milkmen still keep their cattle and sell the milk, while the Potters sell pots in the markets of Asansol and Domahani.

The Bauri laborers were brought in by the Milkmen, years ago, to labor in the latter's fields; Bauris reside in a para separated from the main village para. Koras, a so-called tribal people linguistically and culturally related to the Santals, live separately too, and work as they can in colliery and field. The other five jatis live together in the main village para. Bauris of Gôndôgram have relatives in this village, and the Jele who works Dhopa Pukur lives in Charpukuria.

TABLE 5   *Village 3: Gopalgram*

Stratum	Jati Name	Number of Households	Persons
Upper	Śutrodhôr (Carpenter)	35	400

One hundred years earlier, the land around the present village of Gopalgram was *daŋa* (wasteland), grazed by the herds of wandering Goalas. Four families, representing four different jatis (Kanauj Brahman, Carpenter, Milkman and Washerman), originally settled the village. Bauris were brought in as laborers and settled in a separate para. Only the Carpenters prospered, however; the other families variously died without issue, sold their land, or moved away. Carpenter families, however, attracted by the notion of a village entirely of their own kind, as well as by the possibility of employment in nearby collieries, moved to Gopalgram. There are fifteen different gotrô names among the Carpenters of Gopalgram, indicating the minimum number of immigrant families.

Today, the Carpenters raise some rice for home use (on not more than sixty bighas) and keep, altogether, about 150 head of cattle. For the most part, however, they derive their income from their traditional occupation, providing carpentry service for many villages of the district, and by working in factory and colliery. The rest of the land around the village is owned and cultivated by Kanauj Brahmans from a number of nearby villages.

Gôndôgram is only about a half-mile away, to the northeast, and Carpenters of that village spend much time in Gopalgram, where most have many close relatives.

TABLE 6   *Village 4: Tilimunda*

Stratum	Jati Name	Number of Households	Persons
Upper	Ekadôś-tili (Oilpresser)	38	240
Lower	Bauri	10	50

Two jatis make up the village of Tilimunda, with forty-eight households containing, in all, a bit less than three hundred people. For once the records are precise; in 1843 three families (of three different gotrôs) whose descendants identify themselves as of the *Ekadôś-tili* jati, traditionally pressers of oil from cottonseeds, received permission from a wealthy man of Ethora to settle near the pond that still provides water for the village of Tilimunda. Contemporary Oilpressers know nothing of their hereditary occupation and suspect that it was given up long before their ancestors settled and became cultivators and therefore bhôdrôlok.

Together, Oilpressers own six hundred bighas of land around their village (much is owned by men of other villages), of which two hundred is planted in rice, the rest being ḍaṇa for grazing, for the Oilpressers maintain herds totaling two hundred head of water buffalo and cattle. Labor in the fields is performed solely by Bauris, who live in a separate paṛa of their own, and who include relatives of Bauris in Gôndôgram. Though bhôdrôlok, the Oilpressers of Tilimunda are not wealthy, and most seek other forms of income. Some work in factory or colliery, and an increasing number have become interested in maintaining teashops (such as the one on the outskirts of Gôndôgram). A few Oilpressers own and operate a rice mill in Tilimunda, one of the largest in the district, and polish rice brought to them from many nearby villages.

TABLE 7   *Village 5: Kriśnapur*

Stratum	Jati Name	Number of Households	Persons
Upper	Kanauj Brahman	22	125
Lower	Bauri	11	35

Kriśnapur—the main settlement of Kriśnapur mouja to the north of Gôndôgram—has two jatis with a total of thirty-three households and approximately 160 inhabitants. The Brahmans belong to the same marriage-circle as do those of Gôndôgram (indeed, the malik or leader of the marriage-circle resides in Kriśnapur) and the Bauris of the two villages also intermarry. The founding of Kriśnapur was related earlier.

At the time of the study, of the seven hundred bighas surrounding Kriśnapur some four hundred were under rice cultivation and the rest were wasteland. Many of the Brahmans, however, own additional parcels of land around other villages, such as Gopalgram. The Brahmans own altogether some two hundred head of cattle and water buffalo. All agricultural work is performed by the Bauris, while the Brahmans supervise. Many of the latter, in addition, work in collieries or factories, in office positions.

TABLE 8 *Village 6: Goalagram*

Stratum	Jati Name	Number of Households	Persons
Upper	Goala (Milkman)	50	300
Middle	Poddar (Goldsmith)	2	10
	Napit (Barber)	1	5
	Dom	1	5
Lower	Bauri	30	120

Goalagram is in Salanpur thana, the one to the west of Baraboni thana (which contains Gôndôgram). There are five jatis here, with eighty-four households and approximately 440 inhabitants. The Milkmen, who are bhôdrôlok and part of the same marriage-circle as the Milkmen of Charpukuria, are all descendants of the original five or six founding families. Settlement occurred some six generations ago, as far as anyone has any knowledge; wasteland was made available to the original Goalas by some wealthy person, now forgotten, who lived in Ethora. The Goalas cleared the land, grazed their cattle, and raised their families. Eventually, they became interested in agriculture, bringing in Bauri laborers to work their fields. A Barber family was invited to live in the village, and Doms and Goldsmiths were permitted to settle.

The Bauris live apart in their own para, while the other jatis live together in the main para—although the Dom household is clearly on the periphery. More than five hundred bighas were planted in rice and some other crops, but most of the land around the village was grazing land, supporting more than five hundred cattle and water buffalo raised primarily for milk which was sold in the market towns west of Asansol. Doms work as laborers or provide services (music, mostly) for surrounding villages. The Goldsmiths have given up their traditional occupation, as have many of their jati throughout Bengal and the rest of India, and operate small shops within the village.

TABLE 9   *Village 7: Mônôśa*

Stratum	Jati Name	Number of Households	Persons
Upper	Bengali Brahman	65	360
Middle	Goala (Milkman)	40	180
	Jele (Fisherman)	2	10
	Dom	10	40
Lower	Bauri	20	80
	Santal	8	30

Mônôśa—the former site of Haṭ Mônôśa—is about a mile and a half southeast of Gôndôgram. Though it contains only five jatis (145 households, approximately seven hundred persons), it is considered a large village, for it is surrounded by more than three thousand bighas of cultivated riceland and enough wasteland to support the village's one thousand head of cattle and water buffalo. According to village legends, Haṭ Mônôśa is one of the oldest settlements in the area; some say it is two hundred years old and some even five hundred years old. There are ruins near the village of a *vaiśnavite* (that is, dedicated to Viśnu) temple that may well have been built before 1800.

The Brahmans, whose affinities are with Bengali Brahmans to the east rather than with the Kanauj Brahmans found in increasing numbers to the west, claim their earliest ancestors were brought in the distant past to serve as temple priests, and so founded the village. Today, the Brahmans supervise cultivation (performed by Bauris, some Doms and Santals), but some also work in factories and collieries in office jobs. Most of the cattle belong to the Milkmen, who belong to the same marriage-circle as the Goalas of Charpukuria and Goalagram; in Mônôśa, however, they are not considered bhôdrôlok, a term the Brahmans reserve for themselves. Brahmans inhabit the highest-ranking paṛa; Milkmen the next; Fishermen, Doms, and Bauris live in a third; and Santals in the final paṛa of the village. Santals of Mônôśa and Gôndôgram share the same marriage-circle, as do Doms of both villages.

TABLE 10   *Village 8: Śivapur*

Stratum	Jati Name	Number of Households	Persons
Upper	Kanauj Brahman	10	80
Lower	Bauri	20	100

Śivapur, with two jatis represented, containing thirty households
and perhaps 180 people, is on the northeast border of Kriśnapur
mouja. It resembles its sister village, Kriśnapur, in almost every way,
and it was founded at about the same time by a family of Kanauj
Brahmans from whom almost all the present Brahmans (one household is that of a man who has married into the village) are descended.
There are two paras, one of Brahmans and one of Bauris.

The Brahmans cultivate about one thousand bighas of riceland,
with the Bauris performing the actual agricultural labor, and maintain
about seventy head of cattle and water buffalo. Many of the Brahmans work in office jobs in factories and collieries, and a few of the
Bauris have managed to get menial jobs in the bicycle factory. The
Brahmans are part of the marriage-circle which includes the Brahmans of Gôndôgram and Kriśnapur, and the Bauris of the three
villages also belong to a single Bauri marriage-circle.

Kônnôgram is about four miles north of Gôndôgram. It is one of

TABLE 11   *Village 9: Kônnôgram*

Stratum	Jati Name	Number of Households	Persons
Upper	Caśa (Farmer)	66	360
	Bengali Brahman	29	180
Middle	Goala (Milkman)	15	75
	Napit (Barber)	3	15
	Jele (Fisherman)	9	45
	Kamar (Blacksmith)	1	5
	Dom	3	15
	Bôiśnôb (Vaiśnavite)	1	5
	Poddôr (Goldsmith)	2	10
	Tambuli (Shopkeeper)	5	20
Lower	Bauri	33	140
	Camar (Leatherworker)	3	15
	Mæthôr (Sweeper)	1	5

the largest villages in the area, with 13 jatis, 171 households, and, in all, approximately 890 people. It is also considered an old village, if not as old as Mônôśa; both Farmer and Bengali Brahman families claim to be descended from the original founders, and both can name as many as nine generations of resident ancestors. Farmers, however, because of their greater number and generally greater wealth, claim higher socioeconomic status in the village, while admitting to a lower ritual status.

Relative positions of jatis tend to be somewhat unusual in Kônnôgram, in any case. There are, for example, four paṛas. One of them, of lowest prestige, is inhabited by all the Bauris and by the Sweepers. The latter, incidentally, live in the village but do not work there; they clean toilets and sweep floors in one of the factories. The other three paṛas are of approximately equal status, each containing families of the most important jatis, if in different proportions. In the largest, for example—Upôr paṛa—there are fifty Farmer households and only one Brahman, along with most of the jatis with smaller representation. Even Doms and Leatherworkers live in this paṛa, if slightly to one side. In Majh paṛa, there are eight Brahman and ten Farmer households, along with a family of Barbers. All the rest of the Brahmans, along with six households of Farmers and all the Shopkeepers and the Fishermen, live in a third paṛa. The Barbers, incidentally (of the same marriage-circle as those of Gôndôgram), serve only bhôdrôlok; in Kônnôgram this means everyone but Bauris, Doms, Blacksmiths, and Leatherworkers.

Something over seven hundred bighas—owned mostly by Farmers and Brahmans—are under rice cultivation. Bauris, of course, provide the major source of agricultural labor, but Doms and Leatherworkers will work in the fields when circumstances require. Leatherworkers, however, prefer to work their hereditary occupation, skinning dead cattle that have been abandoned in the fields of nearby villages, then curing and selling the leather.

There are some seven to eight hundred head of cattle and water buffalo in the village, owned mostly by Farmer, Brahman, and Milkman households. Land is in short supply, and many must seek work in factory and colliery, even among the bhôdrôlok, but Farmers in particular are sad, saying that if they but had enough land to cultivate they would gladly give up all other occupations.

The Bôiśnôb household represents a family dedicated to the worship of Viśnu; they are considered pious but not of high rank in the village hierarchy since they are landless. The Tambuli households can tell little of their origin; they are Shopkeepers, they say, and they operate small shops in each of the three major paṛas.

TABLE 12   *Village 10: Saldanga*

Stratum	Jati Name	Number of Households	Persons
Upper	Kanauj Brahman	11	60
	Khôtriyô (Kśatriya or Warrior)	1	5
Lower	Śūṛi (Distiller)	2	10
	Bauri	25	100
	Santal	25	80

Saldanga is some two miles north of Gôndôgram. It contains five jatis, with sixty-four households holding some 255 people. There are four paṛas; Brahmans, the Khôtriyô household, and the Distillers live in the one of greatest prestige, while the Bauris live in a paṛa of their own and the Santals are divided into two paṛas. There are more than eight hundred bighas of riceland—owned, as we might expect, by Brahmans and worked primarily by Bauris. Santals prefer to work as coal-miners, and Distillers in some sort of liquor-dispensing establishment, but when in economic difficulty both will turn, with reluctance, to field labor. The Khôtriyô family arrived only two or three years before the study was conducted. They had sufficient funds to purchase a few bighas of land, which they cultivate and so maintain themselves. The Brahmans maintain, in all, some 150 head of cattle and water buffalo. A few of the Brahmans hold office jobs in nearby collieries. Brahmans, Distillers, Bauris, and Santals belong to the same marriage-circles as their counterparts in Gôndôgram.

* * *

The village of Gôndôgram was chosen for the study because of its relationship with the bicycle factory. The nine other villages described above were chosen, as has been indicated, pretty much at random. Yet they are not unconnected with Gôndôgram; they circle it spatially, and have inhabitants of marriage-circles represented in Gôndôgram—or there are people with economic ties to Gôndôgram, like the Jele from Charpukuria or the tea-shop operator from Tilimunda. Still, a completely different set of villages could easily have been chosen, with the same spatial, social, and economic relationships, and as different from those described here as any of them are from each other. They are, in short, as representative, or as non-representative, as any other villages in the area.

The brief survey is intended primarily to give the reader a sense of the district: the kind of villages, with the kinds of castes and occupations, to be found in the neighborhood of Gôndôgram. So let us note that in these ten villages we have found two Brahman jatis represented (but never in the same village), one more common to the east, in Bengal, and the other to the west in Bihar; and the Brahmans of both jatis are primarily landholders, farmers, cultivating rice with the assistance of Bauri laborers. We found Bauri laborers in almost every village (the only exception is Gopalgram, the village of Carpenters). In all, we found twenty-four jatis represented in these ten villages, some—like Bauris—in almost every one, and some represented only once in ten villages. If Brahmans are invariably landholders when they are present, landholders, we have seen, may be of many other jatis, particularly where Brahmans are *not* present. Some ten or more distinctive service jatis are represented, plus jatis whose traditional services have been abandoned.

Gôndôgram, it will be noted, is one of the larger villages in terms of population, but not the largest. Most of the villages have fewer jatis, but two have more and two have essentially the same number. I would argue, therefore, that Gôndôgram is much like any other village of its district. But, of course, no village is exactly like any other village, and some (such as Gopalgram) are distinctive to the point of seeming unique.

Part II

THE VILLAGE AND THE UNIVERSE

1

Good and Evil

Theological questions and other religious matters cannot be discussed with equal facility or profit with every citizen of Gôndôgram. Women defer in such matters to men, and young men to old men. Even among the men, many—perhaps most—have little to offer. They insist they have never thought about such matters and cannot now, suddenly, attempt to compose answers to questions they have never before considered. They urge the interviewer to do what they themselves would do if such a question had occurred to them: consult with the appropriate knowledgeable members of the community.

Most villagers, even including Santals, would agree that Brahmans have a special jurisdiction in religious matters, but the Brahmans themselves indicate only three of their number as being really qualified to deal with religion. One of them is Hôripôdô Dube, who serves—like his father before him—as caretaker of the shrine of Rôkkhô-Kali (Kali, the savior; in Sanskrit, Kāli). Of the other two, one is the oldest Brahman (a Pande) in the village, recognized by all as intelligent and knowledgeable, as well as impoverished and saintly; the other, also a Pande, is a wealthy and pious man, prime mover in most village religious affairs.

While they might agree on the special jurisdiction of the Brahmans, however, villagers of other castes would most emphatically not be prepared to concede to the Brahmans complete jurisdiction or even exclusive or superior knowledge. The men of Ûcu para urge one to consult with the two senior heads of the Deyasi family of the Carpenters. Nor does this mean that there are not Washermen and Distillers with religious standing, but only that there happen to be none such at present resident in Gôndôgram. Bauris can name four of

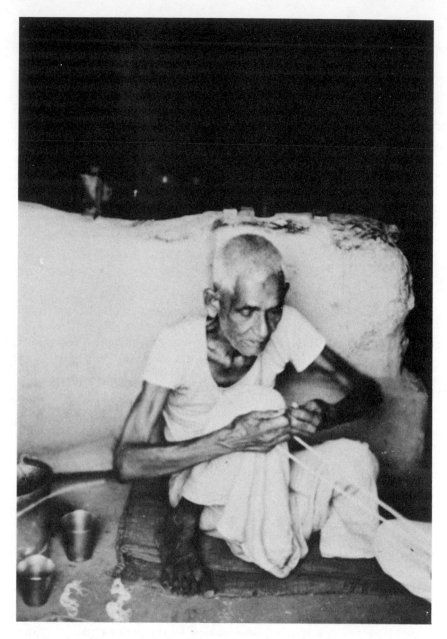

An elderly Brahman making the sacred thread that is worn only by the highest-ranked, or ''twice-born,'' castes.

their caste with knowledge and authority to offer on religious questions: Bamun Bauri (he who was once a Brahman), and three men (two of them brothers who migrated here from a village in Bihar) who perform yearly pujas in honor of the goddess Mônôśa. The Santals refer one to Nando Hemrôm of Śimul Santal para and to Cuna Murmu of Gadhapaṭhôr Santal para: these men each hold the office of *naiki* (religious official) in their respective paras.

For all these religious leaders of Gôndôgram, morality and ethical behavior are perceived as matters between man and man. They are not viewed as the concerns of either the religious leader or of individual divinities, although in the end there is a kind of cosmic retribution for wicked behavior. Further, few if any in the village will attempt a universalistic statement on morality. Rather, as they see it (and explicitly explain it) the human universe is made up of two classes of persons: those people with whom one has a "relationship" (*āttiota*) of some kind, and those with whom one has no relationship. In the case of the latter—the stranger—morality is simply not a relevant issue. Put bluntly, the stranger owes me nothing, I owe him nothing; should he cheat me it is no more than I expect of him, and should I cheat him it is no more than he should expect of me. We impinge on each other and then go our separate ways without further thought of, or concern for, each other.

With those of the first category—the non-strangers—the relationships may be of the kind between equals or the kind between non-equals. People in this category may or may not be viewed as kinfolk; either way they are still āttiota. And among those viewed as kinfolk, there are some relationships that are seen as based upon blood ties, primarily patrilineal. Such relationships are mostly between non-equals—father and son, brother and brother, uncle (father's brother) and nephew. The content of these relationships reflects an assumption of absolute trust and dependability. One's obligations in such relationships take priority over all others and cannot be violated whatever the circumstances. If they are violated at all—even questioned—the relationship is considered broken and recriminations are often vitriolic. The problem is that as the tie becomes attenuated by an increasing number of biological links it becomes more difficult to fulfill the obligations (for one thing there are closer ties and more immediate obligations) and so the possibility of division becomes greater. A man may depend on his sons, but what of his brother's sons? Brothers can be expected to succor each other with more enthusiasm than will first cousins (for each of the latter has brothers, whose claims come first). In principle, however, men who admit to common agnatic descent have obligations to each other which must be met upon call—upon pain of the charge of immoral behavior.

Similarly, one has obligations to one's affines, one's kinsmen through ties of marriage. Here the relationships are between equals,[1] and—interestingly—the trust is not as absolute as it is (or should be) between agnates. Ideally, my wife's brother, my sister's husband, my mother's sister's family, and so on, should come to my aid at time of need. Specifically, I should be able to turn to them for help in finding spouses for the children in my household, and I will be expected to help them in the same ways: locating eligible candidates and investigating and reporting on their reputations and those of their families. We will assist each other at weddings and at obsequial ceremonies. Such relationships are usually not as close as those with agnates; for one thing, they had to begin at some point in time as relationships between hitherto unrelated households. Such relationships begin in suspicion and must prove themselves over time.

Jat-brothers (those referred to as members of the same kutumbô) are also considered to have a relationship based on kinship. Ties of blood and marriage cannot be demonstrated, but they are assumed to exist. Mutual obligation therefore exists, and in this case it is clearly an obligation between male equals. Again, while the sense of obligation is even more attenuated than in the previous cases, and therefore there is greater room for suspicion and hostility, the obligation is nevertheless still absolute. If we are jat-brothers, we owe each other spouses for our children, and we insist mutually that none of our children will be given as spouse to one who is not jat-brother, on pain of expulsion of the entire offending household. From this perspective, expulsion (or "out-casteing") might be viewed as a variant of the basic response to any violation of obligation, severing the relationship. Jat-brothers are expected to aid one another in other ways: economic, social, and political. It is understood, however, that in case of conflict of obligation those with the closest kin ties will receive priority.

In Gôndôgram, however, one may have relationships with individuals who are in no way perceived as affines, agnates, or jat-brothers, but the relationships are considered in principle just as binding and the obligations just as important. Most commonly, such a relationship is between non-equals, that is, between munib (master) and muniś (servant), and this usually between someone of a high-ranked caste and someone of a lower-ranked caste. Such a relationship begins almost inevitably in an atmosphere of suspicion and hos-

1. Apart from the fact that, as we have seen, the man who provides a bride must defer to the head of her husband's household.

tility, and often never leaves it. If a robbery takes place, for example, a servant is the first to be suspected.

Over time, however, a bond is likely to come into being. The subordinate strives to be considered "one of the family." Typically, he addresses the superordinate as "my mother and my father." The obligation of the subordinate thereby precipitates an equal obligation on the part of the superordinate to provide for the needs, not just of the subordinate but of his entire family, not just for now, but into the future and over generations.

These obligations, expressed just now as between master and servant, appear to form the basis of what are usually referred to in the literature as "jajmani" relationships,[2] the ties between men of different castes that constitute the bonding of caste as a socioeconomic system. If my father served your father, as priest or as barber, then you have an obligation to continue the relationship with me. And suppose I am hopelessly inadequate, lacking all the necessary skills? The Gôndôgram villager shrugs off such a question: Suppose a man had an inadequate or incompetent son? Shall he, properly, cast him out on the road to starve? No, just as you have an obligation to care for all your children, so you have an obligation to the son of your father's barber; for better or worse, he is your barber.

Again, it must be emphasized that not all superior/inferior relationships work out this way, nor are all obligations maintained, particularly over generations. The foregoing is a statement of standard, "the way it should be," the way good men should act, not the way bad men, alas, do so often act. Further, the relationship just described may occur on many levels: between householder and servant, between landholder and mahindôr, between regional zemindar and village landholder, and most recently between factory official and factory laborer. In each case, the subordinate addresses the superordinate as "my mother and my father"; in each case he promises fidelity and obedience and hopes in return for perpetual assistance for himself and his family over the generations.

And, finally, a relationship may come into being between two men—neither kinsmen nor yet master and servant—who regard each other as full equals. It is a comparatively rare relationship (many men in Gôndôgram never experience it) and yet it is considered by all a particularly wonderful relationship to have. The commonly used term of reference for the relationship is *adan-prôdan;* the Standard Bengali term for *reciprocity* or *exchange.* Frequently, a villager will refer to a man with whom he has an adan-prôdan relationship as his *āttiô,* the

2. See, for example, Wiser 1936, Lewis 1965, Beidelman 1959, and Kolenda 1963.

term otherwise usually reserved for a kinsman by marriage. Does that
mean the friend is equivalent to a kinsman, or perhaps even really a
kinsman by a tie other than blood or marriage? Perhaps, but as the
villager explains it, the term *āttiô* is being used in its most deepest
sense; my āttiô (atmiya) and I have come to share the same soul—we
reciprocate, we are adan-prôdan.

Among the higher-ranked castes two men who have entered into
an adan-prôdan relationship are of different, but similarly ranked,
jatis. Such relationships are most common, therefore, in Ūcu paṛa,
among Carpenters, Distillers, and Washermen. Men of the same
caste, and of the same village, are likely to be constricted by the ties
of kinship and jati. It can happen, however, that men of the same jati
enter into such adan-prôdan relationships; among Brahmans, they
may be unrelated men usually of another village, sometimes of one's
own. Among Bauris, as has been noted, they are almost invariably
between boys of different villages who meet during their bagal (cowherd) days and decide to become bôndhu-bhai (blood-brothers).

In cases where the adan-prôdan relationship is between two men
of the same jati, they avoid the marriage of their children. Some say it
is because they now view each other as brothers and the children of
brothers may not marry. Others point to the fact that the relationship is
not like that of brothers; it is a relationship between equals, and
brothers are never equals. This, they say, is why they avoid the marriage of their children: two men whose children are married to each
other can never treat each other as equals—the father of the bride must
show deference and respect to the father of the groom. Marriage of
their children, therefore, would destroy the relationship. And so,
whether members of the same jati or not, two men in an adan-prôdan
relationship extend to each other perfect trust and perfect friendship.

We began this excursion into human relationships with an inquiry
into good and evil. Who, then, is the *śarthôpôr,* the wicked person?
The term means "the selfish one"; he is any man who has not lived
up to his reciprocal obligations in any of the relationships just explored—between kinsmen or castemen, between master and servant,
or between any two villagers. Most of all, though, the śarthôpôr is the
man who has failed his āttiô in an adan-prôdan relationship.

But suppose a man elects to become a śarthôpôr, a wicked man?
As we have noted, the Gôndôgram villager has no belief that divine
beings will in any way take offense and impose punishment; the man
will not necessarily suffer for such behavior by any immediate divine
retribution. Eventually, however, he must suffer. To begin with, his
fellows will show contempt for him, and in the end, inevitably, his
soul will undergo suffering.

2

Soul and Spirit

Any inquiry into the Gôndôgram Hindu's concept of "soul" is made more difficult than perhaps need be by the very use of that English term, for the word "soul" in certain ways obscures precisely that which we are trying to clarify. In addition, and as we might expect by now, men of different jatis have different views; we must be careful not to lump the views together indiscriminately.

As the Gôndôgram Brahman theologians relate it, to begin with, a human—any human, like any living thing, like even inanimate objects—possesses a corporeal dimension; he has a visible, tangible body. Further, as they see it, a human shares with all other living things the state of having a *jibatta*. The term is actually made up of two Bengali words: *jib* and *atta*—presumably related to, or derived from, the Sanskrit terms *jīva* and *ātmā*.

We might approximate village usage if we translate *jibatta* as "life-principle"; Gôndôgram Brahmans say that every living thing contains, as a fundamental condition of its being a living thing, a jibatta. The jibatta gives life—*is* life—but it is also "self" in that it serves to separate or distinguish each living thing from every other living thing; the "self" from the rest of the universe. And, further, the human jibatta appears to be in no wise different from the jibatta of any other living thing; the jibatta represents the fact of life and of separate being—it does not represent consciousness or will.

For, the Brahmans say, the human being is different from all other living things in having a *second* atta, this one referred to as a *brômhatta*—a "soul" or "self" bestowed upon the human by *Brômhô* (Skt.: Brahmā; God in the aspect of "creator"). Both jibatta and brômhatta are incorporeal, invisible, intangible, but the Gôndôgram Brahman offers some speculations about them. The jibatta, he suggests, is located in the human somewhere at the base of the spine. The brômhatta is believed to be located in the brain and has the appearance, could one but see it, of a *śôhôsrôdôl pôddô,* a lotus with a thousand petals. The brômhatta, finally—and perhaps most importantly—exhibits the quality of *gæn,* "consciousness," "wisdom," "power of discrimination," among other things. In sum, therefore, the jibatta, by virtue of its presence, bestows life upon the human being and the separate existence that is characteristic of every living thing. The brômhatta, however, bestows on the human being, by virtue of its presence in his brain, consciousness—or awareness of self—and the capacity to discriminate between good and evil and to make choices. Only humans have brômhattas, and so only humans among all living things have both knowledge of, and capacity to choose between, good and evil.

And, say the Gôndôgram Brahmans, since a man has the capacity to know good and evil and to choose between them, he alone among living things must bear the responsibility for the choices he makes. If he chooses evil and turns away from good, he will suffer; that is a law not of gods but of the universe.[1]

The man is not *either* his body *or* his jibatta—he is both, inextricably intertwined while he is still alive. The brômhatta is not so intertwined; it is a divine emanation, residing in the human body during its life and serving, as we might say, as a catalyst, imparting by its presence consciousness and the power of discrimination, but unaffected by anything that happens. At the death of the individual, the brômhatta, believed to be as pure and unsullied as it was when it came into existence at the moment of the person's birth, leaves the body and merges once more with Brômhô, the transcendent and primal creator-divinity. At death, too, the body—which has enjoyed or suffered the experiences of life—becomes nothingness, merging with the universe through the act of cremation. Only the jibatta remains, therefore, to undergo reward or punishment.

All Brahmans of Gôndôgram, at any rate all those who feel they have sufficient knowledge and interest to discuss the matter at all, would be likely to agree with the main points in the foregoing: man consists of a corporeal body, plus a jibatta and a brômhatta. Non-Brahmans, on the other hand, would agree only in part. Carpenter Deyasis profess to know nothing of brômhattas (they neither affirm nor deny the existence of such) but agree that each man has a jibatta

---

1. Which is not to say either that the law is not of divine origin, or that it does not have divine approval, only that it appears to operate independently of the gods.

that lives on after his death and will be rewarded or punished for his actions during his lifetime. Bauri theologians, such as they are, know neither brômhatta nor jibatta, but acknowledge that in each human there is a "spirit" (they use the term "*bhut*") which can, unquestionably, live on after his death.

There is, in addition, considerable disagreement in the village about what exactly happens to the soul or spirit of a once-living person after his demise, and the disagreement is not only between men of different jatis but even among Brahmans. The controversy is by no means acrimonious; a man will deliver his opinion, take note of the fact that others hold substantially different opinions, and shrug it all off with the statement that no one can really know for sure.

Most Brahmans agree that, at the death of any human, his jibatta leaves his body, becoming an ethereal entity (*bayôbiyô sôrir*). For some Brahmans, properly speaking it should no longer be called jibatta (life-principle) but *pretatta* (death-spirit, or ghost). Some prefer, simply, *atta*, self or soul. This atta, then, relict of the jibatta, hovers in the vicinity of its former home, while the living observe the days of their mourning. The Brahmans make the first offering (*pindô*) to the spirit of the dead on the tenth day after the death and cremation. On the eleventh day, Brahmans perform the śaddhô ceremony, which— as has been noted in an earlier section—involves the feeding of as many members of the śômaj as the family of the deceased can afford to invite. The rituals of this ceremony are intended to purify and sanctify the pretatta; with this ceremony the pretatta departs from the vicinity of its former existence and moves on to other experiences, it is believed. With the departure of the pretatta, mourning comes to an end.

Learned Brahmans are perfectly willing to speculate on what happens next, though as has been noted they admit freely to lack of certainty. One said, for example, that the pretatta, after the śaddhô ceremonies, is suspended in nothingness for one full day. During this time, the behavior of the formerly living individual undergoes a kind of cosmic summation and evaluation and a judgment is rendered. Some say no one can know by whom the judgment is made, or how; others say it is arrived at and administered by Jamraja (from Skt.: Yama and Rāja), "Lord of Death." Another Brahman adds that, while the evaluation and judgment take a day, it must be remembered that a day for the gods is a year on earth, and that is why Brahmans make another pindô offering one year after death and some also perform a second śaddhô ceremony called the *sôpindôkôrôn*.

And so, therefore, after that divine "day" of judgment the pretatta goes to its reward—or punishment. Most Brahmans agree that the reward or punishment takes the form of a sojourn either in *śôrgô* (customarily translated as "heaven") or in *nôrôk* (customarily translated as "hell"). For some, śôrgô and nôrôk are simply expressive of human conditions; in other words, they believe that the atta gravitates after judgment into the body of a newborn human and begins a new corporeal existence. If the cosmic judgment was favorable (because in the *purbôjônmô,* the previous life, the individual led a "good" life), then the experiences of the new life will all be good, a śôrgô on earth. If the judgment was unfavorable, then the person will experience much misery in his new existence; he will know nôrôk in his lifetime. It may be of interest to some that while the Brahmans of Gôndôgram speak of reward or punishment in coming incarnations, no mention was made of reward or punishment in the form of being reborn into a higher or lower varna.

Some Brahmans, however, while agreeing that eventually the pretatta will undergo reincarnation, insist that it must experience śôrgô or nôrôk in some celestial dimension first; that these terms cannot merely refer to the experiences of life. As they see it, the pretatta, after undergoing judgment, will go for a space of time to taste the pleasures of śôrgô or endure the discomfort of nôrôk. Only after dwelling in one or the other for some time (and no living human knows how long or short that time will be) will the atta return to earth again and to corporeality.

Students of Great-Tradition Hinduism will of course recognize the sources of many of the foregoing beliefs, distorted though they may be. The Brahmans insist, in fact, that their beliefs are in no way folk beliefs, and in no way distorted, but accurate renditions of Vedic and other Great-Tradition teachings. No man may know for sure, they say, and they admit to contradictions and uncertainties, but they are united and firm in the belief that only Brahmans know whatever man can indeed know, just as, in their view, only the prayers of a Brahman have any meaning. They agree, too, in the basic beliefs that the jibatta is eternal and will undergo, must undergo, reward and punishment after death and in succeeding incarnations for the deeds of the living man.

Carpenter and Bauri religious leaders emphatically dispute the Brahman claim to being the sole human beings with the power to offer up meaningful prayers. Carpenter and Bauri acknowledge the worth of Brahman prayers (they concede that Brahmans are all hereditary "priestly" folk), but they insist that any man of any caste may pray.

Both do concede one special advantage to the Brahmans: the Great-Tradition—its written literature, classic prayers, and powerful *mantrôs* (formal liturgy). The prayers of Carpenters (for the most part) and of Bauris are unwritten; they are transmitted orally down the generations. In addition, their very knowledge of the nature of the universe, of the significance of death, and of the behavior of spirits derives from oral accounts and thus, even in the eyes of Carpenter and Bauri theologians themselves, these lack the status of Brahman discourse on these matters. Nevertheless, Carpenter and Bauri refuse to accept, in all cases, Brahmanical explanation and interpretation, arguing that no living human can know for certain.

Carpenters refer in the discussion of religion to *atta* and *pretatta,* and—when asked—acknowledge readily that jibatta is simply another name for the same thing. They profess, however, to have no knowledge of brômhatta ("Ask the Brahmans about that," they advise). After death, they say, the pretatta experiences sôrgô or nôrôk and eventually undergoes rebirth, and will in the new life experience fortune or misfortune in accordance with deeds in the previous life. In all this, they admit agreement with Brahmans.

But Brahmans, as Carpenters see it, are much too certain about exactly what happens and when. Though, as we have seen, Brahmans do profess uncertainty (at least to a visiting anthropologist) and do not claim that reward or punishment in reincarnation must take the form of being born higher or lower in the caste structure, Carpenters present a different perception of what *they* believe to be Brahmanical beliefs and teachings. Brahmans, Carpenter Deyasis insist, claim to know exactly how and when reward and punishment is administered after death, and also believe, say Carpenters, that one's position in the varna system is part of that reward and punishment. Carpenters utterly reject this supposed Brahmanical view and insist that their uncertainty about what happens after death is superior to the Brahman's certainty.

The Bauri theologian, on the other hand, admits both to having little knowledge and to having undergone little effort at speculation. He too is convinced, however, that in essentials Brahmans really know little more than he, despite their learning. They may know more mantrôs than he, simply because they can read, but they know no more than he about the nature of the universe.

He professes to know nothing of attas of any kind, nor—he claims—has he ever heard anything of reincarnation. What he knows is that there are bhuts about, most of them spirits of those who were once alive. Bhuts are malevolent; they can cause illness and death, and the living must be protected against them. Why are they malevolent? Because they are the spirits of those who were evil in their lifetimes, and so they continue to be wicked after death. What happens to good people when they die? He is not certain; perhaps there is a śôrgô for them, as he has heard, perhaps their spirits perish in peace with their bodies. Bad people, however, become bhuts.

Santals, we have seen, are separated socially and spatially from the Hindu population of Gôndôgram. It should not come as a surprise, therefore, to learn that the Santals have two types of religious officials: one (the naiki) concerned with transcendental issues, and the other (the ojha) concerned with the pragmatic. And, since to the Santals what others view as a paṛa is seen as a gā (gram, or village), each Santal hamlet must have its own naiki, and does.

This naiki is indeed the religious leader charged with transcendental responsibilities; to him falls the task of performing annual ceremonies, including sacrifices, in propitiation of major divinities. In actual practice, his role is quite complex. The naiki, like other Santals of Gôndôgram, considers himself to be a Hindu; he treats the cow with respect,[2] and he will attend—or at least look at—religious ceremonies conducted by Brahmans, Carpenter Deyasis, and even Bauris. As he sees it, all these ceremonies are valid—at each, some important, but different, divinity is propitiated—and in just such a way the ceremonies *he* performs are valid Hindu ceremonies; who else but a Santal naiki would (or could) propitiate the great god Cādu Boṇa?

Thus, the naiki propitiates Cādu Boṇa, and other divinities, as his people have always done, and in so doing he maintains the stability of the universe and obtains insofar as anyone can the goodwill of the divinities for the Santals and for all the people of Gôndôgram. On the other hand, while the naiki is not concerned with the solving of personal and mundane problems, such as illness, neither is he disposed to philosophize about the nature of man, death, and the universe. He is, after all, a Hindu, he points out, and leaves such matters to the Brahmans.

Questions about such matters as reincarnation, therefore, or the nature of the atta, elicit no response from the naiki; he claims to know nothing of such matters. When asked about bhuts (spirits), however, he brightens and refers one to the other Santal religious official, the ojha, for bhuts are (in the Santal view) clearly in the jurisdiction of the man who wrestles with mundane problems, such as illness.

The ojha (and there is only one for the two Santal paṛas of Gôndôgram, for the office requires years of training and few are qualified) is happy to talk of bhuts and related matters, but shrugs off queries about transcendental issues. Though, like the naiki, he is only a part-time practitioner, supporting himself through labor in the fields and

2. Gôndôgram Santals do not castrate bull-calves, but have the job done for them by a member of a low-ranked group called *Bôcka* who live in the Dumka district of Bihar. It should be remembered, however, that to the other inhabitants of Gôndôgram, including even the Bauris, the Santals are definitely not accepted as Hindus!

mines, he considers himself a professional and practical healer—and not a religious official.

For him, the sole issue of interest is: Why do people become ill? As he sees it, the problem has three levels of explanation. The proximal, and simplest, explanation of illness is that the world is infested with quantities of a minute creature called *tejo*. When pressed for a description of the tejo, he said it was something like the *poka* (a Bengali word for "insect") but tiny to the point of invisibility. It is the cause, by its very presence in the human body, of all diseases. Tejos penetrate the body through orifices such as mouth and nose, or through wounds (particularly if the latter are touched by flies), and precipitate all the symptoms we observe as disease. His account of the tejo, its appearance and effects, certainly sounds as if he had been exposed to a lecture on the Western germ theory of disease, but the ojha insists that his approach is the traditional Santal one.

The ojha is interested in why tejos invade one person and not another. Sometimes it is accidental, as in the case of the flies and the open wound, but often no such accidental cause can be discovered. In a family, one person becomes ill, another does not; of two persons with the same illness, one may have a mild case and the other become deathly ill. One must search deeper, he feels, for cause and effect. If an illness does not respond immediately to the obvious medicines (whether his or those of the non-Santal doctor), then the tejos have invaded the body at the behest of a bhut, a malevolent spirit, or perhaps even a *bôd-debta,* an evil divinity of greater power and scope than the bhut.

And why, the ojha asks, should the evil spirit attack one person and not another? Sometimes, again, for accidental reasons: a person has stumbled inadvertently upon the locality of the bhut or in some other way brought on its displeasure. A displeased bhut or angered bôd-debta will cause the tejo to afflict the person. He, in turn, can attempt to mollify the spirit in some way. A common Santal solution is to pack up and move from the neighborhood of the malevolent bhut. It is said, for example, that Śimul Santal para was founded by a refugee from Gadhapaṭhôr Santal para who had removed his family from their former home because they were coming down with illness too frequently and experiencing too many inexplicable accidents. He and the ojha concluded that the family had somehow offended a bhut who dwelt in the vicinity of Gadhapaṭhôr Santal para and that they would be better off elsewhere, since a bhut, apparently, tends to stay put.

But most of the time, the ojha believes, a bhut is moved to inflict tejo and therefore disease upon a person through the machinations of a living, evil person. A person who has the power to influence bhuts to visit illness, disaster, or even death upon some human victim is known as a *dan,* if male, or *daini,* if female. The latter (witches, we would call them) are considered to be much more prevalent and according to many informants much more dangerous than their male counterparts.

The belief in dans and dainis is by no means peculiar to the Santals; men of all jatis in Gôndôgram and in the surrounding villages share the Santal fear of inimical old men and women. Sometimes specific individuals are suspected, but more often the daini is totally unknown. She (or he) is out there somewhere in the threatening world beyond the web of kinship and obligation, sometimes even in one's own village. Brooding over real or fancied wrongs, these wicked folk know the *môntôrs* (or so the Santal ojha calls them, in an obvious metathasis of "mantrô") that can bind the bhuts to them. On almost every house of Gôndôgram, of every jati and in every paṛa, hangs a *môndira,* a protective amulet containing such items as a piece of broken pottery, part of an old broom, part of an old shoe, and a withered fragment of a plant, often of a cactus. The môndira guards the house against the *kharap-lôjôr,* the evil-eye or malicious inclination, and it is the daini and her attendant bhut that villagers fear most.

The Santal ojha, therefore, knows that all illness is caused by the invisible tejo. If, in a given case, it is simply tejo at work and nothing more, his medicines or Western medicines can usually take care of it. All such medicines are worthless, however, if the tejo is actually a reflection of a bhut or daini at work. As he sees his work, therefore, his first task is to determine the ultimate cause of the illness. If, as in most cases, he detects the presence of dan or daini, incantations and special rituals will be necessary in addition to the medicines.

There are many men, he notes—even of jatis other than Santal—with knowledge of how to combat the work of dainis. But dans and dainis vary in their power, and not all men can counteract the most powerful. He is, he says, one of the strongest ojhas in the district, although even he has come into conflict with dainis stronger than himself. He has had, in other words, patients he could not cure, and has had to send them on to even more powerful ojhas. Still, his clientele is large, including many non-Santals in Gôndôgram and other villages.

When a patient, afflicted by tejo, bhut, and daini, is finally cured by him, he expects the patient or his family to bring him a goat or a pair of pigeons after one year. These he will sacrifice to *Surjô-debta,* whom he identifies as the same god of the sun worshiped by all Hindus, including Santals. If the patient prefers to have the sacrifice made to Kali, or some other divinity of the patient's choice, the ojha is happy to oblige. Whatever the name of the divinity to whom the sacrifice is offered, he—the ojha—keeps the meat for his own family as his payment for successful services.

3

Gods and Gôndôgram

For the Brahman of Gôndôgram, all that is divine, all that pertains to the gods, may be summed up as Bhagôban, the transcendent divinity, also known as Iśbar (Iśwāra), who is lord of the universe. Bhagôban is truly all-encompassing and transcendent, without form or personification, not to be prayed to or propitiated. The very appellation means only "providence," "fortune," or "fate." Bhagôban, nevertheless, is to the Gôndôgram Brahman the true overarching divinity, incorporating all the others. Mortal man, say the Brahmans, cannot be comforted by such an awesome concept of divinity and must approach it only in terms of component aspects. These are personified; they have names and can be represented. They are the Hindu trinity: Brômhô (Brahmā), the creative aspect of divinity; Śib, or Śibu (Śiva), the destructive aspect of divinity; and Biśnu (Viśnu), the supportive or maintaining aspect of divinity.

These divine persons, say Brahmans, are the particular concern of Brahmans. Brahman men of Gôndôgram pray regularly (some daily, some weekly) to Biśnu and Śibu. Few Hindus, it is said, pray to Brômhô. Every Brahman household has a sacred location in the courtyard at which prayers to Biśnu and Śibu are offered; this is a low altar of brick and mud, regularly plastered with cow dung, usually with a few *tulśi* (basil) plants growing from the top. Every morning, every male in the Brahman household, upon his return from his bath, kneels before this tulśi-môncô, pouring water and offering a brief prayer for the continuing favor of the divine. In many Brahman houses there is in addition a special shrine or room dedicated to Biśnu or Śibu. The Pandes once supported a common shrine to Narayôn (Nārāyana), another appellation of Biśnu.

145

A tulśi-môncô in a Brahman courtyard. It is the customary locus for daily familial Brahman prayers. Tulśi-môncôs are occasionally seen in the courtyards of other castes, especially of Carpenters.

Prayers to Biśnu and Śibu are representative of the transcendental dimension; they are supportive and universe-maintaining, requesting essentially that the divinities not turn their faces from their worshipers. Rarely are they requests for divine intercession in human affairs, though they can be, and sometimes are, if the individual wishes to make such a request. To put it succinctly, it was my impression that a Brahman prayed to Biśnu and Śibu as part of his regular obligatory worship; when he had a request to make for divine intercession he tended to address the request to some other divinity.

Brahmans in Gôndôgram pay particular attention to the classic Great-Tradition divinities, such as the three already mentioned, plus Śôrôśôtti (Skt.: Saraswatī), the divine personification of learning and the arts; Lôkkhi (Skt.: Lakṣmī), personification of good fortune; Ganeś (Skt.: Gaṇeśa), personification of success in undertakings; and so on. In addition, they offer prayers to Durga, (Skt.: Durgā), acknowledged throughout Hindu India as the fierce consort of Śiva, but who is worshiped in Bengal, in effect, as a major overarching divinity in her own right.[1] Gôndôgram Brahmans also offer prayers to Kali, another female divinity, whose exact position within the Great-Tradition scheme is even more difficult to analyze.

While Kali is known throughout Hindu India, attitudes toward her vary sharply from district to district. In much of south India and central north India she is dismissed by Brahmans as a low-caste divinity, one of the many such Little-Tradition "godlings" (Marriott 1955) who are worshiped by non-Brahmans as bringers of, and protectors from, illness and disease. In such areas, the Brahmans will not go so far as to deny her divinity (they rarely deny divinity to any personification worshiped by anyone) and consider her, given her jurisdiction, a local manifestation of Śiva, or divine destruction. She may even be considered by the Brahmans as a consort of Śiva, along with all the other such female Little-Tradition godlings. Only in two major regions of India, however—Kerala and Bengal—is Kali accorded what can only be termed Great-Tradition status.

True, she is fearful and frightening in her representations; usually she is portrayed as garbed only in a necklace of skulls and a girdle of severed human forearms, while blood drips from her tongue and from the weapons in her many arms. In Western writings it is customary to refer to her as "dark," partly because of her color (she is usually represented as black, or dark blue) and partly because she is asso-

---

1. At ceremonies in honor of Durga, it is customary to include a tiny picture of Śiva somewhere on or near the massive, full-bodied representation of Durga, in acknowledgment of the fact that she is, after all, his spouse. The prayers at such times, however, are all addressed to Durga.

ciated with such things as death, destruction, and animal sacrifice. The *Columbia Encyclopedia* ends its entry on Kali with the sentence "Kali was the patroness of the Thugs." (Bridgwater and Kurtz 1963). Undoubtedly she was, but for an understanding of religion in Gôndô-gram and perhaps in all Bengal, it is necessary to focus on the fact that she is *ma*—to everyone.

To her Bengali worshiper she is "mother," stern and frightening when she is angry and punishing her wayward children, but most of all benevolent and protective to her obedient children. Bengalis are her children, they feel, and they have nothing to fear from her. Going into battle, Bengalis will shout her name; they are certain that all her terrible wrath will be directed against their enemies and that she will show only her maternal protectiveness toward her own children. Their attitude is surely intelligible if we remember the particularistic values referred to earlier: there are obligations to one's family and kinsmen, among others, but none to aliens or strangers. Kali is ma.

It might seem that the widespread worship of Kali might pose a contradiction for the Brahmans of Gôndôgram, but they perceive none, although they admit readily that all is not easily explained or understood: There are ambiguities. Kali's power and jurisdiction seems equivalent to Śibu's. Is she then the same as Śibu, or an alternative to Śibu? No, Śibu is god, one of the three main aspects of godhood. He represents destruction in the universe. Kali is the divine mother; she can and will destroy whatever offends her. Then what is her relationship to Śibu? She is a consort of Śibu; when we pray to her, we are really praying to Śibu, just as when we pray to Śibu we are really, or ultimately, praying to Bhagôban.

Not all agree among the Gôndôgram Brahmans; some say Kali is another name for Durga, who in turn is another name for Parbôti (Skt.: Pārvatī). Others say no, Kali and Durga and Parbôti are separate and distinct divinities. One Brahman will explain: Kali created the universe; that is why she is "mother." But was the universe not created by Brômhô? Of course, and yet in a different way by Kali as well. Beyond a certain point, it is explained earnestly, explanations simply cannot be satisfactory. If all could be simply and clearly explained, wherein would be the mystery and inaccessibility of the divine?

The ambiguities of divinity do not reside solely in their relationships with one another. Are Kali and Śôrôśôtti and Ganeś and others to be viewed as transcendent deities, concerned with the maintenance of the universe, or are they "godlings" to whom one may appeal for pragmatic aid? It all depends. It depends upon the circumstances and upon the individual divinity concerned.

The nature of *divinity* itself seems to vary from case to case. Even to be a Brahman means, in Gôndôgram, that one is partially divine. At the very least, the Gôndôgram Brahman conceives that he alone among mortals can offer up prayers that will reach the overarching divine and thereby help to maintain the universe and the well-being of mankind. It is in this sense that he will smile at the efforts of non-Brahmans to offer transcendental prayers. A tulśi-môncô, he says, in the home of anyone but a Brahman simply has no meaning. A non-Brahman may pray if he wants to—and who these days can stop him?—but his prayers go nowhere. On the other hand, Brahmans concede that a deity, any deity, may hear the prayers of any human asking for immediate personal assistance. In fact, the prayers of some people, in such situations, may be more effective than those of others, even if the latter are Brahmans. But these are viewed more as petitions; prayers are after all the jurisdiction of Brahmans. Therefore, any individual with a pressing personal pragmatic need may petition any deity for assistance.

On the whole, however, it is wiser to ask the assistance of one who is skilled in such petitions, and it is sensible to address the petitions to the particular deity most likely to be concerned with the particular problem. One could, if one wished, pray to Biśnu to help a poor student improve in his studies, or to Śibu to prevent the death of an ill person. One could, and some do, and who knows but what such august divinities may even respond occasionally. It is wiser, however, to address the petitions to those most likely to intercede.

And so, the essential ambiguities of the gods appear to be that they are one (Bhagôban) and yet multifold, that they are transcendental and yet pragmatic. These ambiguities must always be borne in mind, for a Hindu deity is never "either-or" but "both." Only Bhagôban (fate, fortune) would appear to be completely transcendental; no one in Gôndôgram would pray to Bhagôban to intercede in some mundane affair. To a slightly lesser extent, Brômhô is a purely transcendental deity; few would pray to him for mundane reasons, but there were those who would insist that it was theoretically possible. Biśnu and Śibu are transcendental, but clearly more accessible, and all other deities unquestionably have both transcendental and pragmatic dimensions.

This holds as well for the Little-Tradition deities (or godlings) such as Mônôśa, she who presides over snake-bites. She may be worshiped primarily by Bauris, she may lack any place whatever in the Great-Tradition pantheon; but still the Brahmans of Gôndôgram acknowledge her as divine, as a manifestation of "God as destroyer" and even therefore as some low-ranking consort of Śibu. Further, like most other deities known in Gôndôgram, she is worshiped regularly at an annual ceremony that is essentially transcendental in nature, as well as irregularly, for pragmatic reasons, when an appropriate emergency arises—most particularly when someone is bitten by a poisonous snake.

Nor can one even say that in Gôndôgram a deity may be approached *either* in terms of the transcendental (at a fixed annual ceremony) *or* in terms of the pragmatic (at a special ad hoc ceremony). In many cases, the relationship with the deity exhibits much more complexity than that. As an example, let us examine the relationship between the Gôndôgram villagers and the goddess Kali. She is accepted by all in the village as a major deity, and as such is accorded an annual ceremony of propitiation, which will be discussed more fully later in this work. For now, let us note only that the annual Kali puja of Gôndôgram is sponsored primarily by Bauris, though others in the village, including Brahmans, observe and some even participate.

Brahmans admit to difficulty in explaining why Gôndôgram Bauris have sole responsibility; they are aware that in many other villages in the district the Kali Puja is sponsored by the dominant castes, including Brahmans. They point to the fact that they are busy with other ceremonies, that they cannot afford to support so many, that the Bauris wanted to sponsor this one and would resent Brahmanical interference. And, as a few Brahmans will add, it is also true that they are Kanauj Brahmans, originally from farther west, where they know Kali is not as highly regarded. They suggest that, while the Brahmans of Gôndôgram accord full honor to Kali today, perhaps their ancestors did not.

The point is that Gôndôgram Brahmans today do accord Kali full honor, but no annual puja. There is, in Brahman paṛa, in the Dube neighborhood, a shrine to Kali, and it is the exclusive property of Brahmans, specifically of one Dube family. The shrine, a low brick altar, is on the south side of a mango tree at the west side of the school yard. South of the altar area is imbedded a *khūta,* the forklike device, carved out of wood or stone, for facilitating animal sacrifice. In this case the khūta is a log, cleft at one end (the end rising some eighteen inches above the ground), with an aperture between the two prongs just wide enough to admit the neck of a goat. A metal pin is then inserted through the prongs just above the animal's neck to hold it in place.

The present keeper of the shrine, Hôripôdô Dube, was fifty-five years of age at the time of this study. In his father's young manhood, he relates, a dreadful intestinal illness ravaged the district, and many people were dying. He does not know the year or the exact nature of the disease. It happens, we may note, that there were particularly bad local outbreaks of cholera in 1907–1908 and again in 1917. In any event, the elder Dube dreamed at the height of the epidemic that the goddess Kali was in his room. She said that she had come to save him and the people of his village if he would but build a shrine in her honor.

The next morning he set up the shrine, and he and the other Gôndôgram Brahmans sacrificed goats there in honor of the visit of Kali. It is said that though many died in surrounding villages, Gôndôgram was spared the worst effects of the epidemic. In gratitude, the Dube maintained the shrine, and each year on the anniversary of the first offering he and the other Brahmans made and continue to make regular sacrifice. At the annual ceremony, a *murti* (icon; a statue or painting—in this case a statue) made by the Gopalgram Carpenter śilpi (artist) at the cost of about eight rupees is set up. It is a representation of Kali, about three feet high, similar to the ones used at other Kali pujas. For this ceremony, however, she is known as Rôkkhô-Kali (Kali the savior).

Interestingly, there are other shrines to, and annual ceremonies in honor of, Rôkkhô-Kali in the surrounding area. Two occur in nearby villages, and the three dates of annual ceremony are not identical but within a few weeks of one another. In each case, an ancestor of a villager had a dream at the time of an epidemic (they may well not have occurred during the same epidemics) that Rôkkhô-Kali had come to him. The Rôkkhô-Kali puja of the village of "Cincuria," in fact, is one of the major annual pilgrimage events of the district. Hundreds of people come; there are shops and children's rides and a carnival atmosphere. At the Cincuria puja I attended in 1964, about one hundred goats were sacrificed, and the sponsors of the ceremony (Brahmans of Cincuria) claimed that in some years as many as two hundred goats have been sacrificed.

At the Gôndôgram Rôkkhô-Kali puja, about a month later, the participants were for the most part inhabitants of Gôndôgram, primarily Brahmans and Bauris, with perhaps two or three visitors from neighboring villages. Fifteen goats were sacrificed (Hôripôdô Dube had predicted about twenty, but noted that he never knew the exact number in advance). Of these, five were of the category called *koulik*. A koulik is an annual offering, usually of an animal for sacrifice, to a deity in memory of some past favor. It is not really a payment anymore, nor is it in expectation of a specific future favor from the divinity. While it derives from a specific payment for a specific mundane intervention, a koulik is an offering that really now verges on the transcendental: we thank the deity for past favors, we hope for future blessings, but mostly we express gratitude and obligation—our sense of being bound in perpetuity—to a particular deity. The other ten offerings were *manśiks:* a manśik is understood to be a specific return for a specific service rendered.

These manśiks reflect the fact that the Rôkkhô-Kali shrine of Gôndôgram is in regular use throughout the year. Rôkkhô-Kali, after all, has demonstrated that she can intercede to save villagers from illness and death deriving from intestinal complaints. Anyone of the village (or of any village in the district) seeking aid for a family member suffering from such an illness may come to Hôripôdô Dube and ask him to seek the intercession of Rôkkhô-Kali. Many come throughout the year.

In July of 1963 the six-year-old son of Nirmal Bauri of Gadhapaṭhôr developed diarrhea and other signs of severe intestinal illness. Nirmal is one of the Bauri men who sacrifice to Mônôśa, but he explained in an interview some months later that he believes that Mônôśa is not as likely to be as effective as Rôkkhô-Kali in such a situation. He ran to Brahman paṛa, fearing his son was dying, and awakened Hôripôdô Dube. The latter led him to the shrine before the mango tree, where Nirmal knelt and, as instructed, recited the following manśik, or promise: "*He ma amar cheleke bācao ar ami tomake admuṛo ar śolô-ana dubo*" (O, Mother, save my child and I shall give to you one lopped-head and sixteen annas.).

The "sixteen annas" (one rupee) went to Hôripôdô Dube for his services. He also provided Nirmal with powder derived from a dried plant (the Dube guards his secret, giving only the name of the powder: *dôibo ośudh*). Nirmal returned home, administered the powder as directed, and the child recovered. The young Bauri then saved his money for months, eventually purchasing a young ram goat for twelve rupees (a figure which he recites with pride and awe) in fulfillment of his manśik.

Most of the people who feel indebted to Rôkkhô-Kali provide the manśik goats sacrificed to her at the time of the annual puja. That is sufficient; the debt is considered paid—but for some people, a special relationship has come into existence between their families and the divinity who has personally interceded in their lives. Such people will continue to provide a goat, as a koulik (a goodwill offering without anticipation of specific gain) at least throughout the lifetime of the person aided. It is not uncommon for the koulik offering to become a permanent practice, continuing over the generations.

One of the koulik goats at the annual Gôndôgram Rôkkhô-Kali puja is paid for, by subscription, by all the Brahmans of Gôndôgram, in memory of the original visitation of Kali and the protection she gave the village at that time. Among the contributors is a family of Pandes who claim, in private discussion, to disapprove of animal

Holding the sacrificial blade, a young Brahman stands in front of the
Dharmôraj temple. Beside him is a wooden fork that is used to restrain the
animal during the sacrifice.

sacrifice of any kind. They would much prefer, they say, to discontinue their contribution—clearly as a matter of principle, since the contribution is a tiny one, much the smallest of their many religious
expenditures. They say they cannot, partly because it would create
bad feelings and hostility in other Brahman families, and partly also
because it is wrong to discontinue participation in a religious ceremony in which your father and grandfather once participated.

In the case of Nirmal Bauri, he preferred not to wait for the
annual ceremony for the completion of his manśik, but brought the
goat to Hôripôdô Dube as soon as he could afford to purchase it. The
details of the sacrifice were much the same as at the annual ceremony, and indeed at all animal sacrifices in Gôndôgram, although at
special, individual sacrifices such as Nirmal's no representation of the
deity is set up.

As is the usual custom, Nirmal's goat was bathed—made ritually
pure—in a nearby pukur, and śindur (vermilion) was marked on its
head, between the budding horns. The sacrifice was performed by
Hôripôdô Dube himself, with the assistance of his nephew. Hôripôdô
Dube has no sons of his own and has been training his brother's son,
a young man in his early twenties, as his assistant and eventual successor. These two men perform, together, all the sacrifices to Kali in
the village, even at the annual puja sponsored by the Bauris.

On this particular occasion they were assisted by the Carpenter
priest, the Deyasi, who happened not to have any pressing engage-
ments that day and so volunteered his services. The Deyasi performs
all animal sacrifices in the village in the name of the deity Dharmôraj,
but he and the two Dubes have a friendly working arrangement, essentially one of professional courtesy and assistance. Both the Deyasi
and the Brahman, for example, possess a khôrgô (sacrificial blade, or
sword), but they exchange freely, since the blades are not identical.
The Deyasi khôrgô is barely two inches wide (reminiscent of a cut-
lass) and more suitable for smaller goats. The Brahman's khôrgô is
heavy and cleaverlike, more than six inches at its widest (reminiscent
of a scimitar, which is, indeed, one of the translations of khôrgô) and
must be used for the larger goats being sacrificed.

The goat readied, Hôripôdô Dube knelt and prayed briefly before
the mango tree and the shrine of Rôkkhô-Kali. As is the practice in
prayer to most deities, he faced north. For the sacrifice, both Dube
men were bare above the waist, save only for their sacred threads.
Below the waist, each wore a short workingman's white dhuti, with a
red kerchief (gamca) knotted like a girdle about the waist—the customary garb of a man performing an animal sacrifice. After prayers
and an offering of flowers, the goat was brought forth and its head,

facing north, was placed in the *khūta,* or fork, and the metal pin inserted to imprison the head. The Deyasi crossed the animal's fore-legs behind its back, tying them in place, while the young Dube gathered the hind legs in his hands and leaned back, pulling on them. The body of the goat straightened, suspended horizontally about one foot off the ground. The Deyasi placed a bundle of rice straw under the neck of the goat to prevent the blade from being dulled or chipped on the ground. Hôripôdô Dube sprinkled a few drops of water on the goat's head as it projected from the khūta, and all was in readiness. The Brahman stepped to the left side of the goat and raised the blade above his head. His nephew pulled with all his might on the hind legs, his heels dug deep into the ground, in order to separate the neck vertebrae of the goat and so permit an easier passage for the blade. Hôripôdô Dube cried, *"Jôe ma!"* (Victory to the mother!) and brought the blade down swiftly, slicing the head off cleanly with one blow, as indeed he must if the sacrifice is to be considered accepted by the deity. All the onlookers, raising their hands in prayer, echoed his cry, and his nephew fell backward with the jerking headless body.

The ceremony was over. The Deyasi and the young Dube made the final arrangements and dispositions while Hôripôdô Dube knelt a moment more in prayer. The head was the property now of the man who had performed the ceremony, Hôripôdô Dube, who carried it off home as a contribution to the evening meal. It always goes to the man who performs the decapitation, although at major annual ceremonies, such as the hecatomb at the Cincuria Rôkkhô-Kali puja, there are far too many for one man. The Brahman pujari (officiant) there sells the excess, as choice cuts of meat, at four to eight annas apiece.[2]

The Deyasi also severed the right foreleg with the khôrgô, using the blade delicately, like a butcher's knife. This he gave to the nephew as his reward for services rendered, and turned the rest of the carcass over to Nirmal Bauri who dragged it home by one hind leg. There, it would be cut up, to furnish a feast for all the families of the Bauri para. At the annual Rôkkhô-Kali pujas, other dispositions may be made of the goats, particularly those offered as koulik. One koulik foreleg may go to a favored relative or guest, or to someone whose family made a particular contribution to the ceremony or to the shrine. The bodies of the goats (kouliks) are frequently cut up and cooked on the spot, and all comers are welcome to the feast.

We see, therefore, that while the manśik of Nirmal Bauri is

2. Four annas equal twenty-five naya pais, under the post-Independence decimal coinage system that everyone knows and uses but hardly anyone in rural areas ever refers to. A villager gives and receives prices in terms of annas, at sixteen to the rupee, but pays in the only currency available, paisa at one hundred to the rupee.

clearly entirely within the pragmatic realm,[3] the annual Rôkkhô-Kali puja exhibits elements of both pragmatic and transcendental dimensions. One sees this ambiguity again and again. One Pande family, for example, performs an annual ceremony in honor of Ganeś, the elephant-headed Great-Tradition god of successful endeavors. Once, about twenty years before, the wife of the head of the household (herself the female head) became mentally ill. Household members, including the lady herself, cannot identify the illness with any greater accuracy—they speak of depression, about confusion about her own identity and that of others—but they are convinced that the illness was in her mind. Other Brahmans and religious specialists (but no medical doctors) were consulted as weeks went by without signs of improvement. It was finally decided that Ganeś was the appropriate deity to turn to for help in alleviating mental illnesses.[4] Ganeś was prayed to, the woman recovered, and in gratitude she offered prayers to Ganeś for three years on the anniversary of her recovery.

Her prayers during those three years were not just in thanks for her own recovery; she also prayed to Ganeś—who had already helped her family once—to grant them financial success, for they were at the time undergoing misfortune and financial difficulty (all of which may well help to explain her previous "mental illness"). The family began to prosper in those three years and concluded that the prosperity emanated from Ganeś. They therefore considered themselves obligated to perform, in perpetuity, an annual puja in honor of Ganeś, and they do so.

Ganeś, as a Great-Tradition deity, cannot be propitiated with animal sacrifices. Instead, at considerable expense, the Pande family provides a feast for relatives and neighbors. A murti, a small statue, is made each year by the artist from Gopalgram. It is set up, garlanded with flowers and other decorations, in the entrance to the family's puja-room, the chamber permanently set aside for religious purposes.

The cooking for the feast is done each year by two Brahman cooks resident in Asansol. The purohit for the Gôndôgram Brahmans, a Bengali Brahman from the village of Ethora, conducts the ceremony—a lengthy one, taking up three full hours. The primary guests, those that are fed first in the evening, are Brahmans of their own sômaj; for the most part in-laws, but also others from Gôndôgram and from one or two neighboring villages. Carpenters of Gôndôgram are

3. Hôripôdô Dube was amused when I asked whether Kali might not be even more gracious if she received the offering in advance of the cure: "Do you usually pay for something you haven't yet received?" he inquired. "Well, we don't!"

4. The Santal ojha, as a matter of fact, considers himself to be most efficacious in removing mental illnesses brought on by dainis and bhuts. Brahmans are reluctant, however, to turn to Santals for aid, at least as a first resort.

fed in the second shift, and Distillers after that. Bauris wait patiently outside the courtyard during the night, as the others are all fed, but eventually they receive whatever is left in the pots. Beyond the Bauris are clusters of beggars, who drift into the village from all over the district, knowing that a feast is in progress. They receive whatever food may be scraped from the leaf-plates of the guests, for nothing edible is wasted.

4

Little Tradition:
Transcendental and Pragmatic

While Brahmans in Gôndôgram may believe that the prayers of a Brahman have a sort of special potency, at least when addressed to the Great-Tradition divinities, we have noted that the non-Brahman inhabitants of the village would never agree that only Brahmans can offer meaningful prayers. Many of the Carpenters have tulśi-môncôs in their courtyards, and offer daily propitiation and prayer. Some Distillers and at least one Bauri are talking about constructing tulśi-môncôs of their own, though none but Brahmans and Carpenters have as yet done so. All in the village, however (apart from the Brahmans) insist that any man, of any caste, may pray to the gods in any form or manifestation with fully equal propriety and meaningfulness.

On the other hand, all in the village, *Brahman and non-Brahman alike,* appear to agree that certain *individuals* have better access to particular deities than do other individuals. When the Bauris sponsor the annual Kali puja—paid for by primarily Bauri subscription, in a temple they built and paid for themselves—they bring in Hôripôdô Dube of Brahman para to perform the ceremony and sacrifice. After all, as keeper of the Rôkkhô-Kali shrine, he is unquestionably the man in Gôndôgram with the greatest affinity for, or strongest relationship with, the goddess Kali.

Similarly, all in the village (including Brahmans) acknowledge the special relationship between the Carpenter Deyasi family and the god Dharmôraj. Dharmôraj is a rather obscure divinity, for the most part unknown outside of rural Bengal, and certainly not part of the Great-

Tradition hierarchy. Some writers (see Peterson 1910: 57–58)·have speculated that Dharmôraj (the name means dharma-king, or perhaps "lord of the right way") is all that remains of the once widespread Buddhism of Bengal. It is certainly true that the annual Dharmôraj puja takes place on the same day that Buddhists elsewhere, particularly in Southeast Asia, observe as sacred to the Buddha. There are a very few elements, too, in the puja proceedings (such as the presence of the representation of a lotus) that tend to support the argument that it derived, long ago, from a ceremony in honor of the Buddha. The Deyasis, however, along with their relatives and fellow villagers, appear to know nothing of the Buddha and his worship. Dharmôraj, they insist, is a purely Hindu divinity, for they themselves are Hindus, and nothing else. The name, the Deyasis say, is simply an appellation of Jam (Yama, the god of death in the classic religious literature). There is nothing of Yama in the temple of Dharmôraj, nor is he ever represented or referred to during the worship of Dharmôraj.

The Deyasi family relate that once, many generations ago, in a village they no longer remember, an ancestor of the family dreamed that Dharmôraj was appearing in person before him, with instructions to institute, thenceforth, regular annual worship. The next day, the original Deyasi (then, of course, merely a Śutrodhôr, or Carpenter, like all of his family) went down to the pukur for his morning bath. There he found, as it had been foretold in his dream, certain tortoise-shaped (and sized) stones, and a few tiny gold objects. These, he believed, were representations of Dharmôraj, and he took them home. He built a shrine to Dharmôraj, and sacrificed a goat. Ever after, the family—taking the name Deyasi (religious officiant)—considered themselves dedicated to the worship of Dharmôraj.

Though they have migrated from village to village since that time, they have kept the divine representations and continued the worship. Today, in Gôndôgram, there is a temple near the Deyasi family home, dedicated to Dharmôraj. It is the oldest temple in the village, constructed at least thirty years before this study was undertaken. Before the coming of the factory it was the only temple in the village. It is said that a few Brahmans made small contributions to the original fund for the temple, but Carpenters and Distillers made the greatest combined contribution, as they relate it, and they consider the temple as belonging to them and to their para.

Though interest in Dharmôraj is said by some to be on the decrease, there are many other temples to Dharmôraj in the district, perhaps as many as to any divinity with the possible exceptions of Śibu and Durga. The priestly families who maintain the other temples of Dharmôraj are by no means solely Carpenter (many other castes are represented among them) but I never encountered a Brahman family as priests of Dharmôraj. The Gôndôgram Brahmans say, in fact, that Dharmôraj is a deity favored by non-Brahmans, though not necessarily the lowest castes.

It is said of Dharmôraj, as of all divinities, that he may be petitioned for help with any problem. It is universally believed, however, that Dharmôraj (lord of the right path, Jam, ruler of the underworld, as he is variously known) is more likely than any other deity to come to the aid of women suffering the problems peculiar to the female. Barren women and women who have borne only female children turn to Dharmôraj and pray for children, most particularly sons. Women with diseases and illnesses of the uterus—and, in short, with any physical problem associated with female physiology—come to Dharmôraj for aid.

Many prefer to offer their petition on the day of the annual Dharmôraj puja. At the one I attended, a half-dozen women—of different castes, and most of them not residents of Gôndôgram—huddled in a special place before the temple of Dharmôraj, close to the sacrificial khūta, or fork. At each sacrifice they leaned forward to dip the middle fingers of their right hands in the spilled blood. And, at the same puja, there were four other women, heavy with child, who were there in gratitude for answered prayers. After the representations of the deity were carried to a certain pukur for ritual ablution on the morning of the puja, the four pregnant women followed the procession of Deyasi men home from pukur to temple, each measuring the entire distance with the length of her body, in repeated prostrations.

But anyone may offer prayer and mansik to Dharmôraj at any time of the year, and many do. I counted five goats sacrificed to Dharmôraj during a six-week period, and the Deyasis say that, on the average, two to four goats per month are brought to the temple in fulfillment of promises. No goats are accepted, however, for the two months preceding the annual puja; the contributors are asked to keep the goats (or, occasionally, sheep) for the puja, to swell the number sacrificed then.

All sacrificial animals must be male, as at Rôkkhô-Kali pujas, and the garb of the pujaris, in this case, three men of the Carpenter Deyasi family, is the traditional one: abbreviated dhuti and red gamca (kerchief). Families representing all castes and numerous villages come to the Dharmôraj temple of Gôndôgram to offer mansik. One man I interviewed, now resident in the area, had in fact been born in Bihar.

Bauris will come to Rôkkhô-Kali, as we have seen, for intestinal complaints, and to Dharmôraj for female complaints and fertility problems. For cure of snakebite, however, people come to the Bauris for aid, for they are believed to have particularly good relations with Mônôśa, the goddess at whose bidding snakes will bite or withhold their venom, and who can, if she wishes, cure a person affected by snakebite. Villagers point out that Bauris, as field laborers, run the greatest risk of contact with poisonous reptiles. After them come fishermen. The Bauri and Jele—quite understandably, say the villagers—are more concerned than any other jati with the propitiation of Mônôśa. Three Bauri men of Gôndôgram (one of them the Nirmal Bauri earlier described as consulting Rôkkhô-Kali) perform regular annual sacrifice to Mônôśa, each near his own home. In addition, during the year, each may expect to pray and offer a manśik for one or two people, from this village or another, bitten by poisonous snakes.

Brahmans admit the special relationship of Bauri and Mônôśa, and are content to see Mônôśa pujas performed regularly for the protection of the village. In time of actual emergency, however, most Brahmans of the village would be reluctant to consult a Bauri pujari for aid. This reluctance is unformulated by them, but it is clearly present. One may speculate that it reflects distaste for Bauri customs and lack of ritual cleanliness; or doubt as to Bauri knowledge, intelligence, and expertise; or perhaps unwillingness to become indebted to someone with whom the relationship is normally the obverse.

We have seen, for example, that Brahmans afflicted with mental illness in the family chose to pray to Ganeś for aid, in preference to a visit to the Santal ojha renowned for his ability to fend off bhuts and dainis who afflict the mind. No doubt, had prayers to Ganeś failed, they would eventually, in desperation, have turned to the Santal, as other Brahmans have. In desperation, too, some Brahmans have turned to Bauris for aid in curing snakebite. Happily for them, however, there is a Brahman family in the village of "Durganôgôr," not too far away, who have set up a shrine to Mônôśa and who are believed, if only by Brahmans, to have a good relationship with her.

Years ago, before the birth of the oldest Brahman of Gôndôgram, a boy of the Durganôgôr Brahman family had been bitten by a poisonous snake and had lapsed into unconsciousness. According to the Brahmanical account, the family had in fact consulted a Bauri ojha, without success. The unconscious boy was then placed in a room of the Brahman house, left there, and the door was locked from the outside. The boy's mother knelt in prayer to Mônôśa, having set up offerings of food and flowers as she would to any other deity. Her prayer, again according to the Brahmans, was more of a threat than a propitiation—unusual, but perhaps understandable in the case of a lordly Brahman woman addressing a deity associated with lowly Bauris: "*Amar chele jodi aj môre jae tomar pôkôri-tôkôri sôb tule pukurer jôle phele debo. Ta na hôle, amar chele bæbôstha kôro*" (If my child dies today I will take all your things and throw them in the water of the pukur. So that this may not happen, see to my child.).

The boy, it is related, recovered consciousness and lived. No one speculates as to whether Mônôśa responded favorably out of intimidation or out of kindheartedness; the point is that she did respond. Since then, that Brahman family has maintained the room as a shrine to Mônôśa, praying there regularly, and keeping there a quantity of water. A drink of that water is said to cure snakebite, or so Brahmans claim. Members of other jatis obviously prefer to consult Bauri specialists. Brahmans say, further, that Mônôśa is actually a sort of "adopted doughter" of Durga; one pointed out that her very name, Mônôśa, tells us that she was created by the mind (*môn*) of Durga. He added that the Bauris, of course, know nothing of such matters.

Santals of Gôndôgram have no similar shrine; they worship Cādu Boŋa, the Santal supreme deity, at his annual ceremony, and at time of illness they consult their ojha. They have been known, however, to bring a bad case of snakebite to the Mônôśa pujaris of the Bauri paṛas. Further, those who can possibly do so attend the great Santal mela (fair) at the village of "Śātaibhil" every year on the first day of the month of Magh. At the occasion of the mela during my study, in fact, there were only three persons to be found in the Santal paras of Gôndôgram, all of them elderly and infirm.

While it is called and considered a Santal mela, people of many other jatis attend, buying sweets at the stalls and giving their children rides, and many also participate actively in the religious ceremony. In fact, the two men who perform most of the goat sacrifices (and at a gathering of thousands of people the sacrifices run well into the hundreds) are both Bauris, and are called deyasis.

The shrine at which they perform sacrifices, and which they care for during the rest of the year, is actually a well or spring at the bottom of a depression some three feet square. A flat stone slab, rounded at the top and vaguely tonguelike in appearance, projects upward from the water. About one foot of its length is above the water, and it inclines sharply to the east. The slab has become heavily encrusted, through the years, with a thick coat of dried vermilion. Behind the slab, on the eastern side of the well, there is an enormous heap of broken figurines, mostly of horses and elephants, all of red fired clay. On the western side of the slab there is a cleared space large enough for the two deyasis to stand, feet in water, as they make a brief presentation (to the slab and the deity it represents) of the next goat or sheep to be sacrificed. Above the depression (again, to the west) a khūta is set in the ground so that the animal to be sacrificed may be held with its head facing toward the stone slab.

On the day of my visit, about one hundred male goats (including a handful of male sheep) were sacrificed, along with about fifty cocks. People who wish to make an offering at the shrine, but who cannot afford an animal for sacrifice, buy two clay horses at one of the neighboring stalls at one anna each and break them on the heap behind the slabs. It was said that hundreds of clay horses (*sædom,* in Santal; *ghôṛa* in Bengali) were sacrificed each year.

The shrine and attendant offerings are all in the name of Śātai Buṛi. The word "*śātai*" means "Santal" in local pronunciation, and "*buṛi*" is the common Bengali word for "hag," "crone," or "old woman." Most of those interviewed at the mela agreed that there were in the district seven similar shrines, of which this was one, each dedicated to a specific buṛi and each taking its name from either a nearby village, the jati most associated with it, or some similar factor. The seven buṛis are considered to be "seven sisters" by all. There is disagreement, however, as to the nature of the buṛis. For some they are just buṛis—"old women"—and nothing more. For others, the buṛis are also dainis—witches. And for a few, the "seven sisters" are in fact actual goddesses (*debis*). For all, there is agreement that the buṛi can be propitiated and the offerings are mansiks for favors previously granted and for the maintenance of the goodwill of the buṛi. She is petitioned for recovery from illness—any illness—and also by women who lack male offspring.

Gôndôgram itself has one other shrine of importance, that of the *gram debi/deb'ta,* located in a small grove of trees on the south bank of the Dhopa Pukur. Actually, the grove *is* the shrine, or sacred spot, although there is a fragment of ancient statuary (apparently a rough representation of a lotus) on the ground in the grove, at which prayers are offered. Villagers seem to use the terms "*debi*" (goddess) and "*deb'ta*" (or "*debôta,*") god) in free variation for this deity, and claim that either term is perfectly acceptable. The gram debi, it would therefore seem, is the village guardian spirit, or genius, perceived as not having a personal name or sexual attributes.

For the most part, the shrine is visited by girls of the village just before departing for their weddings; they pray for a happy marriage, long life, and many healthy children. Some Brahmans say that they prefer to have the girls of their families pray at more private shrines; within many Brahman compounds there is a place sacred to the *kulôdeb'ta* (the guardian spirit of the household) and this is where Brahman women are expected to pray. It was to be observed during the year of this study, nonetheless, that Brahman girls about to get married prayed to the gram debi, whatever other prayers they may have offered elsewhere.

Anyone may pray at the shrine of the gram debi at any time, and some of the old men and women make a point of pausing occasionally on the way home after bathing. The village in a body also comes for prayer, but this only rarely, as when drought or blight seems to threaten the continued life of the village. Only Santals ignore the gram debi, even at the time of a girl's marriage.

5

Calendars, Clocks, and Rounds

For the inhabitants of Gôndôgram, like those of villages elsewhere in the world, the year is made up of predictable rounds of events. Some of these are statistically predictable; there will in any year be births and deaths and marriages, though none can predict the exact days they will occur. Some rounds, such as the agricultural, are tied to climatic and other environmental changes: the times for planting and for harvest. The religious round, however, can often be specifically delineated: on such an hour of such a day of such a month we will engage in such a ceremony. The anthropological researcher, eager to penetrate and encompass the totality of village life, seeks everywhere the local calendrical round, the cycle of festivals and ceremonies in which the members of the village engage.

In India, or at least in rural Bengal, this is not as easy to accomplish as it may be elsewhere. First of all, the units of time (year, month, day, hour, and so on) differ from their Western counterparts sufficiently to require some explication. Second, given the nature of community as expounded in this work, we must inquire as to the locus of the round: is it "village" as it is in so many studies, or is it in some other dimension of the Bengal "community"? If, as it shall be argued here, the round is not "village" but something else, how can we delimit the round of the "villager"?

Let us consider first, however, the units of religious time in rural Bengal. The Brahmans of Gôndôgram relate that we live today in the "*Kali Yuga,*" the age of degradation and impending dissolution. I never heard anyone in Gôndôgram, of any jati, dispute this statement, and it is likely that most Hindus in India would agree.

If we inquire, however, as to the exact year and month of that

165

age, there is no universal agreement to be found throughout the sub-
continent. According to the Bengali calendar, the time of my study
(1963–1964 of the Christian calendar) overlapped the years 1370–
1371. Villagers informed me, as did others in Bengal, that this represented the number of years since the reign of one raja Bikrômadittô.
He would appear to be the same king (Vikramaditya, king of Ujjain)
referred to by Underhill (*The Hindu Religious Year,* 1921: 14) as
establishing the Samvat, the present calendrical era of India, in com-
memoration of "his victory over the Saka kings in the year 3044 of
the Kali Yuga (57 B.C.)" (*ibid.*).

The difficulty is that while Bengali Hindus, like their colleagues
throughout India, claim to follow the Samvat, the Bengali calendar
appears to date from about A.D. 593, a time far removed from Vikramaditya of Ujjain. Why, therefore, is he referred to at all? After all, in
1963–1964 there appeared to be few in any part of India who considered the date to be 2020 (since 57 B.C.).

Perhaps we may find in this the working of a familiar Indian
phenomenon. Little-Tradition deities, known only to the inhabitants
of a circumscribed district or region, are articulated with the Great
Tradition by being given a Great-Tradition name, or by being in some
other way identified with a Great-Tradition deity (see Marriott 1955),
as in the case of the Brahman identification of Mônôśa, referred to
earlier as the "adopted daughter" of Durga. In much the same way,
perhaps, Hindus throughout India have maintained their local calendrical eras—actually dating from some time of importance locally—
but articulated with the Great-Tradition Samvat and therefore presumed to date from the reign of Vikramaditya. In Bengal, in the last
decades of the sixth century, it would appear that the throne of Gauḍa
was held by Sasanka (Majumdar 1943: 59 ff.), and one may, if one
wishes, speculate that this event marked the actual beginning of the
present calendrical era.

In any event, the Hindus of India agree as to the name of the
calendrical era and its founder, although they disagree as to the actual
year. And, in addition, they do not always agree as to the name of the
month in which they find themselves. Underhill, for example, after
discussing the complexities of a calendar in which solar (or zodiacal)
phenomena interdigitate with lunar ones (1921: 16–23), does point to a
cycle of twelve months, of lunar origin, beginning with Chaitra and
ending with Phālguna. Underhill claims that this calendar is in use
throughout Hindu India. While this is true in principle, perhaps, there
are important regional variations; in Bengal, for example, the pan-Indian months are all known, but the year begins with the month of
Vaisākha (the *second* month of Underhill's calendar) and *ends* with

Chaitra! Furthermore, New Year's Day, 1371 in Bengal (that is, the first day of Vaisākha) fell on April 14, which was the twenty-fifth day of Chaitra for many non-Bengali Hindus of northern India.

The months of the Bengali year, in order and in Bengali pronunciation, are: Bôiśakh, Jôiśthô, Aśaṛh, Srabôn, Bhadrô, Aśin, Kartik, Ôgrahayôn, Pouś, Magh, Phalgun, and Côitrô.

Given the foregoing disagreements, it may seem astonishing if not contradictory that many, perhaps most, religious holidays are celebrated throughout India on exactly the same day. They are, however, and the reason for this may be simply stated: The era, the year, the month, and even the day of the week are all irrelevant to the calculation of the occurrence of religious events. Rather, the times of religious observance are determined with the aid of zodiacal calendars found throughout India. Only two steps are involved: determining the correct lunar period (waxing or waning of the moon) and then within that the exactly correct "moment" in time for the ceremony.

In Bengal, for example, the months enumerated earlier have each about thirty days, according to the calendar. These "calendrical months" (as we may perhaps term them) are viewed by religious leaders as no more than guideposts to the months that really matter: the "lunar months," the actual appearance in the sky of New Moon, Full Moon, and New Moon again. The New Moon is called *ômabôśśa* and the Full Moon *purnima;* the period of "waxing" (from New Moon to Full Moon) is called *śuklôpôkkhô* and the period of "waning" (from Full Moon to just before the appearance of the next New Moon) is called *kriśnôpôkkhô*. Each Bengali ceremony is set in a particular śuklôpôkkhô or kriśnôpôkkhô of the yearly lunar cycle.

It is sufficient, therefore, for a religious leader of Gôndôgram to know that the ceremony he wishes to perform occurs, say, in the śuklôpôkkhô of the calendrical month of Bôiśakh. He begins his computations from the first New Moon of that month. His counterpart elsewhere in India may be told to perform the event in Chaitra—both men will seek the same New Moon and perform the ceremony on the same day.

Unfortunately, it must in passing be noted that matters do not always work out as smoothly as this. Since the calendrical month and the lunar month are not exactly congruent, they tend to wander apart over the years, and it is the custom in India (as elsewhere where lunar calendars are in use) to add an intercalendrical month to a year periodically to bring zodiacal events and lunar months back into association. If two religious groups or communities, hitherto following the same calendar, disagree as to the necessity for adding an intercalendrical month, it may well happen (as it did in Bengal in 1963) that one will add the month and the other will not. There will then be disagreement between the groups as to the name of the current calendrical month.[1]

In any event, the person wishing to hold a religious ceremony must first determine the appropriate lunar period. He must then determine the exact moment in time for the ceremony to take place—and this too depends upon a special system of reckoning. The calendrical month in India, as elsewhere, is made up of weeks, days, hours, minutes, and seconds. The astronomical, or sidereal, lunar month is of course made up of twenty-seven days plus some hours, minutes, and seconds. For religious purposes, however, Hindus divide this lunar cycle into thirty equal segments, each called a *tithi,* and so there are exactly fifteen tithis in each period of lunar waxing or waning. A tithi, it will therefore be observed, is somewhat shorter in duration than a terrestrial day; it is composed of twenty-two hours plus a specified number of minutes, seconds, *pal, bipal,* and *anupal*—each of these being one-sixtieth of the preceding subdivision.

A ceremony or festival, then, is supposed to take place at a particular moment during a particular tithi during either the śuklôpôkkhô (waxing) or kriśnôpôkkhô (waning) of a lunar period associated with one of the named calendrical months. Just as a lunar period resembles but is not identical to a calendrical month—so that the two may coincide or vary considerably in their times of occurrence—in much the same way a tithi resembles a day, but is not necessarily congruent with it. A tithi may begin at any time of the day or night, as determined by the appropriate calculations and recorded in almanacs, and it will end not quite twenty-three hours later.

A second reason advanced earlier for the difficulty the ethnographer experiences in determining the calendrical round has to do with the problem of determining the locus of the round. Underhill, for example, in the work referred to, provides a comprehensive chart of all holidays and festivals described in the book (1921: 136–159). The chart is useful as an introduction to the pan-Indian Great Tradition, but it obscures rather than clarifies regional variation. And given the

1. Presumably, in a year or two the reluctant group will make the same calendrical adjustment, bringing the calendars back into alignment—but they may not. Presumably, too, the ceremonies performed by the members of the two groups will occur on the same days, since both are observing lunar rather than calendrical phenomena—but, again, sometimes shifts occur and what was once an identical ceremony performed by two groups on the same day becomes two different ceremonies performed a full lunar cycle apart. In such cases, is a new rationale developed—the ceremonies attributed different significances or directed to different divinities? What happens when the now "different" ceremonies are adopted by the other groups? These are questions worth pursuing, but not in this work.

varied Little Traditions of the Indian countryside, Underhill's chart serves only as the grossest of guides; in a particular village anywhere in India it can even be severely misleading.

Anthropologists, by and large, have adopted an alternative approach: the fieldworker charts, month by Indian month, the festivals and ceremonies observed in his particular village of study. Such studies are unquestionably of great interest and utility, but they cannot necessarily be interpreted (as they can elsewhere in the world) as providing an account of the normal religious round of the average villager. Who, after all, is the *average* villager? In Shanti Nagar, Ruth and Stanley Freed tell us (1964), only Kumhars worship Durga in the month of Chaitra, or celebrate the Jeyth ka Dusehra with a ceremonial bath, while only Brahmans fast and go without water on the eleventh day of the month of Jyesth. In Kishan Garhi, Marriott reports, the Car Festival (*ratha yātrā*) is not observed (and therefore not listed in the village yearly round) but villagers travel to a nearby town to observe the festivities (1955: 194).

The difficulties we see derive from the fact that the Indian village is rarely a "small community" in the Redfieldian sense; rarely do we find an aggregation of equalitarian farmers as in some Western village. Rather, there is (at least in the case of Gôndôgram) a collection of distinct clusters, each cluster of families representing locally a far-flung marriage network claiming membership in a particular regional jati. And, as we have seen throughout this chapter, jatis of the same village share many of the same religious elements, but they can also differ from one another.

The "village calendar," it therefore follows, runs a strong risk of being a construct of the anthropologist, imposed from without and not derivative or reflective of the structure. For, through propinquity and long familiarity, any villager of any jati is likely to be aware of the ceremonies observed in his village by all the jatis represented in it. If queried, he can help construct a chart of the village's "yearly religious calendar." True, he probably knows best those ceremonies in which members of his śômaj are active participants, but he has some acquaintance with other ceremonies, sponsored or performed by jatis other than his own, to which members of his jati may come as spectators. His knowledge of religious events in the village at which members of his jati are not customarily in attendance is often superficial and even erroneous, but he can certainly itemize them, and the fieldworker can get more data from other informants.

It is interesting to note, in fact, that this villager can, if queried, often provide much more accurate information (as against the last category) about certain ceremonies performed by members of his śômaj in other villages nearby—in which he has often participated—and never performed in his village at all. These latter ceremonies, of course, would have no place in our chart of the village round, although they may be referred to somewhere in the accompanying text.

What emerges, in other words, is a clear intimation that, given the nature of the Indian community, a listing of religious events occurring in a given village may be meticulously accurate, but it may in fact not represent the actual religious cycle of *any* member of that village!

An alternative, of course, would be to construct a yearly religious calendar jati by jati. Though this might prove a bit cumbersome and more than a little repetitious, it might certainly provide insights the other approaches do not. It does share with the other approaches (the regional and the village) the weakness of not providing us with any sure guide to the religious round of activity of any actual persons. Jatis do not exist in vacuums; the individual families that comprise a śômaj reside in villages which almost always contain representatives of other jatis. People observe and even participate in ceremonies sponsored and conducted by members of other jatis.

A high-caste man in one village, therefore, may observe or even participate in ceremonies sponsored by a lower-ranked jati that happens to be represented in his village. This high-caste man's cousin, who resides in another village where that particular lower-ranked jati is not represented, may know nothing of that ceremony. As an example, the Kanauj Brahmans of Śergôr Śômaj do not perform the annual Kali Puja of Bengal. They note, in explanation, that they are of Bihari provenience, and the Kali Puja is confined for the most part to Bengali jatis. In Gôndôgram, however, the Bauris sponsor an annual Kali Puja, and Hôripôdô Dube, he of the Rôkkhô-Kali shrine, actually conducts the ceremony and performs the sacrifice. Many members of the śômaj, however, live in villages where the Kali Puja is not performed, but where other ceremonies, not known in Gôndôgram, are performed.

We must accept the fact, therefore, that neither "village" nor "caste" alone (nor even in combination) can provide us with an adequate representation of a "yearly religious calendar." We must bring the côkrô (the district, or circle of villages) into the question.

There is, we may say, a total set (or pool) of ceremonies in a given circle of villages. There are *intra-* as well as *inter-*caste rules governing participation in and observance of those ceremonies. The actual ceremonial events take place, of course, in particular villages of the district, but not necessarily in all of them. The history, social composition, and interaction patterns of a particular village conspire to make the ceremonial event slightly different from the same ceremony performed in another village, even if by members of the same jati.

Each villager draws upon the totality of religious events available in his district. He is guided in his choice (to a considerable extent, even controlled) by the rules and the status of his jati. Put another way, we may observe that for the villager calendrical religious events fall into three categories: (a) those in which members of his śômaj customarily participate; (b) those at which they may be observers; and (c) those which members of his jati do not attend, either because they are not welcome or because their own rules preclude such attendance. These categories apply to all the villagers of the district. For any given villager, however, we would have to know, in addition, in order to explore his yearly religious calendar, something of the composition of his particular village. And finally, after all that, there is the element of personal (or familial) choice: some Dubes in Gôndôgram participate in the Bauri-sponsored Kali Puja; some Dubes will not go near the event.

One approach to the problem posed in the foregoing would be to catalogue and compare all the calendrical religious events taking place in the côkrô, or at least those I observed or heard about. Such an account would overburden this work and would in the end serve to distract from its original intent and focus.[2] I shall therefore condense the data, taking as my guide (as I list the religious events month by month) the concerns of the inhabitants of Gôndôgram: the events that are of particular interest to them.

2. Moreover, Lawrence Babb, in his book *The Divine Hierarchy* (1975), has already provided us with an account very much on this order, if for a region in Madhya Pradesh.

6

A Community Calendar

Bôiśakh (H.: *Vaisākha*)—April–May

It is the custom throughout the côkrô for women to cook enough food on the last day of the old year to feed the family on the first day of the new one; the old year should begin to feed the new, and the first month is viewed as an extended period of thanksgiving to Biśnu (Viśnu) the Preserver, and he is invoked in the names of many of his representations.

The honoring of Biśnu occurs most commonly in the form of group singing. In each village a *dôl* (band of singers) is formed, and in some villages there may be more than one. The dôls wander through the streets during the night, sometimes from sunset to sunrise, stopping in front of houses and singing *kirton* (a religious poem in honor of Biśnu) after *kirton*. In Bôiśakh, people say, the most significant religious event is this *nôgôr-kirton,* the village-wide kirton-singing.

In small villages there may be one dôl made up of men of all jatis. In large villages, each dôl may represent, exclusively, men of only one jati. In general, men of the dominant (or at least higher-ranked) jatis tend to predominate in kirton-singing, and men of the lowest-ranked jatis are least in evidence. In Gôndôgram there have been traditionally two dôls; one serenading only in Brahman para and made up only of Brahmans, and one in Ūcu para made up of Carpenter, Distiller, and Washerman men. A third dôl had been forming in the years just prior to my study, made up of Bauri men from two of the Bauri paras, and serenading in those paras only. It did not assemble every night, nor did it extend to Gadhapathôr or the Santal paras. The existence of this dôl was known in Ūcu para, but Brahman informants never mentioned it; when asked, they categorically denied all knowledge of it.

Jôiśthô (H.: Jaistha)—May–June

The monsoons customarily arrive in Bengal during this month and villagers throughout the côkrô are busily engaged in agricultural pursuits, most particularly in the planting of rice. In few villages, therefore, is there much time for festivals or major religious ceremonies. Gôndôgram is normally no different from its neighbors in this respect, but it happened that in 1964 the annual Dharmôraj Puja, which is usually observed on the purnima (night of the full moon) of Bôiśakh, was observed this year on the purnima of Jôiśthô.

A calendrical adjustment of the kind discussed earlier had been made in Bengal during 1963, and so many pujas were moved temporarily from the months in which they usually occurred. To complicate things, not everyone accepted the calendrical revisions and so in some neighboring villages identical festivals were being celebrated in different months. This happened with Dharmôraj Puja, but the celebration in Gôndôgram had always been one of the largest and most important in the Gôndôgram segment of the côkrô, and it is fair to say that for Gôndôgram villagers and most of their neighbors Dharmôraj Puja in 1964 was associated with the month of Jôiśthô.

There are some indications that interest in Dharmôraj and his puja is diminishing in the côkrô. A number of villages have apparently abandoned the puja within the memory of living inhabitants. Where it is still performed, it is associated primarily with "middle" or "laboring" jatis, among whom it continues to be fairly popular.

In Gôndôgram, the puja was performed in front of the Dharmôraj temple, in Ūcu para. The ceremonies were of course presided over by the Deyasi family of the Carpenter jati. All Carpenters of the village contributed and participated, along with many members of their śômaj from other villages. Washermen and Distillers of Gôndôgram also contributed and participated. A few Gôndôgram Brahmans, mostly of Dube families, gave contributions and some even observed part of the ceremonies. Bauris participated as *bhôktôs* (devotees), fasting for two days before the puja. Each such bhôktô is sponsored by a man of wealth, frequently a Brahman, who thereby acquires merit without personally having to undergo the inconvenience of fasting.

A large crowd was in attendance, made up of people from many villages and of many different jatis. Many of the people were planning to make supplication to Dharmôraj, and some were engaged in the annual pilgrimage out of gratitude for past services rendered.

Aśaṛh (H.: *Āsādha*)—June–July

In all the villages of the côkrô people are busily engaged in agricultural pursuits during the month of Aśaṛh, claiming they have little time to spare for festivals. There are a few villages, however, containing representatives (among their "dominant" castes) of jatis deriving from Orissa and other points to the south. In such villages the *rôth* festival (*ratha yātrā*) is observed with much ceremony. Villagers from all over the côkrô travel considerable distances to see Narayôn (Nārāyana, or Viśnu) paraded in a cart (rôth) through the streets.

There appears to be increasing interest in the festival; in many villages men report that they would not miss the event, though they are aware that it was unknown in the district a few decades back. In a few villages, I have even heard tentative discussions about the possibility of inaugurating rôth festivals of their own. It is not performed in Gôndôgram, nor was its institution contemplated, but villagers of all castes went off to attend the annual festivals.

Srabôn (H.: *Srāvana*)—July–August

Agriculture still occupies men's time in this month. Villagers point to the need to propitiate Mônôśa (she who controls snakebite) particularly for those now laboring in the fields. In most villages of the côkrô (Gôndôgram is an example) men of "laboring" jatis such as the Bauris perform the ceremony. In the village of Kônnôgram, however, where the dominant jati is Caśa, whose traditional occupation is "farming," they perform Mônôśa Puja as a major village festival, and in two villages where Goalas (Milkmen) are dominant they too perform the ceremony and even exclude local members of the "laboring" jati from sponsorship and direct participation.

In Gôndôgram, there are three small separate ceremonies performed, one in each Bauri para for the people of that para. The pujas occur at the same time; though all three pujaris are illiterate, they consult with each other and with a friendly Brahman. They know, in fact, that the ceremony must take place on the last day of the month of Srabôn and need only to be apprised of the imminence of that date a week or so in advance so they can begin preparations.

Bhadrô (H.: *Bhādrapada*)—August–September

In a number of villages in the district, at least at the time of this study, Mônôśa Puja was celebrated in the month of Bhadrô. The pattern, though not without a few exceptions, seemed to be that in villages in which the puja was sponsored and celebrated by "dominant" jatis the event took place in Bhadrô. In villages such as Gôndô-gram where Mônôśa is propitiated primarily by "laboring" jatis, the event tended to occur in the preceding month of Srabôn. Gôndôgram villagers of all castes, however, felt free to visit the ceremonies of other villages during Bhadrô.

In Gôndôgram itself, the only holiday of importance during Bhadrô (apart from *jônmaśtômi*—celebration of the birth of Kriśna on the eighth tithi of the śuklôpôkkhô [moon's waxing] of Bhadrô—which tends to be a minor event in this côkrô) is the Biśśôkôrmô Puja on the last day of that month. Visvakarma, the architect and weapon-repairer of the gods, is little known in the côkrô, except among a few artisan jatis. In the factories and technological institutes of the area, however, his puja is the most important religious event of the year. There is no work on this day; the buildings are scrubbed, all machines are cleaned and decorated with flowers and *alpona* (rice flour-paste designs), and a puja is performed complete with presiding Brahman purohit and a murti of the deity. All villagers (of Gôndôgram, or wherever) who work in the factory make a point of attending the puja at the factory, for this is the day when a man who works with tools must honor his tools.

Aśin (H.: *Āśvina*)—September–October

This is the month of the Durga Puja—the celebration, so important in Bengal, of the victory of the mother goddess over the buffalo-demon, Môhiś-aśur. It takes place during the sixth to tenth tithis of the śuklôpôkkhô (moon's waxing). Since a large, expensive murti must be constructed, and there are many other costs to be borne, many of the poorer villages of the district simply cannot afford to sponsor such a ceremony; in five of the ten villages surveyed it was in fact not performed, and in Gôndôgram it has been performed only since the coming of the factory. I was assured, nevertheless, by men of all the villages surveyed, of every jati, that they tried never to miss a Durga puja; everyone who is able travels to the nearest village where a ceremony is held to observe the festivities.

In Gôndôgram, the best artist in the district was engaged to construct the murti, and the puja was held in the still-unfinished Durga mondir (temple) slowly rising between Brahman and Ūcu paṟas. Participation in the puja reflected the extent of participation in the subscription for it: all Brahman households are represented throughout the ceremonies, and Carpenters and Distillers more infrequently. Bauris and Washermen, joined by a few Santals, observed the proceedings from outside the temple but did not participate in any way.

Kartik (H.: *Kārtikka*)—October–November

The puja in honor of the goddess Kali is cited by villagers throughout the côkrô as the most important religious event of the month of Kartik. It occurs on the last day—or more accurately the final tithi—of the month, at the time of ômabôśśa (appearance of the New Moon). The celebration usually, but not invariably, involves animal sacrifice, and there is in fact considerable variation in many elements of the puja from village to village. Kali is viewed by all in the côkrô as being the particular concern of Bengalis; in those villages, therefore, in which men of jatis of Bengali origin (whether Brahman or whatever) form the dominant or elite element, the puja is celebrated with all the detail and expense of any Great-Tradition event.

In villages in which such externally derived jatis as the Kanauj Brahmans are dominant, the puja is either not held at all or a much abbreviated version is performed by men of "middle" or "laboring" jatis. In one village not far from Gôndôgram, inhabitants proudly report an interesting compromise: a large expensive Kali Puja is performed, sponsored by almost all the jatis of the village (there are many, all of Bengali provenience), and all are permitted to attend, from Brahman to Bauri. Villagers say that while all participate some are understood to direct their prayers to Kali, some to Durga, and some to Mônôśa.

Gôndôgram is of course dominated by Kanauj Brahmans, and no Kali Puja was ever held in the village until a few years after the establishment of the factory. Until that time, Brahmans say, they—like their jat-brothers in similar villages—never attended Kali Pujas. Men of Ūcu and Bauri paṛas did, however, make a point of journeying most years to some nearby village to observe Kali Puja festivities.

Two or three years before my study, the Bauri men of Gôndôgram assembled and decided to sponsor and hold a regular Kali Puja in the village. They took up a subscription among all Bauris and among all the jatis of Ūcu paṛa. Contributions were also solicited from officers of the factory, but Bauris deny that they solicited either Brahmans or Santals of Gôndôgram, although there are a few Brahmans who insist that they did in fact contribute, and upon request. A small Kali mondir began to go up in the southernmost Bauri paṛa, and sacrifices to Kali were performed in front of it each year.

The member of the Bauri community who had been inducted into it many years before, claiming to have been an expelled Brahman—Bamun Bauri—was put in charge of arrangements because of his presumed ancestral expertise. Hôripôdô Dube, the keeper of the village Rôkkhô-Kali shrine, was invited to conduct the ceremony. Once he began the puja—inside the temple built by Bauris, in front of a murti purchased by Bauris—no Bauri (including Bamun) was permitted inside the temple. The Bauris all squatted in front of the mondir watching as much as they could through the open door. The Brahman concluded the ceremony with the sacrifice of two goats, keeping (as is the custom) the head and a foreleg of each goat for himself.

The Bauris of Gôndôgram turned out in force and were joined by relatives from nearby villages. Many men of Ûcu para drifted by, though few stayed for the entire ceremony, and a very few Brahmans (mostly Dubes) were to be observed in the crowd, along with a few officers from the factory, who had dropped by, they claimed, out of curiosity about village customs.

Ôgrahayôn (H.: *Agrāhāyana*)—November–December

This is usually the time of the rice harvest, and people say they are too busy for festivals and ceremonies. Most landholders, however, do take the time to perform the *nôbannô*, or "first-fruits" ceremony. They tend to perform it quietly in their homes, and in only two villages surveyed did informants consider the ceremony sufficiently important to be included in the catalogue of village religious events.

Pouś (H.: *Pausha*)—December–January

This is another month in which, for Hindus, there is little in the way of religious ceremony, apart from a special ritual bath on the day of the winter solstice. Everyone knows, however, that Pouś is the month of the year's major festival, or *pôrôb*, for Santals and related peoples such as the Koras. Even though the Hindu inhabitants of Gôndôgram claim that they and their families have nothing to do with the Santal event, they are all aware of it. And the fact is that young men of every jati do manage to wander past the Santal para at one time or another during the festival, most particularly when the Santal girls are dancing. Dancing girls convey an erotic image in the côkrô, even when they dance as sedately as do the girls of the Santals, and even though they no longer dance with their breasts bare, as Santal girls once did, a decade or more earlier, when the adult men of the village (who now claim to ignore the festival) were boys.

A former Brahman, now a Bauri religious leader, observes a ceremony taking place inside the Kali temple. When a Brahman priest is officiating, Bauris stay out of their own temple.

In Gôndôgram, this Santal Bādhna pôrôb takes place in the Gadhapaṭhôr Santal paṛa, with many additional Santals from Śimul paṛa and other villages in attendance. The ceremony and sacrifice ushering in the pôrôb take place traditionally in a field to the north of the paṛa. The field is owned by a Brahman family of Gôndôgram, who have given permission for the ceremony since their ancestor first permitted ancestral Santals to settle in Gôndôgram. At the end of the pôrôb, on the first day of Magh, Santals from Gôndôgram and from all over the district journey to the great "Santal Mela" (fair) at Śātaibhil.

Magh (H.: *Magha*)—January–February

The *pancami* (fifth tithi) of Magh is allocated throughout the côkrô (barring a few villages involved in calendrical disputes) to the worship of *Śôrôśôtti* (Skt.: Saraswatī), the goddess of learning and the arts. Śôrôśôtti is everywhere considered a Great-Tradition deity—never to be offered animal sacrifice, but only gifts of prayer, fruit, and flowers. In this côkrô, she is nevertheless considered the primary concern of schoolchildren only.

In Gôndôgram it is said that only perfunctory attention was paid to Śôrôśôtti until recent years when, as a result of the measure of prosperity brought by the factory, many boys, particularly of Brahman, Carpenter, and Distiller jatis, began to go on to secondary schools. The boys of Ūcu paṛa (primarily Carpenter and Distiller) now regularly construct a temporary canopy under which Śôrôśôtti Puja is performed. It is said that the boys must save their own money for the purchase of the murti and the other puja items, but many of course turn to their families for aid in raising the contribution. Only a few Brahman boys participate in this puja; most prefer to conduct one of their own in the home of one of the wealthly Brahman families. There is another Śôrôśôtti Puja in the village, a small one antedating the others, held in the schoolhouse and supported by contributions from some of the Brahmans.

Phalgun (H.: *Phālguna*)—February–March

Throughout much of India, this is the month in which Holi (or Holika), the popular and colorful Saturnalialike festival, is celebrated. In the côkrô around Gôndôgram, however, it passes almost unnoticed. Only in the industrial center of Asansol and in the compounds of factory workers—where the population is largely alien to the côkrô— are there noticeable festivities. In a few villages, including Gôndô-

Santal drummers lead a group of dancing girls at the annual Sātaibhil ceremony, while men of many castes look on. The bicycle is a product of the local factory.

gram, there is some minor celebrating for one day (the purnima of Phalgun), but only by small boys armed with packets of pink powder.

Few other significant religious events occur in the côkrô during this month, but for Gôndôgram and the villages in which Brahmans of the Śergôr śômaj are dominant, this is the month in which a special annual kirton-singing takes place, sponsored by the śômaj and hosted by the Brahman families of a different village each year. All Brahmans of the śômaj attend and participate in the singing, and people of other jatis residing in the hosting village attend as observers.

Côitrô (H.: Chaitra)—March–April

Two religious events are everywhere cited as noteworthy for this month: Rôkkhô-Kali Puja, and Śibu Puja. Rôkkhô-Kali Puja, as was noted earlier in this chapter, refers to a village memorialization of a supposed intervention by Kali, at some time in the past, to protect the village from the ravages of some epidemic, possibly cholera. The epidemics (and interventions) thus memorialized vary from village to village, and so of course do the occasions of Kali's appearance; the puja does not always even take place in Côitrô. It does take place in Côitrô in Gôndôgram, however, and in three other of the ten villages of the côkrô surveyed. While it is clearly a Little-Tradition ceremony of local provenience, sponsorship and participation is for the most part by "dominant" jatis.

Śibu Puja (worship of Śiva) is observed on the last day of the month. In most villages where the puja is observed the celebration is seemingly a minor one: prayers in a temple (if there is one, or if not, in a few wealthy homes) offered by a few old men of the "dominant" jatis. Actually, however, the puja constitutes one of the most important events of the year, particularly for young people and particularly for those of "dominant" or "middle" jatis. These journey, on foot and by vehicle, in great numbers to the few villages in the côkrô where great melas (fairs) are held on this day. For the young people of Gôndôgram and the neighboring villages, the favored object of pilgrimage is the village of Marickota, where the côkrô-wide Côndrô-cur Mela goes on throughout the night.

7

Structure, Process—and Maya

Brahman priests constitute the most noticeable category of religious leaders in Hindu India, but they are not the only ones. Srinivas (1955) pointed out that every caste in his Mysore village boasted religious leaders of its own. In Gôndôgram, we have seen both Brahman and non-Brahman priests.

There are subtleties, however, that we cannot ignore. Everyone in the village recognizes that Brahmans—all Brahmans—have a special relationship with the sphere of the divine. For the most traditional of Gôndôgram's Brahmans, this common recognition is expressed in the belief that no prayers but those of Brahmans have any meaning. For the most embittered and alienated men of other jatis, the common recognition is expressed in statements implying: The Brahmans are supposed to be holy, priestly people—but look how they behave!

The village Brahmans, therefore, are in charge of most religious events in the village, and act as advisers at those events they do not sponsor or control, such as the Dharmôraj and Kali pujas. The economic dominance of Brahmans in the village certainly enhances their prestige, but is not the basic source of it. In neighboring villages in which Brahmans are not dominant, more religious events are sponsored by other jatis, but Brahmans are still advisers and consultants.

When such questions arise as: What rituals must be performed? What may be left out? What is the significance of the ritual? Who is right in a theological dispute?—almost invariably, a Brahman will be consulted. In other words, religious leaders in other jatis (while in no way denying their own ability and authority) recognize the special competence and knowledge of Brahmans in religious matters.

This is true even for the Bauris, who are farthest from the Brahmans of the Hindus of Gôndôgram. Thus, Bauri pujaris customarily consult Brahmans to learn exactly when to conduct ceremonies in honor of Mônôśa. And when Bauris decide to sponsor the village Kali Puja, direction of the event is put in the hands of the Bauri man who was once cast out of the Brahman jati; he may be a drunkard and an object of mockery at all other times, but he was a Brahman once and so none would dispute his religious expertise.

But if Gôndôgram Brahmans share with all their varna the universal attribute of "priestly folk," this does not mean they are willing to "serve" as priests. The Brahmans of the Śergôr śômaj are primarily landholders; they supervise the raising of crops for market on their fields and they will engage happily in other occupations of a managerial or supervisory nature. Somewhat less happily they will—when pressed financially—engage in other occupations, such as working on the factory assembly lines, but they will not act as family priests even for other Brahmans.

As they see it, a Brahman should, by virtue of his varna, spend much of his time in prayer. He must do that, however, at home or in temple—out of obligation or righteousness, but never for remuneration. Brahmans who sell their services as family priests, therefore, are viewed as somehow sullied, religiously as well as socioeconomically a degree below the Brahmans who do not sell their services as priests.

Brahmans who serve as priests for other Brahmans, however— officiating at their marriages, upônôyôns, and other family events— consider themselves (and are so considered by other Brahmans) superior to Brahmans who serve non-Brahmanical jatis, and they maintain a distinct marriage-circle. And among Brahmans who act as priests for non-Brahmanical jatis, there are still further distinctions and separations, reflecting the tasks they are willing to perform and the ritual purity of the jati or jatis they serve. No Brahman in the district will serve as family priest for a Bauri. Specifically, no Brahman will officiate at a Bauri marriage. Bauris turn, therefore, to some old, respected man of their jati, referred to as a *murubbi,* and he officiates at marriages and other ceremonies.

Santals, as we have seen, have their own religious leaders, too, but they express no desire to exchange them for Brahman priests, even if the latter were available. Bauris, on the other hand, are bitter about the refusal of Brahmans to serve as their priests (they tell a legend of how Brahmans once served as their family priests but because of a Bauri man's bad behavior this former right was withdrawn). Murubbis clearly serve in lieu of Brahmans, just as Bauris go to nondescript roadside barbers only because the village barbers refuse to serve them.

To sum up, all Brahmans are "priestly folk" but only certain Brahmans, and none in Gôndôgram, serve as family priests, or purohits. Such Brahmans have their own marriage-circles, and are separated and graded among themselves in terms of the degree of religious purity of the jatis they serve, from Brahmans on down. Bauris are among the jatis considered too impure for even the lowest-ranked Brahman purohits to serve, and so have their own officiants, wise and respected old men of their own jati.

The jatis of Ūcu para (Carpenters, Distillers, and Washermen) can find Brahman purohits (though not always the same ones) to serve as their family priests, but for ceremonial and other religious leadership they tend to turn to the Deyasi family of the Carpenter jati. The Deyasis consider themselves a "priestly family" but freely acknowledge the special aptitudes of Brahmans, and frequently turn to the latter (particularly to Hôripôdô Dube, the keeper of the Rôkkhô-Kali shrine) for advice and assistance. There is jati separation in religious matters, but at another level we see complex interaction and interrelationship—except for the Santals, who keep almost entirely to themselves.

In addition to the Brahman purohit, there is another kind of religious personage who finds his way to Gôndôgram, the *gurudeb*. Every family in Brahman para, and most families in Ūcu para—but none in the other paras—has a religious adviser it can turn to. The purohit is called to perform marriages and other ceremonies; the gurudeb is called for advice, instruction, and consolation. He is an astrologer, casting horoscopes for the members of families he services, and he also reads their palms. He instructs the children (and sometimes adults) in morally correct behavior, gives them prayers to recite, and offers both comfort and explanation in times of trouble and disaster. The gurudeb is often a Brahman (though of a marriage-circle ranked below those of any purohit), but apparently he need not always be of that varna.

The gurudeb and his services provide an important key to the question raised earlier: how can the pragmatic and the transcendental exist side by side in the Indian village without any indication of contradiction or conflict of belief? It was pointed out, the reader may remember, that not only do such practices and beliefs exist side by side—worship of transcendental divinities and belief in karma; and propitiation of local deities capable of major interference in the lives of man—but they in fact often occur in the same individual! The contradiction, it would seem, is in the eye of the beholder, who perceives the two syndromes synchronically, rather than in their actual diachronic relationship. In order to demonstrate this, let us follow the response to misfortune in a Gôndôgram family—*over time*.

It would be helpful for our analysis if we distinguish certain obvious stages in the progress of misfortune: the *Onset,* when members of a family first perceive and begin to react to misfortune; the *Continuation,* when the misfortune has been with them for some time and has come to be recognized as a factor in their lives; and the *Culmination,* from the time the misfortune has brought about its final disaster.

For people of Bauri and Santal paras, one might say that misfortune is part of their normal lives and that therefore there can be no perception of *Onset.* Such a statement would not be entirely true, of course, but it is true that the sequence of responses to be outlined here holds least of all for the poorer villagers and is most characteristic of the wealthier inhabitants, those of Brahman and Ūcu paras.

The Onset. Misfortune comes in many guises. Illness in a member of the family is the most obvious and common one; not just a common cold or mild fever, but something more deep-seated and troubling, something that does not seem to be responding to home remedies or even a visit to a doctor.

Other misfortunes, for the people of Brahman and Ūcu paras, might be conflict with some relative or neighbor over ownership of a piece of land, or the observation that a child is doing poorly in school, particularly when he is one of those few village boys in secondary school. A young bride who has not become pregnant during her first year of marriage is a source of concern for the family, as is a woman who bears children, but only girls.

The point is, the heads of the family are disturbed and worried; they feel endangered. At the next visit of the gurudeb (and if they are anxious, they will summon him), the head of the household informs him of the problem. The gurudeb reads the appropriate palms and casts horoscopes. He is likely to note a dangerous sign somewhere: a crack in a lifeline, a disturbing conjunction of planets, and so on. Events affecting a wife may be noted in her husband's palm; danger to children in the palms or horoscopes of their parents. It is possible, then, that the gurudeb will acknowledge the danger and indicate its source, in palm or stars. In such cases he is likely to counsel caution; one should not, for example, engage in new or risky financial enterprises if one's horoscope is not propitious.

Let us suppose that the gurudeb has provided such an explanation for the present problem, thus reducing anxiety, and has advised the family on how to deal with, and overcome, the misfortune. Let us suppose, further, that the family takes his advice and that in a reasonably short period the trouble disappears. The ill person recovers; the wife becomes pregnant and is delivered of a boy; the problems in school are cleared up; or the land dispute is settled amicably. No further thought is given to the matter, beyond an increased dependence on and confidence in the gurudeb. After all, he pinpointed the source of the problem and showed them how to overcome it or at least correctly predicted that it would disappear. In such a case, it is obvious, no discussion of karma or divine retribution is necessary, and none is likely to take place.

The Continuation. But let us now suppose that the misfortune does not go away. The boy continues to do poorly in school and seems likely to fail completely; the dispute over the piece of land has become more bitter and may be heading for the courts. Much more serious, of course, is the case of the continuing illness, or the woman who continues to be barren or to give birth to still another female child.

The villager responds in such situations very much as he does with more mundane problems; he seeks the aid of someone with influence and power. The unemployed Bauri, for example, prostrates himself before a Brahman landholder and begs for patronage; if he receives it he is the latter's follower forever, even voting as the Brahman directs. The Brahman who wants a new road to the village prostrates himself, in exactly the same way, before someone he considers more powerful—the "Maharaja of Kaśipur" in bygone days, and the factory Works Manager today—and acknowledges the perpetual authority of the petitioned with the formal: "You are my mother and my father."

As the villager sees it, however, certain continuing and substantial misfortunes (such as barrenness and illness) require divine, not human, intervention. Throughout the district there are temples to many different deities, and shrines and sacred places of all sorts. Listening to everyone's advice, based upon personal experiences, hearsay, and local legends, the head of the afflicted household visits temple after temple, shrine after shrine.

As we have seen, certain places have reputations for efficacy in certain kinds of misfortunes: Rôkkhô-Kali shrine in Gôndôgram for intestinal complaints and the Dharmôraj temple for the misfortunes of women, such as barrenness. Ganeś is propitiated by high-caste people for aid for the mentally afflicted. Deities have their specialties, and their shrines attract large numbers of those so afflicted, but we have seen that one can appeal to any deity for aid with *any* misfortune. The pattern, obviously, is to turn first to the deity (and at a shrine near home) associated with one's misfortune. If the divinity fails to help, one turns, in increasing desperation, to shrines further and further afield.

The details of the supplication and propitiation vary, but there is a basic similarity. One communicates the nature of the problem to the officiating priest or shrine-keeper. He instructs the supplicant in the form the petition must take and the time and manner of presentation. Basically, the supplicant abases himself or herself before the deity, calls the deity "Mother" or "Father," and promises offerings if the petition is answered. For some deities the offerings will be in the form of animals to be sacrificed (particularly goats) and for others flowers, prayers, and monetary offerings will be promised.

After the prayer for divine assistance, the supplicants return home to await results. If within a reasonable period after the petition (usually no more than a year and often much less) the misfortune ends, it is assumed by all that there has been a miraculous divine intercession. The court case was won, the child successful in school, the ill person recovered, the barren woman pregnant, and so on, because the deity answered the prayer—and for no other reason.

As we have noted, the favored family thenceforth feels a special and continuing obligatory bond to the deity and his or her shrine. Not only is payment made in the form of the promised offering but the family is likely to visit the shrine or otherwise make an offering every year thereafter on the anniversary of the miracle. If the divine intercession resulted in the birth of a male child, he may be named after the deity or the temple and be required by the family to offer appropriate prayers throughout the rest of his life. This response does not merely reflect gratitude and the fulfillment of a promise; the family now feels they have a divine friend in high places. A Bauri who has a wealthy patron is justly envied by his neighbors, as is a village landholder who has the ear of factory or government officials—and so is a villager of any status who has called successfully upon divine aid.

Such a villager, if queried, does not know for certain the source of his misfortune, now happily past. It may be that his gurudeb was right and there was some unfortunate planetary conjunction in his horoscope. Or perhaps the misfortune reflected a punishment for misdeeds in another existence. Perhaps some malevolent spirit or person wished him evil. Who can know—and in the end, what does it matter? What does matter is that he and his family were facing disaster but were successful in finding a deity powerful enough and friendly enough to change the scheme of things, converting misfortune into good fortune.

The Culmination. But now let us suppose the family has not been so fortunate. The months stretch into years, the pilgrimages and prayers mount, but all is to no avail. The case in court is lost and the family is stripped of its land. The boy is expelled from school and becomes a ne'er-do-well. The ill person dies, the wife arrives at menopause without ever having borne a live male child. Disaster is complete and irrevocable.

In any village in India (as indeed in any place in the world) one meets people who have experienced such total disaster. In Gôndô-gram there is, among other such unfortunates, an old Pande, in his seventies at the time of this study, whose wife had died when he was still a young man, leaving him three daughters to raise. He had made good marriages for them in distant villages, selling his land to pay for weddings and dowries. Now, penniless and alone, he lives in a crumbling hut, dependent upon grudging gifts of food from distant relatives in the village.

It is his "kôrmô," he explains to the visitor, and listening neighbors nod sadly in agreement. He must have been a wicked man in some previous existence, all acknowledge, though he has been a saintly one in this life. His punishment for previous sins is to find himself alone and beggared, without family and most of all without sons, in his old age. He says he had hoped to die years before, but even this comfort was denied him. His reward, however—all his neighbors agree—will be a truly wonderful life the next time he is reborn.

And so we see that the transcendental concerns are finally invoked, but only when all else has failed, when disaster is complete. The nature of the universe, the cycles of rebirth, the meaning of karma, and the orderings of destiny all have relevance now; they enable an old man to surmount total tragedy, to make his peace with harsh reality and live out his remaining days with some measure of dignity and even hope.

There is no conflict, then, between pragmatic and transcendental beliefs and practices in Gôndôgram. The issue is one of sequence, of process. Similarly, there is no conflict, we have seen, between villagers holding widely differing views on religious questions. Ambiguity is the relevant structural principle; there is never one possible cause of misfortune but always many possible sources, and until the source is determined it is difficult if not impossible to effect the cure, though the problem may be solved by divine intervention.

The Santal ojha, as we have seen, must determine whether the illness derives from tejo, bhut, or daini, or some combination of the three. This element of ambiguity runs through the entire belief system of the Gôndôgram area, and, in important measure, makes it possible for the system to function as satisfactorily as it does. Given this ambiguity, moreover, one begins to see why the villager perceives none of the apparent contradictions discussed earlier.

For the Western observer, the villager's representations about the very natures of the divinities express this same ambiguity. What at first appears to be contradiction and inconsistency turns out to be complexity and multidimension.

This complexity, in turn, appears to reflect the social complexity: there is, after all, not one simple system of beliefs, but a system of systems, reflecting, quite clearly, the complexity of relationships between and within the jatis of the village. In one village, we have seen, men of different jatis may address prayers to different deities at the same ceremony! Though the systems—belief or social—interrelate, the fit can never be perfect. Where the fit is not perfect, one can perceive contradiction—or ambiguity. The Gôndôgram villager opts for the latter: even the Brahman priest, faced with an apparent contradiction, refuses to say that one way is Hindu while the other is not. Each is correct, for the man who follows it. He smiles, and says in explanation: "Don't you see? In the end, all is *maya*." "Maya" is usually translated as "illusion," but perhaps, in this context, "ambiguity" would serve much better.

Part III

THE VILLAGE AND THE FACTORY

1

Riceland and Bicycles

It would not be correct, as we have seen, to look upon Gôndôgram as having been an isolated, purely agricultural village at any time in its history. From the time the first Dhopa settled on the banks of the pond, hoping for work washing the laundry of mining employees, Gôndôgram has interacted with the industrial world surrounding it. A few Brahman men, of the wealthier families, have had clerical positions at one or another factory or mine around Asansol. Carpenters plied their trade in mine and mill as well as village. Bauris and Santals worked as industrial laborers, when they could, and Distillers sold their product to industrial and colliery employees. The market of Asansol superseded the local haṭs . . . and in so many other ways Gôndôgram reflected the fact that it was firmly imbedded in and a part of subdistrict Asansol.

But, for all of that, rice agriculture remained the paramount influence on village life, on economic, social, and ritual relationships. This changed radically and definitively only after 1951, with the establishment of the "Das-Walters" bicycle factory. Established just outside Gôndôgram, on land in large part belonging to men of that village, it was viewed from the first as an alien intrusion. The factory is indeed alien to the village, but it is of course a complex of foreign (primarily British) and Indian (but Westernized) elements.

To begin with, the Das-Walters Company is an affiliate of the parent British company, which in fact controls all aspects of production and manufacturing quality. All such matters are supervised personally by one senior official, the "Works Manager," who was, at the time of the study, a British engineer appointed by the British home office and directly responsible to that office and to no one else. He was the only non-Indian in the Table of Organization, as far as I was able to determine. Otherwise, the staff was Indian, and most of the senior officers were either members of the Das family, or of the same jati, the Bôiddô (Vaidya) jati. All these officials had lived (before the partition at the time of Independence) in the part of Bengal that was to become successively East Pakistan and then Bangladesh.

Legend in and around the factory has it that the Das family, a few generations back, owned a roadside store dealing in used bicycles, the kind of shop one sees in the poorer streets of Asansol. Whether or not there is any truth to the story, it is certainly true that the Das family, by the time of Independence, controlled the sale and distribution of the British-made "Walters" bicycle throughout South and Southeast Asia. When the parent company decided to permit production of the bicycle in India, for distribution in that part of the world, the Das family took over responsibility for production as well as distribution.

Actually, the members of the Das family, while major stockholders and occupiers of all important positions (with the exception of that of Works Manager) in the company, still appear to concentrate most of their attention on sales and distribution. The details of the legal and financial relationships between the parent company and the Indian affiliate would of course take us far beyond the scope of this work. We might pause in passing, however, to glance at the role of the Works Manager, for it does seem to reflect a pattern much older in India than contemporary investment and industrial arrangements.

The factory is, as we have noted, in many ways an independent entity; an Indian institution under Indian supervision, with most decisions made by the Das family and by the other Indian shareholders and their representatives. Production, however, is controlled absolutely by the Works Manager; he determines quality and the details and conditions of manufacture, and makes (or supervises) all decisions affecting production, including selection and promotion of key personnel. He holds the somewhat difficult position of being at the same time the expert (but foreign) adviser to the Indian factory owners and administrators—and responsible to the parent company in Britain for the maintenance of their standards of quality and productivity. His role is therefore strikingly reminiscent of the British Residents in earlier times, appointed by the British but serving as advisers to nominally independent local Indian princes who were in fact ultimately "subject to the paramountcy of the British Crown" (Moreland and Chatterjee 1957: 325).

As a result of negotiations between government authorities and Das-Walters officials leading to the decision to establish a factory in the Asansol area, certain promises were made to the company. Local representatives of government would enable the company to acquire land and would provide necessary power and transportation facilities. Power lines were brought in without too much delay or difficulty, and a railway spur to the factory site was ready at about the same time the factory went into operation. This provided a means for bringing in the basic production materials, most particularly steel tubing.

The promise of a new paved road, however, linking the factory to the Grand Trunk Road directly to the south, turned out to be more difficult to fulfill. The road was in fact not completed until some twelve years after the opening of the factory; until then the trucks carrying away the completed bicycles had to find their way along the inadequate, potholed and circuitous older rural roads.

The promise of aid in the acquisition of land was carried out, but also not without difficulty. The land around Gôndôgram may be inferior and sparsely inhabited when compared with other sections of Bengal, but every inch of the land desired by the factory was nevertheless owned or claimed by someone, and no claimant was at all eager to relinquish it.

The factory management discovered, to its grief, that while it was true that rural land was cheaper than town land, other factors were present to bring up expenses. As we have seen earlier, inheritance patterns are complex in Gôndôgram and its neighbors; not only do all sons (and, in law, all daughters) inherit equal shares, but they must inherit equal proportions of different kinds of soil or terrain, both good and bad.

From the point of view of the heir, the disadvantage of owning such scattered property is satisfactorily offset by the knowledge that he has shared exactly in the quality of the inheritance; if there was a section of particularly fine land anywhere, he has his piece of it. The scatter might be said to have an ecological advantage, too; with scattered holdings, the farmer is less at the mercy of a particular local disaster—whether a windstorm or subsidence or a fire in the fields, or whatever.

For the factory, however, the system of inheritance could precipitate only headaches. No man wanted to sell any of his land, but if he were forced to, each one wanted whatever money was coming to him. The factory found it could not purchase large parcels of land from single owners; in most cases it had to buy assortments of tiny fragments from many owners.

The basic problem was that the owners were reluctant to sell—at any price. From the perspective of almost every villager of whatever jati, land is far more desirable than the money it can bring on even the most favorable market. Money is ephemeral; it can be used only once and then is gone forever. Land remains in the family over generations. A man who owns a bigha or two of land can hope to grow, even in a bad year, food enough to keep his family alive. Members of the factory management insist that compensation for land was more than generous; villagers dispute that claim, but admit, bitterly, that even if princely payment had been offered most villagers would have preferred—if given any option—not to sell.

Opposition and conflict in the village increased to the point, apparently, where senior members of the factory management felt obliged to try to do something about it. They attended a meeting of village men and announced that they considered themselves, henceforth, to be "sons of Gôndôgram." A job of some kind in the factory, they promised, would always be available for any boy of the village. The factory would assist, too, in efforts of the village to improve itself.

As factory officials recount the meeting, they appear to have viewed themselves as addressing the "village"—all the men, that is, without observable internal social distinctions; but the village response varied, jati by jati. Brahmans were impressed by the offer of assistance in improvement efforts; this offer meant nothing at all to men of most other jatis, who make no reference to it in their accounts of the meeting.

On the other hand, Brahmans dismissed the offer of jobs with some irritation. As they tell it, they saw themselves at the time as farmers, producing crops for market, not as laborers. What they needed, in their opinion, was land for cultivation, not menial employment. Carpenters (who, along with Pande Brahmans, tended to own most of the land required by the factory) did not consider the offer of jobs adequate compensation for the lost land, but had no intention of spurning the offer.

Distillers were also interested in the possibility of jobs, but even more intrigued by the opportunities for income in other ways, particularly by providing liquor for factory workers. Washermen, too, hoped for the opportunity to ply their traditional jati occupation. Few if any Bauris were present at the meeting or were ever aware of any promise of employment; only one or two expressed the belief that the promise actually applied to Bauris. Santals apparently had no interest whatever in the factory, or any awareness of promises to the village.

Eventually, the necessary land was purchased and all claims satisfied. Numbers of laborers were hired by the contractors who undertook to build the factory and the quarters surrounding it, as well as the railway spur and (much later) the new road. The official date of founding of the factory is given as March 25, 1951, but it was many months after that before the plant was in anything like full operation.

At the time of this study (1963–1964), the factory employed approximately 2,790 persons in the manufacture of bicycles. Of these, 2,135 were in the category of "semi-skilled operators"—those who worked on the assembly lines or performed the other basic manipulative tasks of production and assembly. All other employees of the factory, from senior management to the most menial of sweepers, numbered 655.

A partial breakdown of employment categories, educational requirements, and remuneration would be useful at this point.

TABLE 13 *Factory Employment*

Division	Positions	Persons Employed	Wages, per Month (in Rupees)
Office and Administration	Officers & Comm. Ass'ts.	30	450 (and up)
	Clerks	185	190 (average)
	Peons	27	115
Works and Technical	Tech. Ass'ts., Managerial, etc.	62	425 (and up)
	Supervisors, Charge-hands	103	265 (average)
	Semi-skilled Setter, Worker, or Operator	2135	210 (average)
	"Mazdoors"	248	110

Table 13 shows that 242 persons were employed, at the time of this study, in "Office and Administration." Twenty-seven of these, those in the lowest category, were "peons"—the Indian category which translates best into English as "office boy" or "messenger." Peons assist clerks and officers in their work, carrying messages, bringing records from office to office, serving tea, and so on. They are expected to be able to read, in English, up to "Class VIII Standard" (roughly equivalent to American eighth grade, or at least to completion of elementary school). They received an average monthly wage of 115 rupees each. There were 185 "clerks" receiving an average remuneration of 190 rupees per month. They were expected, at minimum, to have attended secondary school; for advancement to "senior clerk" some intermediate certificate had to have been achieved. The rest of the staff ("commercial assistants" and "officers") were required to have graduate and/or professional training and received salaries from 425 rupees per month on upward to undisclosed high sums.

In "Works and Technical" 2,548 were employed. Of these, 248 were unskilled laborers, categorized in the records as "mazdoors," who carried supplies and materials to the various production departments and carried away the completed work. They were expected "to be able to read and write" (though the issue was rarely put to the test) and received an average monthly income of 110 rupees, or slightly less than peons.

Some 2,135 persons were covered by the category "semi-skilled worker, setter, or operator" and received wages averaging 210 rupees per month. A reading ability "up to Class VIII Standard" was formally required, but in practice, sufficient ability to make out instructions and directions on machinery (with assistance) was adequate. Over them were 103 "supervisors" or "charge-hands" who averaged 265 rupees per month and were expected to have secondary school as well as work experience. The rest of the staff, from "technical assistants" through "foremen," "superintendants" to "managers" were expected to have increasing levels of engineering training and experience, and were paid accordingly, from 425 rupees per month on up.

In addition to those employees described above, there were a large but shifting number of people employed in various menial or minor capacities, on a limited or part-time basis. These included sweepers, domestic servants of various kinds, and canteen employees. They numbered about one hundred persons, male and female, and rarely earned more than 100 rupees per month; they were also rarely, if ever, eligible for leave of any kind or for promotion.

Other people were employed in activities generated by the presence of the factory, though their incomes did not derive directly from the factory (but rather indirectly, through one or two removes). About five hundred people, mostly road-gang laborers, were employed by various contractors for work in and around the factory— building and maintaining roads, putting up new workers' quarters, and so on. About fifty people, it was estimated, operated (or were employed in) the various shops and stalls acceptable to the factory and located in its vicinity.

And then there was the unacceptable (or frowned on) periphery: purveyors of illegal locally distilled liquor, prostitutes, beggars, thieves, and so on. The number as well as the individuals in this last large category were subject to continual change; in theory none were present at all, and were actually in the neighborhood because of the ignorance (real or feigned) of factory and local police. Periodically, because of an increase in illness, crime, or absenteeism, the factory management complained to the police, who came into the area and chased out such unwanted persons. In a few days, most of them (or people just like them) were back at their old activities.

Although there was some intention, at the time of the establishment of the factory, to employ local people, this plan was largely ignored during the succeeding decade. At the time of the study, it was estimated that fewer than three hundred of those directly employed by the factory were "local people," that is, from the surrounding villages. Some of the reasons for this change in expressed policy will be explored in the following pages. For now, I would note only that most employees at almost all levels are obtained, under the Employment Exchange Compulsory Notification Act of 1961, from governmentally administered "Employment Exchanges." Of the 2,790 persons officially employed full-time by the factory, 1,976 came from the state of West Bengal (this included the 300 or so "local people"), 473 from Bihar, and the rest from Orissa, Madhya Pradesh, Nepal, and East Pakistan (now Bangladesh).[1]

All strangers to the area required housing, and even the very poorest housing was in extremely short supply around Asansol. Approximately 800 units of housing quarters had been constructed near the factory, and 300 more were under construction, with long waiting lists. Of the 800, 200 were set aside for "staff." For the higher staff, those earning more than 425 rupees per month, the quarters consisted of attractive cottages set off in a special compound located about halfway between the factory and Gôndôgram. Most of the rest of the quarters were rows of identical concrete buildings, each containing a number of small apartments. Some were occupied by a single family; most contained a number of individual workmen (their families back in their home villages far away), crowded together partly because of the shortage of living space, and partly to save as much money as possible.

While the factory was being established, the demand for such quarters was less intense than it became in later years. The management of the factory even offered to provide apartments for some Gôndôgram villagers (that is, for the families of the few Brahmans who had office jobs) who wished to take advantage of them. No villagers accepted the offer, but some were sorry later when they visited the

1. Most of those from East Pakistan had come as refugees at the time of separation of India and Pakistan; they were mostly relatives and friends of the management, altogether, some 89 people.

dôgram, unfortunately) but rapidly disappearing everywhere. The children of even Gôndôgram villagers, I was assured earnestly many times, would exhibit none of the caste prejudices of their elders. Meanwhile, it was explained, the present "villagers" expressed these caste sentiments by refusing to associate with—eat with or even work alongside—men of other castes.

In a similar simplification, factory officials viewed traditional village religion as a naive adoration of Viśnu, Śiva, Durga, and other divinities with offerings of flowers and food. Such officials could sometimes be seen, in their Western clothes, standing at the outskirts of the crowd during such ceremonies as Kali and Dharmôraj pujas, faces expressive of disbelief and disgust at the animal sacrifices and other rituals.

The "villager," they go on to say, thus may have led an idyllic and unspoiled life in days gone by, but the coming of the factory "spoiled" him, and he has proved a burden for the factory. They remind the visitor that the factory management, at the time of the founding of the factory, promised to help the inhabitants of Gôndôgram to improve their lot—and also promised jobs to them and to their sons.

Assistance, they say, was intended and has indeed been given. What was not intended was for the village to become dependent upon the factory, demanding everything and doing nothing for themselves. "They kiss our feet and call us their 'mother and father,' " reported one official in disgust, "and then ask us to pave their roads, provide electricity—they want everything done for them."

The officials insist, however, that the offer of jobs was a sincere one, much as some regret it now. They were interested in the idea that local people might come to work while residing in their home villages, thus obviating the need for workers' quarters. They assumed, further, that the local "villager" would be no worse, if no better, than any other employee of equivalent training and education. As they see it, everything has worked out most unfortunately. Three reasons are advanced in explanation of their dissatisfaction with the local "villager" as factory employee:

(a) *Laziness and Absenteeism:* The local Bengali "villager," say officials, is an indifferent worker at best. He exhibits no interest in his equipment or his work; he does the minimum required of him and shows no initiative. Even more serious, they say, is his lack of dependability. Absenteeism, the officials claim, is much more troublesome among local people than it is among those from outside the district, who are recruited through the labor exchange and who reside in the workers' quarters.

Some of the officials, when questioned closely, acknowledge that when they speak of laziness or of indifferent workers they have village Brahmans in mind; they admitted they had no complaint to make on that score about Carpenters or members of other jatis. Brahmans (said those officials who were willing to make the distinction) were as a group reluctant to work in the factory at any manual job and were always requesting transfer to some office work, even when they were manifestly unfit for it.

If there was some disagreement among officials about the matter of laziness, there was none whatever about absenteeism: *all* men of Gôndôgram—of *whatever* caste—and indeed *all* men from any of the local villages, had unsatisfactory attendance records when compared with non-local employees. This was advanced as a major reason for the reluctance to employ local people in greater numbers, admittedly a reversal of the original factory intent.

Some officials attributed the absenteeism to a greater debility among local people, arguing that the area around Asansol is particularly unhealthy; others said it was just another example of "the villager's" general laziness, but one official did note that the local "villager" is of necessity more susceptible to importunities to stay home and help with planting or harvest.

(b) *Caste Exclusiveness:* Indian officials of the factory insist that they themselves subscribe in no way to the notions of "caste"; they add, too, that the laws of India proscribe the maintenance of caste distinctions, and that British-born officials in any factory are totally uninterested in anything having to do with "caste." And finally, they point out, caste restrictions and observances interfere with the flow of modern business and factory maintenance. For all these reasons, they say, "caste" is officially ignored in the factory; no factory representative or form ever inquires into caste identification, and some officials insist that evidence of such curiosity on the part of any officer might well be grounds for dismissal. Requests for particular employment (or restriction from particular employment) couched in terms of caste preference or caste restriction are likely to be refused.

Even more, recognizing that men of the same caste may tend to congregate together, officials try, as a matter of policy, to separate men of like caste and mix together those of different ones. This, they admit, can only be done when they have some intimation of caste identity; given the official policy on this, officials rarely know, or admit to knowing, caste identification.

Despite all this, to the deep dismay of the officials of the factory, there is a noticeable tendency for people of like caste to congregate together in the factory. The officials feel that this tendency is particularly noticeable in local people, and most particularly in the

workers who come from Gôndôgram. To a man, officials claim to be
baffled as to how such a thing takes place; after all, the policy is to
discourage the placing of men of the same family or caste in the
same department.

If it is difficult to detect them, given the problem of making such
inquiries without breaking the rules, it should be at least as difficult
for the new workers to be assigned to departments where relatives are
already employed. Such requests, it is pointed out, are usually not
honored and new employees are assigned in terms of need and vacancy, unless the new employee happens to have previous skill and
experience. And yet, again and again, factory officials discover to
their dismay that a particular department has come over time to be
constituted by men of one particular caste, often close relatives.

The officials usually become aware of the state of things when a
death occurs in the household of one of the employees in the department. As we have seen earlier, a death in the family imposes many
restrictions upon a man for the period of mourning, and the period of
mourning may be anything from ten to thirty days, depending upon
his jati rules. During this period, his diet is restricted, certain activities are enjoined, and he may even be required to spend his time (or a
large part of it) in prayer and contemplation. An employee in mourning inevitably poses problems for the factory; even when he returns to
work, after a period of absence, he must be reassigned for a time to
other, lighter work, for many jatis hold that injuries—particularly the
shedding of blood—must be avoided at all costs during mourning.
Still, officials perceive the inevitability of the situation, and indeed
share many of the sentiments, and so they do all that they can for the
individual mourner.

They become deeply disturbed, however, when a death occurs in
the household of one employee and most of the members of his department announce that, as close relatives and jat-brothers, they in-
tend to join him in his period of mourning! And it is such an an-
nouncement, with its inevitable attendant stress and confusion as
management attempts to cope with the problems caused by one entire
department dropping out of the chain of production, that is usually
the first intimation the factory has that the department has been taken
over by men of one jati.

The response of the factory, after the initial dismay, is to attempt
to break up the concentration, or at least water it down through the
introduction of new people of different origins. From that point on,
vacancies are filled only by men from other parts of India, presumably of different jati.

Such efforts, officials report glumly, rarely seem to work. For some unknown reason, they say, such new employees turn out to be more than usually unsatisfactory; their quotas remain unfulfilled and the complaints about the quality of their work are many. Such new men tend to be dismissed for incompetence with much greater frequency than average, or they themselves resign or beg to be transferred elsewhere. The point is, say the officials, "they don't stay," and a department once taken over by cousins and jat-brothers tends to remain that way despite all efforts on the part of the factory officials.

While this is a problem at all times, at all levels, and with employees from all over India, officials insist that "local people"—and particularly the inhabitants of Gôndôgram—give the most trouble. Many of the Brahmans of Gôndôgram who are employed in the factory as "semi-skilled operators" work in the enameling department; many of the Carpenters work in the chain department. These two departments, particularly, have precipitated severe crises more than once, because of deaths and the resultant protracted mourning.

(c) *Clamor for Employment:* Given the first two complaints that factory officials have about "local people," it is understandable that they are somewhat reluctant to employ them in great numbers. Nevertheless, the officials remember their early promise to find jobs for "sons of the village" and claim they will continue to do so, if without any real enthusiasm. Unhappily, from the factory viewpoint, these "local people" not only insist upon the jobs promised to them but they cheat, say officials, constantly bringing in outsiders, from villages far from Gôndôgram, and insisting that these are all "sons of the village." "Do you know how long it takes," said one official bitterly, "for a boy to be born in that village, grow to maturity, and then come to apply for a job in the factory? *Two weeks!*"

Again and again, officials say, a man of Gôndôgram will show up, an embarrassed adolescent boy in tow, insisting to all that this is indeed his son, and where had the official received the erroneous impression that he had no more grown sons? Factory officials note that they could make an issue of these frauds (and some say they may have to, in the future), but the villagers are so insistent that in the end, usually, some job is found for the boy.

3

The Village Response

As we have seen, it is difficult if not indeed impossible to typify the Gôndôgram "villager" in any way; it is probably least meaningful of all to attempt to construct one generalized Gôndôgram response to the presence of the factory. Individuals, of course, make idiosyncratic responses, to some extent, but it is possible to speak of a specific jati response; in the main, Brahmans as a body have made one kind of response, Bauris another, and so on.

The Brahmans of Gôndôgram, we noted, were not interested at first in the offer of employment in the factory. One or two men, with sufficient education, applied for and received clerical positions. A few other Brahmans applied for jobs as semi-skilled operators for "sons"—in every case, impecunious distant relatives.

Within a year or two, however, Brahman attitudes underwent a shift. The yearly income of a semi-skilled operator, they discovered, compared favorably with the net income of any but the richest of rice farmers in the neighborhood. Further, such income did not require the participation of the family; presumably, one man could work while the rest of the family saw to the fields, and so his income would be entirely an addition to previous earnings. Brahman men of Gôndô-gram, of all ages and of all degrees of education and family income, began to clamor for the jobs "that had been promised them." The jobs they wanted, in fact, were without exception non-manual. If nothing else were available, or if the Brahman lacked sufficient educa-tion, he would be willing to accept the position of stores clerk—but what he wanted was to work in the office in some kind of clerical capacity. What the factory needed, however, was semi-skilled opera-tors on the assembly line.

206

The factory-related employment situation in Gôndôgram is outlined in table 14. Of the thirty-two Brahman households in Gôndôgram at the time of the study, only six had no representative employed in or around the factory (and of these, five had family members employed in other factories or in some colliery, usually in a staff position). Thirty-six men from the remaining twenty-six Brahman households were in factory-connected employment. Of these, eight held clerical positions of one kind of another (three as stores clerk), one drove a company truck (and thus was classified in a special laboring capacity), one was a "charge-hand," two were employed in a small grocery shop near the factory, and the rest (twenty-four) were employed as operators. And the greater number of these were in the enameling department; only three or four were scattered in other departments.

None of the Brahmans working as operators expressed any real interest in the work (men in the enameling department said they actively disliked it; it was hot and smelly, dangerous, and generally unpleasant). All were disappointed that they had not acquired office jobs. Some blamed their failure on the machinations of other, more fortunate, Brahmans, who kept them out of the office, but most admitted they were simply not qualified; the educational qualifications of older Brahmans are low, particularly in English.

Many still dreamed of being transferred somehow to office or store. One man in particular, scion of a wealthy family and with pretensions to eventual political power in the village and perhaps beyond, made particularly desperate efforts, so far unavailing, to get an appointment as stores clerk. He said he felt he would never be able to hold his head up in the village, or at least have authority with other Brahmans, as long as he continued to work with his hands.

All Brahman men interviewed insisted that things would be different for their children, if it were at all possible to do something about it. Children of Brahmans were encouraged to stay in school, to try for secondary schools. Frequently, the money earned in the factory was put aside in large part (when there were other sources of income) for children's schooling. It was hoped that children would become accountants, senior clerks, engineers, technicians—anything but operators like their fathers and older brothers.

There were, at the time of the study, six Carpenter households in Gôndôgram (but many more in the neighboring village of Gopalgram). Deriving from these six were nine men who worked in or around the factory. One Carpenter was employed as a stores clerk, and one young man had a job in a betel shop near the factory; the other seven were operators—four in the chain department where the links of chain were stamped out, and three in the frame department.

TABLE 14 *Factory-Related Employment in Gôndôgram*

Jati	Total Adult Men	Clerk	Stores Clerk	Peon	Foreman or Charge-Hand	Truck Driver	Operator	Mazdoor	Canteen or Other Menial	Road Gang or Construction	Peripheral Employment	Other Industries or Collieries
Brahman	48	5	3		1	1	24				2	5
Barber	3						1					
Carpenter	14		1				7				1	1
Distiller	17			1			7	2			7	
Washerman	5						1	1			3	
Dom	1									1		
Bauri												
Gadhapathôr	12								2			
Šimul	16*						1	3	4	1	*	
Dôkkhin	8							2	3	1	1	
Santal†	14									†		
Muslim	1								1			

* Two adult women also engaged in "peripheral employment."

† All Santal adult men, and most women, available for seasonal road and construction work.

All Carpenter men over the age of eighteen, and a few under, had worked, prior to the coming of the factory, at their traditional occupation—carpentry. They fixed carts, built doors and window frames, and repaired other items made of wood. For some, the trade represented their sole source of income, for others it was a welcome addition to whatever they made from their ricefields. One Carpenter, we have seen, was a part-time śilpi (artist), sculpting icons in clay for ceremonies.

At the time of the study, only two or three of the older men still worked—occasionally, in their spare time—as traditional village carpenters, and there was one man in the village employed in a distant factory as a carpenter. The young men, however, no longer learned the trade from their fathers, for all looked forward to employment in the factory—as operators, they hoped. There was one boy of a carpenter family who dreamed of being an engineer.

When the factory first came, many Carpenters were deprived of land and took the factory's promise of employment very seriously. A number of the older men sought and received immediate employment in the work of construction. Their job was to erect the bamboo scaffolding as the walls went up. They worked at other construction carpentry tasks as well, and when the factory was ready to open they applied for work inside. Almost all, as has been noted, were assigned to the category "semi-skilled operator" and given the necessary three months training before taking up their permanent duties. Many other members of their śômaj, from Gopalgram and other nearby villages, are employed in the factory, having started out in much the same way in early construction work. The chain department, in fact, was made up almost entirely of Carpenters, and they were substantially represented in the frame department.

Carpenters report that they find the work undemanding, if uninteresting, and the working conditions quite pleasant, particularly when they can work surrounded by jat-brothers. The wages, most attest freely, are far superior to anything they could have hoped to earn following their traditional occupation, and none would voluntarily leave the factory to resume the trade of village carpenter. Apart from the one man whose son shows some promise of eventual achievement in a technological institute or perhaps even an engineering school, Carpenters wish for nothing more than that their sons be given jobs similar to their own on the assembly line, preferably in the same departments.

And yet, having said all this, some Carpenter men go on to express a measure of sadness. Work in the factory is certainly well-paying, they note, but it is also dull and unsatisfying. An operator

performs a series of rote movements in any factory task—the same
ones over and over, days without end. Whether one stamps out the
bits of chain link, or assembles them, or assembles the fork in the
frame, there is really very little satisfaction to be obtained after the
first few days. It cannot compare with the pleasure of repairing a
broken cart, or the deep satisfaction a man could feel when building a
new one, working in the cool morning hours in the yard in front of his
house with the children watching and neighbors walking by, joking
and gossiping. There was true pleasure, a Carpenter will say, in working with the tools he inherited from his father and in teaching his sons
the ancient trade. Now the boys are not interested in learning to
become carpenters, for they—like their fathers—hope they will go to
work in the factory. And, after a hard day's work, who has time to
teach the boys? In many Carpenter homes, the tools are rusty and
neglected. And yet, say the men who have made all the foregoing
remarks, it cannot be denied that the factory wages are excellent, and
no one in his right mind would choose the chancy and inadequate
income of a village carpenter over the factory wages . . . .

There were eight Distiller households in Gôndôgram. From them
came ten men who worked directly for the factory; seven as operators
scattered in various departments, two as "mazdoor" or helper, and
one in "staff"—but in the most menial of all clerical positions, that of
peon, or office boy. Seven other men from Distiller households were
employed in the periphery of the factory. Three of these admitted that
their work consisted of purveying liquor to the factory workers; the
others would say only that they worked in "shops," but it was common belief in the village that they too sold liquor, if illegally.

Many of the Distiller men now working as operators once worked
in liquor shops; they say they prefer their present occupations because factory work is legal, steady, and remunerative, although they
point out that a man who can rise to own his own liquor shop can, if
he is fortunate and avoids trouble with the law, make much more
money in the long run. Only one or two Distillers of Gôndôgram have
ever owned such shops, however, and then only for short periods of
time. Mostly, they work for jat-brothers, for the stalls and shops
selling liquor around the factory (and around other factories and the
collieries) are largely owned and operated by members of their jati.

The attitudes of the Distillers are more difficult to encapsulate than
those of other jatis in Gôndôgram. The man who is a peon is proud of
his status and hopes his sons will follow him into clerical positions. The
operators show no particular pride or enthusiasm for their work, and
those who express the hope that their children will follow them into the
factory wish them to be clerical workers rather than operators. But

most Distillers would prefer, if given the opportunity, to be independent entrepreneurs. Selling liquor is what they know best, but any kind of successful storekeeping would be acceptable.

Meanwhile, more money than ever before is coming into Distiller homes because of the advent of the factory, and a good part of this money is being channeled into education for their children. They have an advantage over Carpenters—as the latter note with irritation—for Distillers in Bengal are a "scheduled caste" officially, and thus entitled under law to apply for the seats in schools and universities and the civil service jobs set aside for members of such castes. Distillers are aware of their educational advantages and are beginning to attempt to utilize them.

In general, unlike Carpenters and Brahmans, the Distillers of Gôndôgram have no regrets for the past; the present has its difficulties, and there will be more in the future, but there are also new possibilities for success and fortune, and the Distillers are seeking them out.

There were five adult men in the four Washermen households of Gôndôgram. Of these, one worked as an operator in the wheel department and one as a menial laborer for the factory. The three others, assisted by the women of their families, washed clothes, primarily for the officers of the factory.

The Washerman operator is of course proud of his position and income, and is respected by other members of his jati. For most members of the jati, however, the coming of the factory represented a wonderful opportunity to resume their traditional jati occupation, that of washing clothes. Before the coming of the factory, the Washermen—landless, and living in a poor village—frequently supported themselves by working as field laborers (both day labor and mahindôr) for Brahman households. They have always considered themselves first and foremost "washermen" but there was little scope for plying their trade. Only Brahmans in Gôndôgram ever gave out washing, and then only special, rarely worn holiday garb. With the factory-induced prosperity, however, some Brahman households are sending out more clothes than heretofore, although never enough to maintain a household of Washermen. But the higher staff officers of the factory, in their compound not too far from the village, have become major customers. Their families, in comparison with village families, wear many clothes and all is sent out—and the Washermen of Gôndôgram have a monopoly on the laundry work.

The Washermen of Gôndôgram, therefore, are completely happy about the coming of the factory. The past, for them, was unpleasant; their ancestors, they believe, lost all the land (and so the factory acquisitions bothered them not at all) and until the factory arrived they had to serve, like the detested Bauris, as field laborers. Now, at last, they can engage in their favorite and traditional occupation—they can feel like Washermen again—and as they see it there will always be work for themselves and their children.

Gôndôgram had one Dom household, containing one adult male; in the past he worked for different men in the village as a day laborer. With the coming of the factory he has been employed, off and on, as an ordinary laborer for various construction contractors, most particularly those who work on the roads.

Of the two Barber households in the village, one was the traditional one whose members had served the village over generations. The eldest son of this household was employed as an operator in the factory and was deaf to all entreaties to return to barbering. His younger brother also planned to seek work in the factory, and so their old father had been forced to come out of retirement to serve his old clients in the village. He had also brought in a young jat-brother from a distant village who now served the village as barber. This last has given no indication, as yet, of a desire to give up the profession for factory employment. The old man is pessimistic, however; he is proud of his family occupation and sorry that his sons will not follow it, but he acknowledges that the money is better in the factory.

The Bauri response to the factory varies slightly from para to para. In Dôkkhin para, there are eight households, each containing one adult male. Of these, two continue to be employed in agriculture in the village, one as a mahindôr and one as a day laborer. The other six are in factory-related employment. Two work as "mazdoors" (helpers) in the factory proper, while three serve in the canteen, an occupation much favored by Bauris in the district. One Bauri is employed peripherally; he works as a gardener for one of the higher factory officials.

In Śimul para there are thirteen Bauri households containing some sixteen adult men. Two men are sharecroppers (bhag-kirśani) for Brahman households, and five others work as laborers (day laborers and mahindôr) for other Brahmans, though a couple of these men work so infrequently because of age and infirmity that they consider themselves retired. The remaining nine men are employed in the factory or near it; one is a laborer for a contractor, four are menial laborers for the factory (three in the canteen), three are "mazdoor," and one—the only such Bauri in Gôndôgram—is an operator in the glazing department. Apart from these men, two women from Śimul para are also regularly employed, as domestic servants for factory officials. Other Bauri women have worked, as necessity demanded or opportunity offered, for short periods of time as day laborers on construction gangs, but these are the only two with steady employment.

In Gadhapathôr para, the most distant from the factory, there are nine Bauri households, containing twelve adult men. Of these, only two men work for the factory, both as laborers. The rest continue to work in agriculture; two as bhag-kirśani, five as mahindôrs, and the rest as day laborers.

It appears, then, that closeness of residence to the factory was an important factor for the Bauris. Men of Dôkkhin para have experienced little difficulty in obtaining regular work in or near the factory, and the men (and women) of Śimul para have done almost as well. Only in Gadhapathôr para are the Bauri men unable to penetrate the barriers to factory employment.

It must be emphasized that few if any Bauri men are in other than factory employment out of choice. True, some of the men engaged in sharecropping profess to be pleased with their work (noting that it is far superior to ordinary agricultural labor), but the majority of Bauri men insist that they have no desire whatever for agricultural employment of any kind; they want to work for the factory. They will accept any kind of factory employment, but most would be delighted to work with their jat-brothers in the canteen. Those, therefore, who give their occupations as mahindôr or day laborer are engaged in such work because no other was available. They visit the factory and the contractors regularly, hoping for some job that will take them forever out of the fields of Gôndôgram.

There can be no doubt, in fact, that in their minds the Bauri men of Gôndôgram have removed themselves from the village and its agricultural way of life. In Gôndôgram, in the past, they were servants—man, woman, and child—working for the Brahmans, without hope of improvement or financial aggrandizement. They were always on the outskirts of village life, excluded from religious ceremony, barred from using the barber or the priests others could summon.

Once employed in the factory, however, even in the most menial of jobs, they are men like other men; for the first time in their lives they have what they regard as adequate salaries, they may eat with men of other castes, drink with them, they are petitioned by labor unions and political parties. The Bauris are almost unanimous in the opinion that they want nothing further to do with agriculture; they want to be employed in industry, and nothing else. They speak for themselves and not for their children (for as Bauris see it, once a boy becomes a man he will of course do whatever he wants without consulting his parents), but it is fair to assume that they expect their children to want the same kind of factory employment. Only one

Bauri—the solitary Bauri operator—talks about the need for education of children, so that they can have advantages not available to
their parents.

At the time of the study, there were eleven Santal households in
Gôndôgram, three in the newer Śimul para and eight in the older
Gadhapaṭhôr Santal para. The three Śimul para households contained
among them three adult males; all of them employed for at least part
of the year as laborers for contractors associated with the factory. All
the men, too, augmented their incomes by working as day laborers for
farmers in Gôndôgram and in neighboring villages. When necessary,
their wives would also work as laborers, in the fields or for road
gangs.

The eight Gadhapaṭhôr Santal households presented an employment picture that was quite similar but differed in one respect. Of the
eleven men of this para, almost all shared the work pattern of their
jat-brothers in Śimul para; nine worked during the year in both agriculture and factory-related contractual labor. Only one man claimed
that he was employed full-time as a contractual laborer (and he was
also the only one who worked for a contractor engaged in a construction project far from Gôndôgram and the Das-Walters factory) and
only one other man of this para claimed to be engaged full-time in
agricultural work.

The difference between men of this para and those of Śimul para,
however, was that the Gadhapaṭhôr engaged exclusively in kirśani
agriculture; that is, they raised crops on fields owned by others utiliz-
ing one or another sharecropping basis. They all estimated that such
work required four months of their time, leaving eight months free for
employment by the contractors. As in Śimul para, women of the
Santal households worked when necessary beside their husbands as
laborers for contractors, and of course the entire household participated in the agricultural work. In one household of this para, there
are no adult men. The two women, a mother (widowed) and her
daughter (separated from husband), work as they can for contractors
associated with the factory.

A decade before my visit, or so I was informed by Santals and
others in the village, I would have found few Santals engaged in any
kind of agricultural work, apart from their own kitchen gardens. The
men had worked, like their fathers and grandfathers before them, as
coal-miners. The collieries in the area, however, have been closing
down; many are uneconomical and others are simply no longer productive. Even in those still functioning at full capacity employment is
off as machinery replaces manual labor.

In desperation, Santal men and women accepted day labor assignments in the fields in and around Gôndôgram. Along with all other jatis in the district, Santals believe that agricultural day labor is the least desirable of all available occupations, for both financial and prestige reasons. Bauris may feel they can hope for little more—that working as a day laborer is even a cut above being a mahindôr—but a Santal could only view day labor in the fields as a misfortune that must be kept temporary, to be replaced by a more dignified and remunerative employment as soon as possible. On the other hand, day labor in a contractor's work gang, while not the most desirable of occupations for a Santal, is certainly acceptable for it does provide a cash income far superior to that of agricultural labor.

What Santals prefer above all else (and they claim they always have, even generations before) is to farm land on their own, on an individual family basis. There is great pride in being a Santal—pride in having their own language, in being cleaner than Bengalis, particularly those low-ranked jatis with which they usually associate—and they are convinced they have the knowledge, intelligence, and industry to be successful farmers.

When, with the coming of the factory, the landholders of Gôndôgram began to find themselves hard-pressed for agricultural labor, the Santals stepped eagerly into the breach. The Brahmans would have preferred to have the Santals simply replace the Bauris as mahindôrs or day laborers, but the Santals absolutely refuse the first category and accept the second only with extreme reluctance. On the other hand, they were eager to undertake sharecropping, and with the entire family participating they could do well at it.

The Brahmans' reluctance gave way before the absence of viable alternative. Also, Brahman men were now working in the factory in increasing numbers, and the raising of a crop with mahindôr or day labor requires, for success, the continual presence of an adult male as supervisor. The only alternative was an increase in tenant farming in one form or another, and the Santals constituted the obvious choice.

The Brahmans' reluctance was more than matched by Santal enthusiasm; most Santal men dream of controlling enough land under one form or another of kirśani so as never to have to work as laborers for others again. And some Santals even dream of someday owning the land themselves, which may help to explain the depression of the Brahmans about the state of agriculture in Gôndôgram.

4

Perspectives, Values, Problems

For the villagers of Gôndôgram, the factory has become a major life factor. In many ways, it has replaced the rice crop as that which determines the state of one's fortune or well-being. It is a direct or indirect source of income for almost every household, and for many it is perceived as an avenue for future advancement for themselves or their children. And yet it is also an alien element, an intrusion upon the old patterns and relationships of life. For some, this fact constitutes a threat, for some it is a source of exhilaration. All, however, must adjust constantly to the factory's presence.

Once, the Brahmans controlled the village. They provided the only means of income and of food—land for the growing of rice—and all who wished to articulate with that source had to do it through them. They were the source of labor in the fields, and of rice and money in exchange for services. All who owned no land and who had no outside source of income (and that was most of the village) had to turn to the Brahmans and thereby recognize and accept their authority. The coming of the factory, however, provided an alternative to the Brahmans, and this of course had its impact upon the authority of the Brahmans in village life. In addition, the factory also provided new opportunities for Brahmans and some of them have been quicker than others to see this.

In their feelings about the factory, therefore, the Brahmans are somewhat divided. All agree that its presence tends to be disruptive of old ways; there is a split as to whether or not this is a good thing. The split tends to be along patrilines, though this is neither absolute nor exclusive. The Dubes of Gôndôgram were the first Brahmans to settle in the village; they have always tended to be more conservative and to look down on the Pande families as arrivistes, as upstarts.

For most of the Dubes the factory is a necessary evil; it cannot be avoided, but it is an evil. They will seek jobs there, and they will join in efforts to pressure the factory to assist the village, but they engage in even the latter effort with some reluctance. Any change is likely to be a change for the worse, they feel, and should be resisted as much as possible. They are not interested in quarters in factory housing, and appear to seek ways to encyst or isolate the factory from village affairs.

Ideally, from their point of view, the factory—since it insisted on coming and will not go away—should provide employment for villagers. Like other Brahmans, they hope to see their children advance to prestigeful and high-paying staff positions. But they hope that everyone, and particularly members of their own families, will return from the factory to the village and continue in all the old and familiar ways of life, from family relationships to religious activities.

Pandes, on the other hand, frequently comment that the factory may be the means for their children to get out of the village into the wider and more promising world. They want their children to make friends with factory officials' children; they are not disturbed at the thought that this may lead to the abandonment of old ways, for many Pandes claim they no longer believe in animal sacrifice or caste restrictions on commensality, and so on. They are careful to observe all the rules (for "we have daughters to marry"—and they know that some Dubes would be happy to see Pandes out-casted), but many say they would be delighted to see their children in a position to flout those rules successfully.

Men of the middle jatis—those of Ūcu paṟa—express no opinion on the impact of the factory on the life of the village; they are content to view it as a source of income and are otherwise neither threatened nor exhilarated.

Bauris, on the other hand, are universally enthusiastic. Apart from employment possibilities, they see the factory as providing them with the opportunity for getting out from under Brahmanical control, something that is stressed as important particularly by the younger men. For them, the factory has introduced a new horizon, unimagined by their fathers. They are no longer circumscribed by village and by agricultural labor; even those who have not yet achieved the success of factory employment, those still locked into the fields as mahindôrs or day laborers, dream only of leaving agricultural employment of every kind behind them and joining the industrial proletariat. The last two words are used advisedly, for the Bauris who have gone to work in the factory have attended meetings, have been approached by union organizers, and have in some cases chosen political sides—and have gone on to recruit among their fellows in the village.

As such men saw it, the Congress Party was the party of Brahmans and other landholders, while the Communist Party (or parties) was for the disenfranchised, the low-caste, and the industrial worker. Bauris in the village who were still engaged in agriculture said that they believed they must vote as their employer directed, but the Bauri who was employed at the factory, or in factory-related contractual work, said that he was now free to vote as he pleased, and often indicated that the Communist candidates would have his support.

But if the Gôndôgram Bauri turns to Communism, he appears to do it in terms of the references and values of Gôndôgram. One young man, for example, told me in a conversation that Bauris had a legitimate source of grievance against Brahmans; once, he said, in the distant past his ancestors (the original Bauris of Bengal) had owned all the agricultural land of Bengal. Somehow, in a way the young man admitted he could not fully explain, the Brahmans had acquired control of all the land—perhaps by manipulation of title deeds, since Brahmans were always literate and Bauris presumably were not. Now the Bauri jati, he said, was without land, but he was convinced that one day they would rise up and take back what properly belonged to them.

It is certainly possible that this tale (recounted by only one Bauri in the village) represents an idiosyncratic revision of the widely held belief that the land of Gôndôgram once belonged to the Washermen, who lost it to the Brahmans. The young man, however, was interested in political matters and had spent much time in or near the factory at political meetings. It is likely, therefore, that he has been exposed to, and has assimilated, a Marxist explanation of the expropriation of property by the landed and governing class. The explanation may have been merged, in his own mind, with the Gôndôgram Washerman's tale. My reason for recounting it here, however, is to note that—whatever the original explanation given to him—there is no place in his account for Washermen or indeed for men of any other disenfranchised jati; as he sees it, the land once belonged to the Bauris, and to the Bauris it must and will return.

Thus, the Bauri who claims—sincerely—to have turned his back on Hinduism and "caste" and other things that he associates with Gôndôgram, remains nevertheless very much a part of his jati; and his jati, manifested in his sômaj, constitutes for him an important boundary of self. Bauris associate primarily with Bauris, partly because few others will associate with them, but also out of choice.

They help each other insofar as they can to get jobs with particular contractors (the Santals favor and are favored by others) and in the factory canteen; Bauris of the Gôndôgram śômaj form an important element among the canteen "bearers" (equivalent, in this context, to the American busboy).

In very much the same way, as we have seen, members of other jatis tend to cluster together in particular factory departments or activities, much to the distress of the factory management. Even those Brahmans who profess a desire to turn their backs on the village—who hope to see their children out and up—prefer to work in those departments (such as the enameling shop) where Kanauj Brahmans may be found in some numbers.

The factory management, as we have seen, confesses itself at a loss to explain how men of the same caste manage to cluster in a given department, given the employment regulations, but the problem did not prove a difficult one to investigate. An older Carpenter of Gôndôgram, one of the first of his jati to work for the factory and to be employed in the chain department, was perfectly willing to discuss the matter.

He explained that while the factory buildings were being set up he had been employed, like others of his jati, in the construction work, setting up scaffolding. When construction was completed, he applied for permanent employment and was assigned, purely by chance, to the chain department (just as the first Brahmans to be hired as operators were assigned to the enameling department). A new man hired as operator is given three months' training in the work of the department to which he is assigned; this means, for the most part, learning to operate the equipment in use in that department. In the chain department, for example, there are punches that produce the chain-link units, and other machines that assemble the links and eventually the lengths of bicycle chain. After the training period, the Carpenter began to work in the chain department, as he had ever since.

Each day, in the early afternoon, there is a work break in the factory for "tiffin" (tea and some food). It became the pattern for a younger brother of the Carpenter to bring the working man his daily tiffin. Sitting near the machine, waiting for work to resume, the employed Carpenter would explain the nature of his work to his younger brother. If no official were around, or if none objected, he showed his younger brother how the punch worked, and even allowed him to work it for a few moments, on occasion.

Then, some months later, when a vacancy occurred in the chain department, the older Carpenter could go to the foreman and point out that he knew of a candidate for the job who would not need the full three months' training, for he already knew how to operate the equipment. His brother was brought in, tested, and was awarded the job.

In similar ways, other relatives were brought in, or transferred to, the chain department. *"Bhalo ache,"* (it is pleasant), say the Carpenters, for jat-brothers to work side by side, at whatever task. And in much the same ways, for exactly the same reason, the Brahmans have come together in the enameling department, the Bauris in the canteen, and so on.

And, as the factory officials have noted, once such a caste concentration takes place, it is almost impossible to break it up, much as they would like to. This is quite true, Gôndôgram men of all jatis admit; if a "stranger" (that is, a man of a jati other than their own) is appointed to a department which some jati has come to think of as its own province, the outlook is bleak indeed.

Men of the ensconced jati treat him rudely or ignore him completely. None will help him or advise him. Sometimes, in fact, they will actively harass him. His personal possessions may disappear or be damaged, his work may show inexplicable errors. The charge-hand (the low-level supervisor only one level above the operators, but responsible for the quality and quantity of the department's work) must for his own preservation protect and support the older workers. Not infrequently, he is in fact a member of the same jati and therefore a leader in the campaign to keep the department a jati preserve. The new man's work is rejected as unsatisfactory more frequently than is usual. He finds himself reprimanded for shortcomings; and the slight relaxations of rules, the winkings at small violations common in such situations, are not for him.

Eventually, almost inevitably, the unwanted new man is separated from the department. He may be fired, because after all there have been many complaints about his work and his behavior. More likely, he will plead for transfer, and it will be granted, not so much for his sake but rather to bring tranquility and good production back to the troubled department. Some men, in such situations, have even resigned and left the factory. One way or another, however, the alien is forced from the department, and the jat-brothers are once again happy in the company of their own.

Factory officials are aware of such caste concentrations where the jatis involved are of local derivation. This is because events in the home villages can have particularly devastating effects upon production. The phenomenon, however, is by no means restricted to local jatis, such as the Brahmans, the Carpenters, and the Bauris of Gôndô-gram. One official, in a discussion of caste in the factory, shamefacedly volunteered the information that almost all the "sweepers" of the factory (those who clean the floors and most particularly the toilets and washrooms) were of the Mæthôr (Sweeper) jati.

Attempts to prevent this segregation, a particularly unpleasant one for educated, sensitive Indians who have taken the teachings of Gandhi to heart, have been uniformly unavailing. The problem is, it was explained, that few but Sweepers apply for such work. And, then, even when a man of some other jati, driven by desperation, does take on the employment, "he does not stay." He lacks the skill and knowledge the Sweepers have had since early childhood, and of course he lacks his own brushes and pails. But, most serious of all, reported the official, he is resented by the other sweepers, who feel he has taken a job that belongs properly to one of their jati. They make life so miserable for him that eventually, just like the men inserted in the "Brahman's" enameling shop and the "Carpenter's" chain department, he leaves in discouragement or is fired.

And if caste concentrations occur on the lowest level of factory employment as well as on the assembly lines, one might expect them to occur in the highest echelons, and they do. As has been noted, the Indian family that constitutes the major shareholder—the Das family—are of Bôiddô (Vaidya) jati. Almost all the higher officers of the factory, and many of the junior ones, exhibit names characteristic of this jati.

Once, before the time of this study (according to a story current in the factory), a number of Panjabi engineers were brought to the factory. It is said that, while their skills were badly needed, there was opposition to their hiring expressed by some officers, who appeared to feel that the skills of engineers to be recruited in Bengal were more than adequate. The Panjabis had been attracted by high salaries, but nevertheless within six months the last of them had resigned and departed from the factory with the bitter comment that "Bengalis and Panjabis don't work well together."

And, finally, it must not be assumed that any of the foregoing is peculiar to the Das-Walters bicycle factory; works managers and personnel managers from many different factories in the Asansol area report exactly the same kinds of "caste" problems at all levels of employment.

Carpenters and Brahmans of Gôndôgram, employed as operators in the factory, are aware of official unhappiness at their attendance records. Some argue that they think the complaints are unfair, since they feel they are not absent from work a greater number of times in toto than other workers; others admit that they understand the officials' complaints, but say they have little choice in the matter.

Interestingly, there is merit to the argument that men of Gôndôgram do not in fact take sick leave more frequently than others. One
factory official, after bemoaning the attendance records of local
people, offered to demonstrate his point and produced attendance
records that he claimed were characteristic. (They are in part repro-
duced here, as tables 15 and 16.) One was the attendance record of a
local person, a resident of Gôndôgram—no better and no worse than
other local men, according to the official—and the other what he felt

TABLE 15   *Record of Attendance—Local Person*

Month	Sched. Work Days	No. Days Present	Casual Leave	Sick Leave	Unauthorized Absence
Jan.	21	17		4	
Feb.	19	17	1	1	
March	20	18	2		
April	22	16		6	
May	22	15		7	
June	23	22		1	
July	20	19			1
Aug.	21	21			
Sept.	19	19			
Oct.	15	13			2
Nov.	19	18		1	
Dec.	25	25			
Total	*246*	*220*	*3*	*20*	*3*

TABLE 16   *Record of Attendance—Non-local Person*

Month	Sched. Work Days	No. Days Present	Casual Leave	Sick Leave	Unauthorized Absence
Jan.	24	8		16	
Feb.	19	2		17	
March	25	23	2		
April	26	26			
May	26	26			
June	27	27			
July	25	25			
Aug.	26	26			
Sept.	23	23			
Oct.	18	18			
Nov.	23	23			
Dec.	25	23	2		
Total	*287*	*250*	*4*	*33*	

was a typical attendance record for a non-local and non-Bengali operator. Both operators had been entitled to a week's "statutory leave" or vacation (not indicated on these tables) and to fifteen days' sick leave per year—five days at full pay and ten days at half pay. Other absences, unless authorized, were without pay.

Given the official complaints, it was startling to note that the Gôndôgram operator had been absent for only twenty days during the year—for which times he claimed to be sick—and for six other days for unexplained reasons; a total of twenty-six absences for the year. The non-Bengali operator, however, had been out thirty-three times during the year claiming to be ill, and four more times for unexplained reasons, for a total of *thirty-seven* absences!

When this was pointed out to the official, he insisted that these were not the significant items in the record; what troubled him, he said, was the *distribution,* not the *number,* of absences. From this perspective, it was true that the two records were very different indeed. The non-Bengali took all his days of sick leave—with and without pay—during the months of January and February, and his four days of "casual leave" were divided equally between December and March. In other words, from the end of December through the beginning of March, he was absent almost continually; part of this was annual leave, part was sick leave with pay, and the rest was simply absence without pay. From April through November, however, he was not absent from work for a single day. The Gôndôgram man, on the other hand, was absent from work for a few days (from one to seven) in almost every month of the year; only August, September, and December showed a perfect attendance record for him.

According to the official, when a non-local person employed in the factory returns to his home for his annual leave, one may be certain that he will not return on time. A letter is likely to arrive, or even a telegram, reporting that he has taken ill (and so must use up his sick leave) or that there is illness or other disaster at home requiring his attention even if he must be absent without pay. The official said that the pattern holds at all levels of factory employment, and he personally attributed it to the reluctance of mothers everywhere to see their sons depart again after only a brief visit home.

Whatever the reason, however, he said that the factory had come to expect the behavior and was not particularly inconvenienced by it; after all, the absent worker had been temporarily replaced for his scheduled leave and the replacement could stay on until he returned without additional expense to the factory or adverse affect upon production. The local man's pattern, on the other hand, was much more disturbing to the factory—even if it did not add up to as many absences in the year—because a man unexpectedly away from his machine for a day or two is simply not replaced, and therefore production in his department will be affected accordingly.

The problem, of course, is that the men of Gôndôgram, like most other local people, live at home. If there is an emergency in the family's fields—at time of planting or harvesting—the man's presence will be demanded. If a child is ill, or someone dies (or even if a marriage takes place in a kinsman's household in some distant village) he is likely to have obligations and responsibilities that will prevent his going in to work. Much the same things are probably taking place at the home of the non-Bengali in his village (say, in Bihar), but he is not at home and so his people must somehow manage without him. Whatever can be postponed, such as a marriage or engagement, is of course put off until he returns on leave, which is another reason he has difficulty in breaking away when his leave is over.

Most of the factory officials understand the true basis of the local villagers' absenteeism, despite the mutterings about laziness and sickliness. But while they understand, they are not prepared to condone. True, there is absenteeism among non-local people attributable to drunkenness, venereal disease, and other factors associated with life in the workers' quarters, while few if any of the local people are troubled by such things. This of course was what the factory had originally expected, but now the management must equate production loss due to such causes with production loss due to local villagers' absenteeism. It was my impression that they preferred the former.

5

Family, Jati, and the Factory

The establishment of the factory has done much more than simply open new avenues of employment, new sources of income, and new perspectives for the future. There has been considerable impact in still other ways upon village life, but to see this properly we must pursue the issue institution by institution, jati by jati.

Interestingly, one of the favorite factory complaints about the villager introduces us to one of the areas of change. As we have seen, officials complain that Gôndôgram villagers are dishonest, that they take unfair and unnecessary advantage of the factory's promise to employ "the sons of Gôndôgram" by bringing in boys from villages all over the district and insisting that these are actually their own sons.

The factory officials are quite accurate in their perceptions of what is going on, and yet the villagers are not really lying! In an earlier section, the patterns of marriage arrangement in Gôndôgram were discussed. It will be remembered that it is the duty of the head of a household to seek husbands for all marriageable girls in that household. Both Brahman and Carpenter heads of households in Gôndôgram report sorrowfully that the coming of the factory has added a new and most awkward dimension to their marriage inquiries.

A Gôndôgram guardian from one of these jatis makes his inquiries as do other men of his sômaj (see Klass 1966), and after the usual formalities he sits down with the father of the boy to discuss the thorny matter of dowry and other gifts. Gôndôgram men report that, more and more frequently, the boy's guardian announces that they need not waste time on the matter; he is prepared to agree to an astonishingly small dowry, and in a few cases has even hinted that he might be persuaded to forego dowry entirely. All he asks is that the girl's guardian take steps—all well within his power—to safeguard the future of the young couple. Since it is common knowledge throughout the śômaj (in the case of both Carpenter and Brahman) that Gôndô-gram men have special access to jobs at the bicycle factory, he asks only that the girl's guardian arrange for employment for the prospective bridegroom. If the Gôndôgram guardian can do that, the marriage is assured. If he fails—and it has become increasingly difficult—the boy's family charges bad faith, and negotiations are often broken off acrimoniously.

The guardian of a prospective bride, therefore, must be prepared to seek out some official in the factory and advise him of "another son" just come of age to work in the factory, under the old agreement with Gôndôgram. The official concludes, somewhat justifiably, that the Gôndôgram man has lied to him and is foisting a stranger on the factory.

The Gôndôgram man, on the other hand, does not feel he has really lied to the official. He argues, perhaps speciously: is not a son-in-law equivalent to a son? Does a father not have an obligation to provide for a daughter and her children, just as for a son and his children? And, in any case, say Gôndôgram Brahmans and Carpenters, matters have reached the point where it is next to impossible to arrange a marriage for a Gôndôgram girl of their jatis without the promise of employment in the factory; a śômaj is a close-knit organization, and information about the good and bad fortunes of any of its members is quickly possessed by all. Once some Gôndôgram guardians were able to secure employment for prospective bridegrooms, everyone in the śômaj knew about it and determined to make the same demand should the opportunity ever arise.

Gôndôgram Carpenters and Brahmans find themselves caught in a painful squeeze. On the one hand, factory employment has become a condition for obtaining bridegrooms. In fact, in an increasing number of cases, fathers of daughters seeking husbands in Gôndôgram have raised the issue of jobs for the *girl's brother!* Some Gôndôgram men resolutely resist this demand (arguing that it is the place of the boy's father to make demands, not the other way around), but some have given in, and there are those who fear for the future. And on the other hand, the factory has become less and less generous.

Gôndôgram men can put up with accusations and even insults; they do need those jobs, however. But what with increases in automation, deceleration of expansion activities, and a growing hostility toward Gôndôgram, the outlook is not good. During the year of the study, men were satisfied if they could obtain jobs for prospective bridegrooms as helpers (though once it would have been as operators only) and a few marriages were delayed while guardians continued desperately to petition the factory. One Gôndôgram Carpenter said gloomily he feared that, should the factory ever turn its back completely, no more Gôndôgram girls would be able to get married. Neither the Santals nor the Bauris had any problem in this regard, since men of neither jati were aware of any factory obligation, and Distillers reported only minor problems.

The establishment of the factory, we have observed, affected members of all jatis with representatives living in Gôndôgram. A Brahman of the Śergôr Śômaj living in a village many miles from the factory may have a son employed in it, and a Distiller from a village equally distant may derive his income from liquor sold to employees of the factory. The Gôndôgram Bauris, by virtue of their employment, have become leaders in their śômaj, and Gôndôgram Santals are demonstrating to men of their śômaj that sharecropping is a viable alternative to labor in the collieries.

The śômaj, in fact, seems to respond with remarkable speed to new opportunities discovered or developed, and proper understanding of such śômaj behavior may give insight into the origins of some traditional "caste occupations." We see today that Brahman children in villages distant from the factory know details of the enameling process, and Carpenter children in similarly distant villages have seen chains made and may even have operated the machines. After all, they return with their mother to her father's house in Gôndôgram, do they not? And when there, what is to prevent them from learning of their mother's brother's occupation, and from dreaming of joining him one day in the factory?

From this perspective, the śômaj takes on the appearance of an amoeba. Under the microscope we watch that amorphous animal thrusting out pseudopods in all directions. If a pseudopod encounters an obstacle, it is withdrawn. But if one pseudopod finds a promising direction—even the tiniest crack—it probes further, and then the entire organism flows *into* the pseudopod.

A śômaj responds to opportunity in much the same way. In the village of Tilimunda, for example, to the west of Gôndôgram, it was noted that there are many households of a jati known as Ekadôs-tili, said to be an offshoot of the widespread Oilpresser jati. The Tilis of Tilimunda have not pressed oil from seeds in many generations; most own small pieces of riceland and augment their income by working, in fairly menial positions, in collieries and factories in the area. When the Das-Walters factory opened, a young Tili of Tilimunda came to it, seeking work. He had no contacts there and knew no special or needed skills, and his efforts were fruitless, though he was willing to accept any kind of employment. Tired, at the end of the cheerless day, he sat down for a moment in a tea shop on the outskirts of the factory area.

The owner of the shop served him a clay cup of tea, and they entered into conversation. The Tili told of his efforts to find work, and the tea-shop owner offered him a job; the shop was doing well and he had more work than he could handle alone. The young Tili went to work in the tea shop, cleaning up, serving customers, and learning to brew and sell tea professionally.

In less than a year, he took his carefully saved earnings and opened a tea shop of his own on the road from the factory past Gôndô-gram. It was a good location; many local men stopped for a drink and a few moment's conversation on their way to and from work. He prospered and took in a younger brother as an assistant. Soon, the brother, with his aid, was able to set up a shop of his own at another location. Other relatives—jat-brothers—have joined them, and there were, at the time of the study, five Ekadôs-tili operated tea shops in the vicinity of the factory, and more planned. If fortune favors them, in a few years there is every reason to suppose that tea-shop operation will have become a significant occupation among members of this sômaj. Others, however, have become interested in operating rice mills.

Not all the changes induced by the presence of the factory, of course, are equally desirable from the perspective of the villager. An introduction to new opportunities is welcomed by all—but the introduction of new customs, new patterns of behavior, is frequently deplored. Men who live in the workers' compounds are particularly susceptible to new patterns; far from home and from the observation of their jat-brothers, many are quick to give up the old rules and restrictions. Former vegetarians and teetotallers take to meat and drink, and officials report (often with amusement) cases of men who returned home to discover that reports of their iniquities had preceded them. It is not uncommon throughout India, in fact, for men who have been away from home for long periods to be assumed to be rule-violators and to be required to undergo appropriate penance and purification upon their return to their native villages.

But new patterns of behavior have their impact even upon those who, like the men of Gôndôgram, continue to live in their ancestral homes. An example of this would be the conflict that occurred between one Rammohan Dube and his eldest son. The older Dube was a landholder, head of his household, and also a clerk in the factory. When his son failed his "matriculation" examination, his father obtained employment for him as an operator. The boy (about eighteen years of age) continued to reside at home. As is the custom in the village, all income of all members of the household becomes the property of the household; the boy gave all his wages, every week, to his father—who, in turn, provided the boy with all the things the father thought he needed.

The boy made friends with other young men in the factory. Most of these were non-local men, living in the workers' compounds. He was introduced to smoking, card-playing, and other pleasures. They mocked him as old-fashioned, for he had no pocket money of his own. The boy found, however, that much as he resented his penniless state, and much as he wanted to keep some of his own earnings, he simply could not bring himself to raise the issue with his father. Eventually, without a word to anyone in his family, he simply disappeared from home, moving in with some of his new friends in the factory.

The frightened father turned to the official for whom he worked for aid in finding his missing son. This man, who recounted the story, had become accustomed to such events, and immediately made appropriate inquiries and found the boy in the quarters of his friends. The official brought the boy and father together, and elicited the boy's reasons for his departure. The father was at first shocked and angry. Was it not the custom for all income to go to the head of the household? And for whom was the family saving if not for the eldest son? And if the boy wanted spending money for any reasonable thing, why could he not ask his father?

The official calmed the father, explaining that there were new customs abroad among the young, that there were things (such as cigarettes) for which a village boy could not bring himself to ask his father, and that a working young man was indeed entitled to some regular pocket money. Reluctantly, the father accepted the official's advice. He and his son agreed that the latter would keep five rupees for himself from his weekly wages, to be spent in any way he pleased, and the boy returned to his home.

Many Carpenter and Brahman men in the village knew about the conflict in the Dube household. Most were amused, because the father was considered unusually stiff and unbendingly traditional, even for a Dube. Most fathers of employed sons in the village managed to adjust to desires for pocket money before any crisis occurred. There can be no doubt, however, that young men in the village are becoming more independent than ever before. They are interested in things beyond the ken of their fathers. They smoke and whisper together, and some seek out the young men of the factory as friends. They go to movies and invest their money in cheap Japanese transistor radios. In addition to popular music, they listen to news of India—and of the world. There have been as yet few incidents of the kind related above, but many of the older men worry about the future.

6

Village Economy and the Factory

With the coming of the factory, Bauris have been moving out of village agriculture and Santals have been moving in. While the foregoing is true enough, it does constitute another example of simplification, for many different kinds of changes are taking place in the traditional economic patterns of the village.

It is impossible, for example, to quantify the effect of the factory's presence upon agricultural production, since no dependable or adequate records have ever been kept by anyone in the village, but owners of riceland are unanimous in the statement that production has suffered adversely. Less land is utilized, they say, and that land which is in cultivation is often less efficiently utilized. There are problems at every point in the process of rice production, and there is less profit at the end.

Many reasons are advanced in support of these assertions. Almost all the land is owned by Brahmans, as we have seen earlier, and most of the non-Brahman land is owned by Carpenters. In almost no household of these jatis in Gôndôgram are there adult men left who are able to devote full time to agriculture; the adult men work in the factory.

But agricultural production requires the constant supervision of a representative of the household owning (or renting) the land. Adult men supervise whenever they can; they are in the fields before they go to work and as soon as they return, and on weekends. As we have noted, at crucial times they even stay home from work. But still their time is limited, and when they are home they are tired.

In most landholding families, therefore, supervision of production devolves upon the very young and the very old males, and upon

230

the females. The very old are, obviously, simply unable to spend sufficient time out in the fields. Young boys and the women lack experience and are impeded by role conflict and pressing demands to be elsewhere, specifically school and home. In sum, households in which the adult males work in the factory simply cannot provide supervisors for agricultural production. Under even the best of conditions, there are no really adequate solutions.

And these are by no means the best of times. In the past, landholders preferred to turn the actual work of agriculture over to agricultural servants; mahindôrs, permanent laborers engaged for the year. In practice, most mahindôrs, before the coming of the factory, rarely changed employers. A man (usually Bauri) worked year after year for the same landholding household (usually Brahman), and, as we have seen, his wife worked in the Brahman house and his son herded the household's cattle. The Brahmans could expect that the boy, when he grew to manhood, would work alongside his father as mahindôr, and eventually replace him.

Landholders say that such agricultural servants, connected with their families for generations, tended to identify with the household, its land and its problems. True, say landholders, the laborers still required supervision and direction, but only the basic minimum, since they knew the land and the tasks since childhood, as did their fathers before them.

With the coming of the factory, Bauris have turned from the fields in increasing number. All dream of factory employment. Even a man who has never obtained work in or near the factory, and who has little realistic hope of ever obtaining it, is reluctant to accept work as a mahindôr; suppose he should accept such a year's contract—and then the coveted opening at the factory appeared? Though the mahindôr's wages have increased substantially since the coming of the factory, it is difficult to find a Bauri in Gôndôgram who will work for those wages. A frequently heard remark of Brahmans in Gôndôgram, when the topic of agricultural labor comes up, is: "Today, when you ask a Bauri in this village to work as mahindôr, he rattles the money in his pants' pocket and says, 'I can hire my own mahindôr now!' "

The Brahman is bitter; he seems to resent the fact that the Bauri wears trousers almost as much as he does the man's unwillingness to work for him. If Brahmans say that "all" Bauris in Gôndôgram are now lazy and unwilling to work, Bauris will retort that local Brahmans are no longer willing to hire them because they can find ignorant impoverished men in distant villages still willing to work for starvation wages. It is certainly true that there are Bauris out of work in Gôndôgram who would accept work in the fields (though preferably as day laborers) and who say they can find no work—while many landholders do employ field laborers (Bauri and other) from other villages, claiming they can no longer find dependable labor in Gôndôgram.

But laborers from other villages are strangers. They require more supervision and there is less available. Landholders find field laborers transient, less tractable, and more expensive. It is understandable, therefore, that an increasing number of landholders have simply given up and have turned their land over to tenants (particularly Santals) to sharecrop.

Few landholders in Gôndôgram own very much land, however, and the land in the area is in general not the most productive. If the Santals are satisfied with their share, the Brahmans emphatically are not, but they have run out of solutions—short of giving up their factory jobs. They may not like the factory work, but the money is good, and so they continue to work there, while rice production decreases and the land is alienated. And, of course, if income from rice production continues to drop, it is even more difficult to contemplate giving up the factory job and returning to agriculture.

No landholder has been able to work out the profit and loss of it, but there is increasing feeling among them that, despite the influx of money from the factory, they are actually losing rather than gaining. Apart from the dwindling of income from rice production, they point to the great increase in food costs, and for inferior food, at that.

With the mahindôr relationship breaking down, trustworthy bagals (cowherds) are almost as difficult to find as plowmen, and with adult males away from the home the cattle have suffered. Many animals have died and many households have been forced to sell off portions of their herds for fear of the effects of neglect. A minimum number of bullocks must be kept for plowing and harvesting, so diminution of the family herd usually means sale of milk cows. Once, it is said, every Brahman household could provide all its own milk (and milk product) needs. Now there are only two or three households in that happy condition. Other households must purchase milk; this is expensive and often unsatisfactory, since the practice of adulteration of milk is widespread in the countryside.

Similarly, landholders point with mixed irritation and amusement to the public-health posters exhibited everywhere urging people to eat brown unpolished rice as more nutritious than the polished white rice. Gôndôgram villagers say that they are perfectly willing to believe that polished white rice is lacking in nutrients; they *know* it doesn't taste as good as unpolished rice. The problem is, they say, they can no longer afford to eat unpolished rice.

Once, before the coming of the factory, all rice consumed in the village was husked in a ḍhēkhi, the classic village husking device described earlier. Two persons are needed to operate it; in Gôndô-gram, these were traditionally Bauri girls or young women. These Bauri young women were often members of the mahindôr family, and if they did receive payment it was only a pittance.

Nowadays, Bauri women, complaining that the work is arduous and dangerous (for fingers are often crushed under the falling stone), charge substantial sums for husking rice by ḍhēkhi. All Gôndôgram villagers agree that the prices are prohibitive, and all who have rice to grind take their grain to the crude rice mill in Tilimunda. When the rice is husked by this machine, the nutritious outer layer of the grain is also removed, and the result is "polished rice." The price, they say, is within their means, even if the rice is less desirable. Some of the wealthier men (perhaps two or three households) still pay to have a portion of their rice ground by ḍhēkhi; such rice is served only on special occasions, such as when there are honored guests. For most Brahmans, indeed, ḍhēkhi-ground rice is so special it is served only to the gods, at pujas.

Carpenters have experienced all of the foregoing problems, but to a lesser degree, if for no other reason than they were always poorer than Brahmans, owning less land and fewer cattle, and employing fewer laborers. They complain about loss of production, labor problems, and so on, but with less overriding concern. For them, the greatest threat of the factory is in another area. The boys are growing up with no knowledge of, or interest in, the traditional occupation of carpentry. It is not so much the sentimental sense of loss (though that is present) as the fear of automation; Carpenters have seen new machines introduced year after year, each increasingly sophisticated and able to do the work of many simpler machines. Many look to the future and see there less need for operators in the factory. What will their sons and grandsons do then, since they will have forgotten how to be carpenters?

For many Brahmans and Carpenters the hope of the future lies in education. Carpenters, as we have seen, would be content to have their sons follow them onto the assembly line—but suppose, a few are beginning to ask, the assembly line becomes more automated? And Brahmans, as we have seen, do *not* want their children to follow them into manual jobs in the factory, but rather to enter into the kind of managerial or supervisory positions that Brahmans feel are more suitable for members of their jati. Distillers, too, are eager to have their children educated, and it is said that a few Bauris have begun to consider the importance of education—although at the time of the study only one parent actively encouraged his children to attend school, and Bauri representation in the school was still minuscule.

Given this growing emphasis on education, there has been a concurrent growing dissatisfaction with the quality of education in the village. Gôndôgram has boasted, for a number of decades, a one-room schoolhouse, located in Brahman para near the Rôkkhô-Kali shrine. The single teacher/headmaster was a man of sixty at the time of the study, related to some of the wealthiest Pandes but himself a relatively poor man, whose main source of income was his wages—made up by subscription—as village teacher.

The student body sitting on the floor of the dark, mud-walled schoolroom has consisted always of all the Brahman boys of the village ranging in age from about six to twelve or fourteen. Most, but not all, Brahman girls attend school for at least two or three years; in recent years the number of girls and the amount of time they spend in school has been increasing. Carpenter and Distiller boys in increasing number (and for an increasing period of time) have been coming to school, though neither group matches the record of Brahman boys. Carpenter and Distiller girls had begun to make their appearance in the school four or five years before the study was made, and two or three Bauri boys had attended for brief periods in the very recent past.

The schoolmaster insists earnestly that he welcomes children of all castes and both sexes, but he must contend with parental ignorance. Most parents, he feels, are afraid to send older girls to school for fear they will associate with boys and ruin their marriage prospects. In any event, he says (and others in the village agree), the common Gôndôgram attitude is that girls really have no need to learn to do more than "write their name" in order to be able to demonstrate literacy to the guardian of a prospective bridegroom. Similarly, while he himself welcomes Bauris—on the matter of caste he considers himself a follower of Gandhi—the problem lies with the parents of the Bauri boy, as he sees it. The schoolmaster says that it is not uncommon, should a Bauri boy find his way to the school, for the father of the boy to order him to stay home with the stricture, "I have followed the plow all my life and so must you." This has been changing, he notes, but not with any real speed.

The main subjects of instruction have been simple arithmetic, reading and writing in Bengali, and "English." Other subjects (history, geography, Hindi, and so on) are introduced to the students, but the emphasis is on the first three, in order to prepare as many boys as possible for secondary school. Of all the subjects, English is considered most important by village parents, and it is the one of which the schoolmaster has the weakest grasp. In the past, few village children were able to pass the examinations that would permit them to go on to higher education, and almost all of those who did pass were the children of parents wealthy and informed enough to arrange for special outside tutoring.

With the coming of the factory and the increased awareness both of the need for education and the shortcomings of the village school, demands increased for a better schoolbuilding, an enhanced curriculum, and more—and better trained—teachers. Apart from Bauri and Santal indifference (the latter jati sends no children to the school, nor do any Santals indicate any desire or plan to do so), all Gôndôgram villagers gave support to the proposals for a new school.

Work on the school, however, was held up for a number of years and had only just begun during the time of the study. A major conflict had developed, not about the need for a school but about the location of the new building. Two factions formed. One was led by the Dube Brahmans, who argued that the school should be erected on land northwest of the village. Most of this land was owned by Dubes, but they were prepared to surrender it to the village because they felt it was vital that the school be constructed as far as possible from the factory.

Dubes argued passionately that the factory was a disturbing and potentially disruptive influence. Already it had brought about a breakdown in traditional ways, in relationships between people of different jatis and even between members of the same families. Put the school near the factory, they said, and the youngest children would become exposed to the factory and its influences. It was even possible, said these Dubes, that some of the factory employees would insist on sending their children to the school—and so village children would make friends with children of strange and distant jatis, perhaps even of no jati at all, and would learn strange and unacceptable behavior from them.

The Pande families leading the opposing faction were equally vehement about the need to place the new school to the *southeast* of the village, as close as possible to the factory. For one thing, they said, a good school was expensive; it required a large building with many rooms, sufficient books and other supplies, and adequate salaries for decent teachers. The factory management—which had promised to help the village improve itself and which had as yet failed to provide electricity, good roads, or running water—could reasonably be expected to contribute handsomely to a new school. After all, the villagers were providing labor and much of the cost of construction, and a request for aid to education was one the officials would be reluctant to refuse. They would be particularly willing, said these Pandes, if the school were to be close to the factory and would provide seats for children of employees.

As for the Dube fear that Gôndôgram children would mingle with the children of strangers, the Pandes said they themselves would welcome such an eventuality! They said they wanted their children to learn more about the world and about India and to make friends who might help them one day to better positions and wider opportunities.

The conflict lasted for three or four years, preventing any work on the school. The Dubes have always been the old wealth and the stronger power in the village, capable particularly of lining up support among Carpenters, Distillers, and even Bauris (when necessary) in a factional dispute with Pandes. They could, therefore, delay the construction, but in the end they could not win: Pandes, Upadhyays, Carpenters, Distillers, and even some Dubes—all saw the advantages in having the school located near the factory. A vote was held in the village and the Dubes were defeated overwhelmingly. The new school began to go up between village and factory.

7

The New Gôndôgram

The Dube/Pande conflict over the site of the new school was of course expressive of the basic conflict in the village since the factory opened, the conflict between those who feared change and sought new opportunities. Dube families tend to be conservative, and Pandes much less so, and so the sides in the conflict were perhaps predictable. Predictable, too, may have been the outcome—more villagers of every jati opted to welcome change rather than to resist it. For most, though, what they wanted to welcome was economic opportunity; changes in other aspects of life are more debatable.

But the effects of the factory are difficult to resist, as we see. Even in the area of religious observance, the presence of the factory has precipitated significant changes. Before the establishment of the factory, the inhabitants of Gôndôgram went elsewhere to observe festivities on the days of Durga and Kali pujas. Villagers simply considered themselves too poor to sponsor such expensive festivals.

Five years after the factory opened its gates, Gôndôgram held the first Durga Puja in its history, and within the same year the new Durga temple began to go up. Pandes were the driving force behind the puja, but all Brahmans contributed and participated, and so did many Carpenters and Distillers. The subscription pays for the expensive murti, constructed as we have seen by the best artist of the district, and for the many other items of the puja.

Interestingly, though the presence of the factory has weakened many village relationships and has damaged in a number of ways the original sense of village cohesion, in this one case it has made a major contribution to that cohesion, for all villagers agree that a village without a Durga Puja is a sorry and impoverished place, while the one that regularly celebrates the Durga Puja is a village of some importance.

A few years after the first Durga Puja, the Bauris sponsored the first Kali Puja seen in Gôndôgram. Again, though one group (the Bauris) have been the driving force, others have contributed, particularly Carpenters and Distillers. Subscriptions have been solicited from factory officials, and even some Brahmans claim to have contributed, though Bauris deny this. To have a Kali Puja is also to enhance a village, but the way in which the Kali Puja is conducted in Gôndôgram—a Bauri event, as against the Durga Puja which is seen as a Brahman event—points up the Bauri separation from the rest of the village and their surfacing resentment against Brahman domination.[1]

Before the factory, worship of Ŝôrôśôtti was confined to the school, where a small murti was set up and worshiped by the small children and their teacher. This puja still takes place each year, but it is quite eclipsed by the substantial Ŝôrôśôtti Puja in Ūcu para, sponsored and conducted by all the teenage boys of the village attending schools outside the village. Brahman schoolboys, it may be of interest to note, participate in the Ūcu para puja, but then conduct one privately in their own para, in the home of a wealthy Pande Brahman.

Again, before the factory few villagers apart from Carpenters had anything to do with the worship of Biśśôkôrmô, the patron divinity of those who work with tools. Even Carpenters say that their worship of Biśśôkôrmô, before the factory, was perfunctory in the extreme. Things have changed now. Biśśôkôrmô Puja is a major holiday, the only one observed *in the factory*. For that day, the buildings—walls, floors, and windows—are made spotlessly clean. Where necessary, new paint is applied. Every machine is cleaned and polished meticulously, and garlanded with wreaths of flowers. Alpona (drawings made with rice paste) encircle the floors around and between the machines. In the technical institutes near Asansol, where boys are preparing for careers in the manual trades, the same adoration is observed.

Prayers are offered to Biśśôkôrmô by all who conceive that their well-being derives from machinery. Hindus of every jati offer prayers, and even Muslims and Christians participate actively in the proceedings. Many of these latter note, in conversation, that their participation derives neither from any fear of ill will on the part of Hindus, nor from any spirit of ecumenism. They say quite frankly that they too are dependent upon the machines and if they do not necessarily be-

1. Suzanne Hanchett (1972) has explored the underlying structural issue in her portrayal of the South Indian village-level festival as a moment "during which the total social structure is confronted by its members."

lieve in Biśśôkôrmô still it cannot hurt to honor the machines once a year and express their gratitude for what the machines have bestowed upon them. Even Sweepers join in these prayers—are they not, too, in the end, dependent upon these same machines to provide the money that pays their wages?

Returning one more time to Gôndôgram, we must take note of the substantial impact of the factory upon those relationships having to do with social control, with dominance and submissiveness, with authority and power. For years, the Pandes challenged the authority of the Dubes. With the coming of the factory, the most important Brahman voices in the village have been Pandes. They have adjusted more easily to change and have found ways to take advantage of it, though it is not always easy even for them.

The Community Development Program, responsible for much change in agricultural practice and in rural politics throughout India, had only recently begun activities in the region north of Asansol. A Union Board was in existence, responsible for the collection of taxes and the administering of local improvements in the area. Gôndôgram participated with other villages in such a Union Board, and elected its own representative.

From the start, the Gôndôgram representative was a Pande, probably the wealthiest man in the village and recognized in recent years as the closest thing to a village malik or "headman." But few Dubes recognize him as malik, and his control over Carpenters and Distillers is limited. In any event, he rarely attends meetings of the Union Board any more because he says it is controlled by men from another village who use its revenues to improve their own village only. Other Gôndôgram men see the force of his argument, for they say openly if they could get control of the Union Board they would use its revenues for the sake of Gôndôgram!

But if Brahmans are still dominant, they have unquestionably lost a good measure of the authority they once had. They are no longer the sole source of employment, nor are they respected as they once were as the embodiment of near-divinity and earthly wisdom. Which is not to say they are not respected and obeyed *at all;* they are influential and they do dominate the village, but simply not to the extent they once did. Once, no one moved into the village without asking their permission; a man of lower-ranked jati sat on the ground in the presence of a Brahman. Not only did Brahmans tell others how to behave, but people freely came to them for advice with every problem and to act as arbiters in every dispute.

On November 29, 1963, an altercation broke out in mid-afternoon on the border between Ūcu para and Dôkkhin Bauri para. The south-

ernmost Ûcu para house (that of Nikkhil Môndôl, a Distiller) is separated by only a narrow alley from the northernmost Bauri house.
Both households kept ducks, which swam and foraged all day in the
great Dhopa Pukur nearby. And there were two ducks, each a particular favorite in its respective household, that were remarkably
similar in size, coloring, and general appearance.

On this day, the Bauri duck had not turned up with the rest of the
household flock when they waddled back to the compound. The Bauris went looking but could find no trace of it, and all assumed that
someone had stolen and presumably eaten the bird. That a duck had
been stolen no one could question, but the Bauris argued that it had
not been proven that *their* duck was the missing one—why could it
not have been the Distiller duck that was missing, while the Bauri
duck was appropriated by the Distillers? Some of the Bauris, who had
caught a glimpse of the duck in the Distiller yard, were convinced it
was their own.

The women of the Bauri household went to the gate of the Distiller house and demanded the return of the duck. The head of the
household, a peon at the factory, was away at work, but the women
of his household refused to turn over the duck, insisting hotly that it
was indeed their own. The women of both sides began to scream
insults at each other: *"Tuder ônek bap: amader ekta bap!"* (You have
many fathers [i.e., your mothers are promiscuous]; while we have
only one father!) *"Amra côr na; tura côr!"* (We are not thieves; you
are the thieves!). As the noise and excitement increased, people came
running from all directions.

In the midst of the excitement, Nikkhil Môndôl came walking
home from the factory. Gently, he quieted the women on both sides,
asking the reasons for the dispute, and listening thoughtfully to the
claims and assertions of both. He smiled at all assembled: Was there
not, he asked, a simple solution? Let the duck in question be returned
to the pukur and let it swim some distance from the bank. Then, let
women from each household go to the bank, but well separated from
those of the other household. Let the Bauri women and the Môndôl
women each call the duck home as they were wont to do. The duck
would return to its accustomed owners, and all would agree before-
hand that the duck was the rightful possession of the household to
which it swam.

All agreed to the test, and the duck was taken to the pond amid
dozens of laughing spectators. The duck was sent out; it was summoned, and came without hesitation to the Distiller women who returned with it in triumph to their home. The Bauri women were turning glumly back to their home when they were interrupted by a

screech of rage—from Nikkhil Môdôl! How dare they accuse his family of thievery, he shouted. He had a good mind to call the police! The Bauri women cursed back, and the fight was on again, but only for a moment. Shouting curses, both sides retired into their homes.

As the crowd dispersed, a Carpenter youth commented to me that in all the throng there was not a single senior Brahman male, and it was true. Most adult Brahman men, of course, were working in the factory or resting at home. But there was a time, said the Carpenter youth, shaking his head sadly, not too many years past, before the coming of the factory, when a dispute such as the one we had witnessed could never have taken place in Gôndôgram. The Bauris would have gone to a Brahman before challenging the Distillers, and the Brahman would have made a judgment long before the dispute reached the shouting stage. And if the dispute had started, a Brahman would have come striding up to find out what was causing discord in his village—and Bauri and Distiller would have deferred to him. Nowadays, said the boy, the Brahmans prefer to stay away. They know that if they interfere both Distiller and Bauri are likely to turn on the Brahmans.

Older people, standing about and listening to the conversation, nodded in agreement. Nowadays, they said, the Brahmans have no power over us; they do not show their faces. Some looked sad, and some looked proud, and it was difficult to tell which was the dominant emotion.

Conclusion:

Changes and Continuities

"Caste sits lightly on Bengal," Bengalis will say with a degree of pride, and I for one would not want to quarrel with them. The people of Gôndôgram, when compared with those of other communities in India, do indeed seem to pay only a minimal amount of attention to issues of precedence, purity, and ritual superiority or inferiority.

Nevertheless, whether sitting lightly or heavily, whether unchanging or in the process of disappearing, caste—in all its intricacies—is very much a part of the Bengal countryside. I began by observing that caste is a basic element in community structure; we have seen caste permeating the very factory table of organization.

In order to understand Gôndôgram, therefore, and what has happened to Gôndôgram, we have had to explore implications and ramifications of this structural phenomenon known as "caste." We learned, for example, that the structural principles of the caste system advanced by Bouglé and again by Dumont—hierarchy, separation, and interaction—are very much in evidence in Gôndôgram.

Hierarchy, as the Bengalis imply, may not be as weighty a principle as it is elsewhere, but it cannot be ignored if we hope to understand the functioning of the system and its response to factors of change. Gôndôgram came into existence, some say, because Washermen found it soul-satisfying to gaze upon Brahmans, while Brahmans were troubled when they found they had to return the gaze. Brahmans will accept neither food nor water from people of lower-ranked castes, but happily they have no reason to do so. The wife of the Bauri mahindôr, on the other hand, has no problem in accepting a plate of cooked food from her Brahman employer. This is fortunate, for Bauri and Brahman—and for the functioning of the system.

Those are examples of hierarchical relationships between people of different jatis; we have seen examples of hierarchy within jatis. In principle, people claim, all men of a jati are fully equal to one another, yet in all but the lowest-ranked Bengali jatis (and among Santals) wife-takers out-rank wife-givers. Among Brahmans there is gramer-nam hypergamy, and among Carpenters some indications of gotrô hypergamy—and among all the feeling that a girl must be married into a family of equal or superior status.

We have seen examples of the working of the principle of *separation,* as well. Bauri and Santal paras are physically removed from those of higher-ranked jatis. In fact, whatever the physical boundaries, separation seems to be almost absolute: for all, from all. No one comes into a Brahman's kitchen in Gôndôgram but a Brahman, and preferably only a member of the immediate family. And no one comes into a Carpenter's kitchen in the normal course of events but a closely related Carpenter—and the same restriction obtains for Distiller, Bauri, and Santal.

One does not eat or drink with people of a different jati, or even of a different and distant sômaj. Most of all, of course, marriage is restricted to the members of the marriage-circle. Violation of the rules of separation, particularly in the case of marriage, is punished by expulsion from the group.

And yet the jatis interact, as we have seen, socially, ritually, and economically. This interaction is of course an inextricable element of caste, but I find it more useful, at least for the purposes of this work, to dwell on interaction and its implications in a later paragraph, when discussing the village and other dimensions of community.

Before turning from this brief review of caste in Gôndôgram, however, I would draw attention to one specific and crucial manifestation of separation as a structural principle. We have seen that each jati, represented by a particular marriage-circle, is autocephalous. Each sômaj, that is, has its own leadership (malik, council, or whatever), and that leadership recognizes no superior authority.

There are of course exceptions, particularly in modern times. There are cases, for example, of jatis joining together to support—and in a sense to constitute—political parties (see Lynch 1969). In principle, however, the sômaj is socially and politically an independent entity, controlling the behavior of its membership through the power of expulsion.

We have reports, for the neighborhood of Gôndôgram, of marriage-circle assemblies punishing those who violate the rule of marital separation, but also—and more significantly for our purposes here—of marriage-circle assemblies attempting to cope with changing times and needs. The Kanauj Brahman marriage-circle met and deliberated about the need to provide dowries. The Bauri marriage-circle was able to impose a new rule on its membership, forbidding certain foods and practices, in an effort to raise the status of the entire body.

We see, therefore, that the people of Gôndôgram and its neighbors are all of them members of discrete, separate, and autocephalous bodies. Each such body makes its own rules and imposes them on its membership. Most of all, the body insists upon the social separation of the group from all other groups in the vicinity.

An inhabitant of Gôndôgram is thus before all a member of his jati. He is identified with it by others, and he identifies with it and is subject to it before he is subject to any other rules. The members are his equals—his *only* equals—his responsibility, and his "people."

And yet, for all of that, the marriage-circle is never, not in principle or in fact, a totally autonomous body. Apart from rare cases such as Gopalgram, where only Carpenters live, villages are inhabited by families representing more than one jati. It may well be that people would prefer to live surrounded only by others of the same sômaj. Whether they would or not, however, the point is that for the most part they cannot.

How, for example, could there be a village made up only of Barbers? How could Brahmans live alone? Who would work their fields or fix their plows? The village we see is a compromise between the urge to be with one's own kind exclusively, and the unavoidable need to have others of different jatis close by, primarily for economic reasons, but for some ritual and social ones as well. It is nice to live alone, like the Carpenters of Gopalgram, but in the end it is much more convenient to live in a village with representatives of many different jatis within call.

Despite all political and social cohesion, the marriage-circle lacks any meaningful economic unity. True, the members may believe they share a common ancestral occupation, as in the case of Brahmans as "priestly folk." In some cases, the ancestral occupation is long-forgotten; few Tilis would know how to press oilseeds. In some cases, as with Carpenters and Distillers, the ancestral occupation is still widely known and practiced. It is even true that men of a sômaj—good jat-brothers that they are—will help one another to jobs and other kinds of economic opportunity; the Tili tea shops are just one example of this. As a result of all this, there is a resemblance or congruence between members of the same sômaj, in terms of occupations and economic status.

Nevertheless, the sômaj does not exist in an economic vacuum to anything like the extent to which it exists in a social vacuum. Remove all other jatis from the neighborhood and the śômaj would hardly be affected in any social context; they might find themselves more secure and more content. Economically, however, they are all inextricably units of a complex, stratified, specialized system. They need each other, and most would be impoverished to the point of disaster were there no other jatis around; at least, as long as present rules and practices were to continue in existence.

The village, we have seen, not the marriage-circle, is the economic productive unit. The land is under the control of Brahmans who, in this case at least, may not themselves turn up the soil or pull a weed. Brahmans supervise the production of a rice crop, but they do not—must not—perform the actions of such production. Nor do the Brahmans know anything about carpentry, blacksmithing, or other such. They may not cut their own hair or deliver their own babies. Under such circumstances, it is apparent that a crop is produced, but not by independent, egalitarian, self-sufficient farmers. Rather, there are those who supervise production, those who perform the activities of production under that supervision, and those who provide necessary (or desired) services for equipment and personnel. All share, if differentially, in the total harvest.

This interplay of egalitarian, separated castes, hierarchically arranged, with village productivity in a complex stratified agricultural society makes India the fascinating place it is for the student of social systems. We must face the complexity squarely; there are few adequate "either/or" explanations or meaningful binary oppositions.[1] Mostly, we find gradations and complexities of differentiation that warn us not to dichotomize or triplicate too soon.

There is, then, no "typical villager" to be studied. Not only is each villager a member of a differently bounded body, the śômaj of his jati, but his very perspectives on time and space are different, and so his responses to new phenomena must be different from his fellow villager of a different jati.

The Brahman, for example, lives in a Brahman para, in the midst of men of his own jati. It may not be the largest or even the most centrally located para, but for the Brahman it is unquestionably the center of the village—everything else is periphery or appendage. He is concerned about everything that happens within the boundary of what he looks upon as "his" village. In a village where the dominant jati is other than Brahman, we find the same attitudes by the men of

---

1. Though there are some: the bhôdrôlok/chôtôlok (literally, "good people"/"small people") distinction, or munib vs. muniś, or the Bauri expulsion which is viewed as "putting outside" as against all the others, who consider the expelled man as "made degraded."

that jati. They are the ones who worry about how to bring electricity into the village or whether the road needs repair.

The men of Ūcu para have a different, more limited, perspective. They also see the village as one unit, but their primary concern is with their own para; the Brahmans, they know, will look after the village and will inform the men of Ūcu para if they need their help. No one expects a Bauri to offer either opinions or help with village problems, and Bauris never do. They see themselves as people apart and people at the bottom. They appear, however, to resent the attitudes of superiority expressed by Carpenters, Distillers, and Washermen. And if they are humble in the presence of Brahmans, there is a touch of Uriah Heep in the humility of some, as we discover when the factory arrives and new opportunities open up.

For Santals, the para is central and all else is peripheral; some even refer to their paras as grams (villages) and they practice para but not village exogamy.

The perspectives on time vary in much the same way. A Brahman can recite his ancestry almost to the full seven generations required of a good Hindu. Brahmans alone remember the name of the first Washerman settler and his son. They claim that the gramer nam is the village of ancestral settlement in Kanyakubja—and in the other direction, they plan carefully for their children's future. Bauris, at the other end of the continuum, avoid only the marriage of first cousins, for who can know if two persons have great-grandparents in common? They have no idea where their ancestors came from, and they make no provision for their children, since they expect children to grow up and go their own ways. Barbers, Carpenters, Distillers, and Washermen occupy positions along the continuum. Family structure reflects a similar kind of continuum, from large Brahman joint families to Bauri nuclear families.

Clearly, this is no homogeneous "little community" and it never was nor could be. Nor is it isolated, either; the village needs the district, the côkrô, for it is incomplete without it. We have seen, for example, that a Barber frequently serves as a ghôṭôk, a go-between, or marriage-broker.[2] For the purposes of this work, this is more significant for what it illuminates about community structure than for what it tells us about marriage procedures.

We find a Barber family resident in Gôndôgram, providing services for that village and for five others—none of which has resident Barbers of its own. Shall we label the other five "part-communities"?

2. Oscar Lewis reports, in his study of Rampur, near Delhi: "It was formerly the custom for Nais (barbers) to act as go-betweens in the arrangement of Jat marriages" (1965: 163).

Are they, in this respect at least, "satellites" of Gôndôgram—as Gôndôgram in turn might be called a "satellite" of Ethora, from whence it draws family priests for Brahmans? It depends, obviously, on whether the phenomenon of "one barber for six villages" is the exception or the rule, and that is why the role of Barber as ghôtôk is interesting.

Barbers whose services are restricted to their own village would make poor marriage-brokers, particularly where intra-village marriages are rare or completely forbidden. The Barber-ghôtôk must be the Barber whose work takes him regularly beyond his home village; even more, in fact, he must be one who has many relatives with similar networks for a truly effective system of marriage-brokerage. One lone Barber with a network of only six villages can hardly be an effective ghôtôk.

It seems reasonable to conclude, therefore, that the activity of barber in the Indian countryside relates more meaningfully to the côkrô (district) dimension of community than to the village dimension. True, the barber and his family reside in a particular para of some particular village (for they must, after all, live somewhere). He provides his services, however, for a network of clients, not for a village, and while the network may in some cases be conterminous with a village—a large village, perhaps—it is more likely that the network will permeate many villages. Only in this way is the widespread role of the barber as go-between explicable.

Côkrô then is an important dimension of community, the dimension of total resource, and cannot be ignored or downgraded; the Bengali countryman is a member of his household, of his para, of his village, of his marriage-circle—and also of his côkrô.

But he lives in his village; we come back to that. And when people live together throughout their lives and for many generations, they must interact, even when their respective jati rules call for total separation. Education is hard to come by in the Bengal countryside, and there cannot be a school for each jati represented in the village. Temples and ponds must be shared, if not always by the entire village at least by substantial segments of it. The world beyond the village, state and national, tends to treat it as a single unit; and so men of different jatis must work together, if at times uncomfortably, in responding to national political parties and Community Development programs.

The major area of cooperation and interaction between men of different jatis, however, with its roots in antiquity, has to do with the production of a rice crop. In minimal terms, the Brahman stands, arms folded behind his back, supervising the work of his Bauri mahindôrs as they labor in the fields. Carpenters repair the Brahmans' ox carts in the street in the front of their houses, while Barbers go from house to house grooming their clients. Blacksmiths, Dom musicians, Fishermen, Milkmen, Brahman priests, and all the others perform their services. It matters not at all whether their residence and service are restricted to the same single village, or whether a service network encompasses many villages.

Services flow inward to those who control the productivity, and he who provides the service and he who receives it are bound to each other over the generations by the rules of the jajmani relationship, though they are of separate and independent jatis. Though they owned no land and knew little or nothing about agriculture, those who provided maintenance services for people and equipment in the village had an abiding interest in agricultural productivity, for they shared in it. After harvest, an agreed-on share went to the Barber, the Blacksmith, and so on.

Men in each jati in the village speak of their jati's uniqueness, of their total separation from all others, but we must not be blinded by these assertions. Despite the separation and seeming independence, we observe patterned interaction and interdependence. Separated, they nevertheless live together and work together, and so have rules for all this interaction. The jajmani relationships are perhaps the most important of these rules, providing for the movement of goods and services, but there are other rules as well.

Villagers will insist, for example, that—whatever the requirements of production and distribution—consumption takes place within the jati, in fact within the household, for there are strict prohibitions against inter-jati commensality. Nevertheless, cooked food may be accepted from those ranked higher in the system, and what this means in the end is that Brahmans may and do make periodic feasts at which they feed not only members of their own sômaj but men of all the jatis in the village. There is no conflict or confusion at such times, for the rules are clearly understood by all: Brahmans are served first, and when they are finished, the jati in the village ranked second by the Brahmans is served, and so on down to the Bauris waiting to scrape the pots and the beggars waiting to take the garbage.

The successive seatings at the Brahmans' feasts are understood to represent hierarchical relationships, but the fact that all have eaten together (if separately), with food provided and often even served by Brahmans, seems in a way to symbolize the village as a cohesive interacting unit. In much the same way, the Brahman upônôyôn ceremony, at which a boy of that jati comes of age and dons the sacred thread, also seems to symbolize the village structure. It is after all a ceremony by and for Brahmans, and so it is not surprising that he should have Brahmanical godparents; presumably they represent the jati and by their actions and approval conduct him into it.

But why the godparents from Ūcu paṛa? Is this a kind of *compadrazgo*[3] in reverse? Perhaps, but it is certainly tempting to see the role of the lower-caste bhikku-baba and bhikku-ma as structurally similar to that of the brahman godparents, to effect the entry of the Brahman boys into their roles as Brahman men *within the village.*

In this context, the behavior of the lower-caste godparents, waiting eagerly outside the Brahman compound for the "first sight" of the Brahman boy, is worthy of a moment's consideration. Having been the first non-Brahmans to see the boy, they will have a special relationship with him from then on, and can even expect his assistance in their old age, should it be impoverished.

Perhaps this makes intelligible the reported desire of the founding Dhopa to "gaze upon a Brahman" and his willingness to invite Brahmans to settle in the village. The most common sight of a Brahman, we have noted, is that of a man standing, hands behind his back, supervising the production of a crop. Gazing upon such a Brahman, we might conclude, is reassuring; it tells one the village is an effective, productive agricultural unit.

With these last observations we have moved into the murky waters of ideology: values and beliefs. It is one thing to provide data on ritual or on numbers and natures of deities; interpretation in this area—of what other men believe and why they believe it and the implications of such beliefs—is difficult and clearly open to dispute. With that caveat to myself, I shall attempt a few observations.

The inhabitants of Gôndôgram appear to relate to deities much as they do to people. Put another way, the dimension of the divine seems to be an extension of the human. Bauris, before the coming of the factory, sought to establish personal and permanent relationships with Brahmans. When a Bauri was successful, he became a mahindôr for a Brahman household, and his wife a house servant and his son a bagal. The family would work for the Brahman household from then on, and they could turn to the Brahmans for help in illness or other emergency.

In the old days, landholders of Gôndôgram made obeisance to the fabled "Maharaja of Kaśipur," and we have seen that contemporary villagers make pronam in much the same way to high officers of the factory. The pattern is the same: seek out someone who has

3. "Godparenthood" in Latin America: In this system, godparents are usually chosen for "practical or prestige advantage" (Redfield 1934; see also Mintz and Wolf 1950).

greater resources than you do, demonstrate your submission to him, and try to persuade him to smile upon you. If he helps you, you are bound to him thereafter; you must demonstrate your gratitude, and if you filfill your obligations you can reasonably hope for further favors.

In exactly the same way, a villager with a problem beyond human aid (illness, barrenness, and other such misfortune) seeks the assistance of a deity, and there are many to turn to. Once there is a favorable response, the villager responds with continuing sacrifice and attention; thenceforth, he and his family have a special relationship with a deity who has performed a miracle in their behalf.

This relationship, including the search for it, constitutes the most significant dimension of religion for most of the people of the Bengali countryside—and so one can see how much comfort there must be in the belief that there are so many deities, possibly even a deity for every Hindu! Deities also exhibit something reminiscent of the hierarchy of the caste system, from the triune divinity at the apex to such deities as Mônôśa, associated primarily with Bauris, subject even to upbraiding and threat by Brahmans.

None of this is, or should be, particularly astonishing. Anthropologists have long perceived significant congruences between the ideological and the socioeconomic spheres. Here, we are trying only to illuminate the congruences in the Indian countryside.

We have seen, for example, that Gôndôgram is not a "little community"in Redfield's terms; it is not surprising that we find no single village priest, no single shrine or temple. We find that it is even misleading to attempt to set up a village calendar of religious events.

Religion, we must conclude, is interwoven with community, and reflects the complexity of that structure in rural Bengal. There are religious events associated with the household, such as the prayers before the tulśi-môncô shrine. Some events are associated primarily with the paṛa; the dôls for kirton-singing are organized paṛa by paṛa. The gram-debi/deb'ta shrine is only one example of the village dimension of religion, and yet each jati has its own restricted rituals and favorite deities. In one village, we saw, three jatis attended the same ceremony and were encouraged to address their respective prayers to three different deities! And finally, there are the côkrô-wide melas, or fairs, attended by people from many different villages and jatis.

Without reviewing all the details of belief and practice presented in the earlier chapter, it does seem fair to characterize religion in Gôndôgram as reflecting the same absence of centricity and consensus, the same intricate variation, we have remarked in the social structure. The very calendar itself, we have seen, expresses all of these.

And if the belief system reflects the social system, we have seen that the values adhered to by the people of Gôndôgram are equally reflective and supportive of that social and economic system. The villager expresses what are primarily particularistic values: be concerned for your own, not for strangers. "Your own" includes not only your household and your jati, but specifically all those with whom you have reciprocal obligations—within your jati and within your village and community. The invariable response to the man who fails to meet his obligations is withdrawal and exclusion. If the miscreant is of another jati, then the jajmani relationship breaks down. If he is of the same jati, he is formally expelled by the membership.

Given the complexity and variation, in both beliefs and in socioeconomic relationships, it is inevitable that there must be inconsistency and contradiction, but the ideological structure provides ways around this. When villagers discover that beliefs are in direct contradiction, their reaction is almost one of amusement; the contradiction confirms what they have always understood about the universe. Men have different beliefs and practices, yet all are partly right and probably no human is fully correct. In the end, all is maya; illusion, or, as I have argued, ambiguity.

Further, there is a processual sequence to be observed, relating the pragmatic and the transcendental spheres of religion, and if the sequence seems to contain inherent contradiction, the point is that the process is not explicit or apparent to the countryman. Indeed, he prefers to ignore much of the process of social and economic life, whether it be the actual interaction of supposedly "separate" jatis, or the sacred bull, released in memory of a deceased Brahman, who fertilizes the cows of the côkrô.

The countryman, indeed, is particularly reluctant to focus on economic process as it relates to the utilization of the cow. And yet the cow, along with the bull and the ox, has a pivotal role in the economy (see Harris 1966), and so we, as observers, have had to try to unravel the process. We have seen, for example, that the oxen so necessary for agricultural production are derived from the cattle herds of the countrymen; bull-calves are sold to specialists, who castrate them, heal them, and then sell them when healthy and strong back to the countrymen for labor in the fields.

So much for the process. The countryman himself is consciously aware only of two entirely discrete events. Reluctantly he sells his bull-calves in a cattle market to "disreputable" individuals who will use the animals for ends the countryman does not know and does not want to know. And then, at some other time, the countryman buys his work oxen in that cattle market. He has no interest in where they came from or how they came to be castrated; he considers the operation deplorable, but since it is done and is manifestly irreversible, he is willing to use the animals in his fields.

Again the farmer expresses horror at the suggestion that he might strike a cow or ox grazing in his ricefield. He, of course, could never do such a thing, and if he did he would be punished by his jat-brothers. So he employs a low-caste herd-boy to care for his cattle, and it is the job of this boy to beat the cattle and drive them away from the grain.

And when the animal dies, mourned by the bhôdrôlok household, the Bauri laborers are ordered to dispose of it. The bhôdrôlok intends that the animal be given a decent burial, but the Bauris are chôṭôlok (lesser folk) and if they decide to eat the animal instead, well, what can one do?

What we see, however, doing justice to the facts if not to the spirit, is that cattle are utilized wonderfully effectively and economically. Farmers sell uncastrated bull-calves to specialists, thereby sparing themselves expense and possible risk. They buy the oxen they need, when they need them. Cattle are not permitted to graze on growing crops; they do not "compete with humans for food." Dead, the cattle provide a major source of protein for the impoverished and undernourished lower castes.

The economic system functions, though the functioning is not manifest to the people themselves, and a crop is produced and people live and work together. Similarly, when they feel in need of divine assistance, comfort, and explanation, the ideological system functions to provide such things for them. They themselves, however, feel no need to work out the sequence we have perceived, from "onset" of misfortune through "continuation" of misfortune to a final "culmination."

So much for Gôndôgram and its community: What happens when a factory intrudes, when changes are forced upon this economic, social and ideological system? At least one aspect of the intrusion seems to affect everyone in the village equally: They are perceived by the factory management as one amorphous body. Ascribed to all are the work habits of the Brahmans and the caste-cohesiveness of the Carpenters.

But we have seen that members of each jati have responded differently. The factory means different things to different jatis, and its effects have been very different. Brahmans are understandably worried, for they are losing control of the village and of the productivity of their ricefields. Some of them, however, see the possibility for important new employment for their children.

Carpenters have a greater monetary income than they have ever known before, but they mourn the disappearance of their traditional caste occupation. Washermen and Distillers, on the other hand, have found in the factory the source of an opportunity to *return* to traditional caste occupations. Bauris and Barbers have been able to opt out of the village economic system; they are giving up traditional socioeconomic relationships for industrial employment. Santals, again, show a reverse movement, from colliery employment to sharecropping.

Still, if there is no typical villager, there is a village, and it has been affected by the factory's presence. The income of the village, the amount of money flowing in annually, has undoubtedly increased, but the village economic life has been impaired: rice production and animal husbandry have suffered. At first glance, religious observance in the village seems to have intensified for reasons directly traceable to the factory. Two new temples have been constructed, and major new pujas (to Durga and Kali) have been introduced. A deity hardly known before—Biśśôkôrmô—has been receiving increasing attention. Actually, however, we have seen that the new temples and pujas also reflect the new disruption and conflict within the village; Brahmans worship Durga, and Bauris now worship Kali and subscribe to an expensive puja to show up the Brahmans and the people of Ûcu para.

If better education can now be provided for the children of Gôndôgram, there is less security in the homes at night, and watchmen have had to be introduced. There are more material goods in every home; many young men even have transistor radios. On the other hand, there is intensifying conflict between the generations in many households, just as there is throughout the village between jatis.

The factory has had an impact upon more than the one village: changes are taking place throughout the côkrô. For the people of Gôndôgram, this too can pose problems, as we have seen. Brahman and Carpenter boys and girls of the village are suddenly more desirable as mates, but at a cost. Guardians of Gôndôgram children are discovering that a job in the factory is the necessary catalyst, without which it may be difficult to arrange a marriage.

Still, marriages are arranged and somehow jobs are obtained, and so boys from villages dozens of miles from Gôndôgram find themselves working in the bicycle factory—if they belong to a jati represented in Gôndôgram. For the winds of change blow in the Bengal countryside along paths long-since laid out.

In some places in the world, particularly in the West, the introduction of a factory into the countryside might be likened to a stone cast into a pond; ripplelike, the changes spread from their source, affecting the nearest villages the most, and then those farther away to an ever-decreasing extent. In Bengal, there is an impact upon nearby villages such as Gôndôgram—and a substantially equivalent impact upon quite distant villages which contain representatives of marriage-circles found in the nearby ones.

On the other hand, the impact of the factory may be negligible in a village only a mile or two from the factory in which no jatis—say of Gôndôgram—happen to be represented. If, however, a man of such a village finds a way to siphon away some of the wealth produced by the factory, then other members of his marriage-circle are likely to be similarly affected. The Tili of Tilimunda who learned to operate a tea shop has introduced a new occupation to his jati. The śômaj, in short, would appear to be a far better conduit of change than the road on the map.

Acculturation, Redfield, Linton, and Herskovits (1936) have pointed out, is often a two-way street. If the factory has affected rural life in so many ways, it should not surprise us to discover that rural ways of life have affected the factory. Most of all, we have discovered, elements of the caste system have permeated the factory table of organization and not just this factory alone. From high management to modest Sweepers, we find, jat-brothers prefer to work together and to exclude outsiders.

The village and the factory now exist side by side, if uneasily, and they interact. The factory has changed the village and its community, and the factory has changed in response to the values of those who staff it. Neither, it would seem, can ever be the same again. In any case, surely the village can not go back to what it was before.

If Gôndôgram was never the isolated self-sufficient entity some have imagined, surely it is less isolated and less self-sufficient than ever before. Dissatisfaction with the past exists on all levels, along with the nostalgia. Pande Brahmans, and even many Dubes, would not want to return completely to the old ways; they want their children to become factory officials.

Bauris, similarly, dream of factory employment and would turn their backs forever on agricultural labor if they could, though it could be argued that, were the factory to disappear, they would have little choice but to return to the fields. Would they give up their new-found political independence, however? Were the factory to be eclipsed, would Distillers, Carpenters, and others begin to call again upon Brahmans to settle their disputes? In a generation or two, could Carpenters and Barbers go back, even if they wanted to, to ancestral occupations? Could they resume traditional jajmani relationships? Would the Brahmans want to? Such questions are perhaps academic, since it would seem highly unlikely that the factory will disappear. On the other hand, however, the future is not all that secure. Factory managers, in Bengal as elsewhere in the world, are aware of the advantages of automation. Some predict openly that, before the century is out, factories such as the one we have called "Das-Walters" will be completely automated, with production requiring the services of only one hundred or so highly trained specialists.

For Gôndôgram, of course, this would have the effect of the disappearance of the factory—except that it would still be there, across the road. In such an eventuality, we can only conclude, traditional values and relationships would have persisted, along with the new ones, and the villagers would make their new responses in terms of all of these . . . and, of course, jati by jati.

Selected Bibliography

Arensberg, Conrad M.
  1961   The Community as Object and as Sample. *American Anthropologist* 63: 241–264.
Babb, Lawrence A.
  1975   *The Divine Hierarchy: Popular Hinduism in Central India.* New York: Columbia University Press.
Beidelman, Thomas O.
  1959   *A Comparative Analysis of the Jajmani System.* Monograph of The Association for Asian Studies, No. 8. Locust Valley, N.Y.: J. J. Augustin.
Berreman, Gerald D.
  1962   *BehindManyMasks.* Ithaca: Society for Applied Anthropology.
Bouglé, Célestin
  1908   *Essais sur le régime des castes.* Paris: Travaux de l'Année Sociologique.
Bridgwater, William, and Kurtz, Seymour
  1963   *The Columbia Encyclopedia;* 3d. ed. New York: Columbia University Press.
Dube, S. C.
  1955   Ranking of Castes in Telangana Villages. *The Eastern Anthropologist* 8: 182–190. Calcutta, India.
Dumont, Louis
  1970   *Homo Hierarchicus: An Essay on the Caste System.* Chicago: University of Chicago Press.
Freed, Stanley A.
  1963   An Objective Method for Determining the Collective Caste Hierarchy of an Indian Village. *American Anthropologist* 65: 879–891.
Freed, Stanley A., and Freed, Ruth S.
  1964   Calendars, Ceremonies and Festivals in a North Indian Village: Necessary Calendrical Information for Fieldwork. *Southwestern Journal of Anthropology* 20: 67–90.

Ghurye, G. S.
1950 *Caste and Class in India*. Bombay.
Gould, Harold A.
1960 The Micro-demography of Marriages in a North Indian Area. *Southwestern Journal of Anthropology* 16:476–491.
Hanchett, Suzanne
1972 Festivals and Social Relations in a Mysore Village: Mechanics of Two Processions. *Economic and Political Weekly* 7: 1517–1522.
Harris, Marvin
1966 The Cultural Ecology of India's Sacred Cattle. *Current Anthropology* 7: 51–66.
Karve, Irawati
1968 *Kinship Organization in India*. New York: Asia Publishing House.
Khare, R. S.
1970 *The Changing Brahmans: Associations and Elites among the Kanya-Kubjas of North India*. Chicago: University of Chicago Press.
Klass, Morton
1966 Marriage Rules in Bengal. *American Anthropologist* 68: 951–970.
1972 Community Structure in West Bengal. *American Anthropologist* 74: 601–610.
Kolenda, Pauline Mahar
1963 Toward a Model of the Hindu Jajmani System. *Human Organization* 22: 11–31.
Lévi-Strauss, Claude
1968 *The Savage Mind*. Chicago: The University of Chicago Press. (First printing, 1962, Librairie Plon, Paris.)
Lewis, Oscar
1965 *Village Life in Northern India: Studies in a Delhi Village*. Vintage Books. (Originally published 1958, University of Illinois Press.)
Lynch, Owen M.
1969 *The Politics of Untouchability: Social Mobility and Social Change in a City of India*. New York: Columbia University Press.
Majumdar, R. C. (ed.)
1943 *The History of Bengal*, vol. 1: *Hindu Period*. Dacca: University of Dacca.
Mandelbaum, David G.
1964 Introduction: Process and Structure in South Asian Reli-

gion. In *Religion in South Asia,* ed. E. B. Harper, Seattle: University of Washington Press.
1970   *Society in India.* Berkeley: University of California Press.
Manners, Robert A.
1960   Methods of Community-Analysis in the Caribbean. In *Caribbean Studies: A Symposium,* ed. V. Rubin, Seattle: University of Washington Press.
Marriott, McKim
1955   Little Communities in an Indigenous Civilization. In *Village India: Studies in the Little Community,* ed., M. Marriott, American Anthropological Association Memoir 83.
1959   Interactional and Attributional Theories of Caste Ranking. *Man in India* 39: 92–107.
Mayer, Adrian C.
1970   *Caste and Kinship in Central India: A Village and Its Region.* Berkeley: University of California Press.
Mintz, Sidney W., and Wolf, Eric R.
1950   An Analysis of Ritual Co-Parenthood (Compadrazgo). *Southwestern Journal of Anthropology* 6: 341–368.
Moreland, W. H., and Chatterjee, A. C.
1957   *A Short History of India.* New York: David McKay Company.
Murdock, George Peter
1949   *Social Structure.* New York: Macmillan Co.
Peterson, J. C. K.
1910   *Bengal District Gazetteers: Burdwan.* Calcutta: Bengal Secretariat Book Depôt.
Redfield, Robert
1934   Culture Changes in Yucatán. *American Anthropologist* 36: 57–69.
1955   *The Little Community: Viewpoints for the Study of a Human Whole.* Chicago: University of Chicago Press.
Redfield, Robert; Linton, Ralph; and Herskovits, M. J.
1936   Memorandum on the Study of Acculturation. *American Anthropologist* 38: 149–152.
Risley, H. H.
1892   *The Tribes and Castes of Bengal,* vol. 1. Calcutta: Bengal Secretariat Press.
Senart, Émile
1894   *Les castes dans l'Inde: Les faits et le système.* Paris: E. Leroux.
Singer, Milton
1958   The Great Tradition in a Metropolitan Center: Madras. *Journal of American Folklore* 71: 347–388.

1976   Robert Redfield's Development of a Social Anthropology of
        Civilizations. In *American Anthropology: The Early Years*
        ed. John V. Murra. 1974 Proceedings of the American Eth-
        nological Society. St. Paul: West Publishing Co.

Srinivas, M. N.
1952   *Religion and Society among the Coorgs of South India.*
        New York: Oxford University Press.
1955   The Social System of a Mysore Village. In *Village India:
        Studies in the Little Community,* ed., M. Marriott, American
        Anthropological Association Memoir 83.

Steward, Julian H.
1950   *Area Research.* New York: New York Social Science Re-
        search Bulletin 63.

Swartzberg, Leon
1970   "The North Indian Peasant Goes to Market." Unpublished
        Ph.D. dissertation, New York: Columbia University.

Underhill, M. M.
1921   *The Hindu Religious Year.* Calcutta: Associated Press.

Weber, Max
1961   Types of Social Organization. In *Theories of Society,* vol. 1,
        eds., Talcott Parsons et al. Glencoe: Free Press.

Wiser, William H.
1936   *The Hindu Jajmani System: A System Inter-relating Mem-
        bers of a Hindu Village Community in Service.* Lucknow:
        Lucknow Publishing Company.

Yalman, Nur
1962   The Structure of Sinhalese Kindred: A Re-examination of
        the Dravidian Terminology. *American Anthropologist* 64:
        548–575.

Index